POLITICAL THEORY

AND THE

PSYCHOLOGY OF THE UNCONSCIOUS

POLITICAL THEORY

AND THE

PSYCHOLOGY OF THE UNCONSCIOUS

Freud, J.S.Mill, Nietzsche, Dostoevsky, Fromm,
Bettelheim and Erikson

PAUL ROAZEN

OPEN GATE PRESS
LONDON

First published in 2000 by Open Gate Press
51 Achilles Road, London NW6 1DZ

British Library Cataloguing-in-Publication Programme
A catalogue reference for this book is available from the
British Library.

ISBN: 1 871871 48 4

Cover illustrations:
The photograph of Sigmund Freud
is reproduced by courtesy of the Freud Museum, London
The potrait of John Stuart Mill by John and Charles Watkins
is reproduced by courtesy of the National Portait Gallery

Printed in Great Britain by Cromwell Press,
Trowbridge, Wiltshire

Also by Paul Roazen

Freud: Political and Social Thought (1968, 1986, 1999)
Brother Animal: The Story of Freud and Tausk (1969, 1990)
Freud and His Followers (1975)
Erik H. Erikson: The Power and Limits of a Vision (1976)
Helene Deutsch: A Psychoanalyst's Life (1985, 1992)
*Encountering Freud: The Politics and Histories of
    Psychoanalysis* (1990)
Meeting Freud's Family (1993)
How Freud Worked: First-Hand Accounts of Patients (1995)
Heresy: Sándor Radó and the Psychoanalytic Movement (with
    Bluma Swerdloff) (1995)
Canada's King: An Essay in Political Psychology (1998)
*Oedipus in Britain: Edward Glover and the Struggle Over
    Klein* (2000)
The Historiography of Psychoanalysis (2000)

Edited by Paul Roazen

Sigmund Freud (1973)
Walter Lippmann, The Public Philosophy (1989)
*Louis Hartz, The Necessity of Choice: Nineteenth Century
    Political Theory* (1990)
*Helene Deutsch, The Psychoanalysis of the Sexual Functions of
    Women* (1991)
*Victor Tausk, Sexuality, War, and Schizophrenia: Collected
    Psychoanalytic Papers* (1991)
*Helene Deutsch, The Therapeutic Process, the Self, and
    Female Psychology: Collected Psychoalytic Papers* (1991)
Walter Lippman, Liberty and the News (1995)

For
Alice Fox

Table of Contents

Preface

The study of political theory is a special sort of undertaking. The proverbial person in the street is unlikely to be able intuitively to understand what it is that a political theorist does. The word 'political' can be as misleading as the term 'theory'. To try at the outset to set the story straight: a political theorist is concerned with the broadest questions of society and ethics, in the spirit of what the ancient Greeks meant by the fullest scope of politics. Traditionally, the way an education should be organized, and how it relates to citizenship, is as key an aspect of political theory as what makes for a just war. When I once was asked to teach a course in ancient political philosophy, which in addition to Plato and Aristotle included Cicero and St. Augustine, I found myself so fascinated by the self-inflicted death of Socrates, and what might have been going on at his Athenian trial that it was only with the greatest reluctance that I moved away from Socrates to get to the more formal writings of others. To my mind so many of the greatest questions in political theory were raised by the last days of Socrates that it would have been enough to make a separate course in itself.

I cite the example of Socrates's demise as an illustration of the kind of problem that political thinkers are characteristically interested in. The death of Socrates is a matter of 'theory' in that there is a wide variety of different possible interpretations that could be advanced to understand it. What was the Athenian polity upset about in his teachings, and why did he decide to drink the fatal cup of hemlock? Perhaps if I mention a comment once made by a tutor of mine at Oxford, Sir Isaiah Berlin, the reader will have a better idea of how

xi

PREFACE

political theorists proceed; he observed that whenever one finds oneself in a social dilemma where it is unclear what might count for or against a different resolution, then one can be sure one is in the realm of political thought. Political theory is, then, more concerned with problems, even the most intractable, than with any sorts of solutions. It has to do centrally with thinking about how we think.[1] Another of my teachers back at Harvard (whom Berlin knew and thought well of) once organized a whole course on nineteenth-century political thought around the issue of what is the good society, and what role should the state play in promoting it?[2]

It has been generally agreed that political theory is made up of a great conversation, a sequence of arguments which have been going on for over two thousand years among the giants of intellectual life. So I have spent my whole life reflecting on different aspects of political thought. And people like myself find it automatic to think in terms of all the possible points of view which have been presented over the centuries on the most basic issues of the philosophy of social life. As an undergraduate I was, like others, drilled in the works of Thomas Hobbes, John Locke, and Jean-Jacques Rousseau which have left a permanent impression; those modern titans expressed such a variety of points of view that a comprehensive understanding of their writings could amount to the work of a lifetime. So whenever I think as a political theorist, there is implicitly in the back of my mind what all the great writers on social thought have been concerned with.

An intellectual dinner party, at which Plato and Aristotle, and all their successors, had been invited, would be the ideal imaginary occasion for a book. If I suggest that for such an event silver should be set out, crystal in place, and china arrayed on linen tablecloth, what I mean is that at some such formal occasion an encounter with the most significant figures in the history of political theory would require an immense amount of preparation and decorum. Although there might be some disagreement about just who should be invited to be an imaginary guest, that would not be the main problem with under-taking such a get-together. And I do not even want to think what kind of topics, the intellectual food, would be suitable for the inevitably different tastes. The variety of languages would entail a bevy of trans-lators for such a gathering. But the job of understanding the various points of view, in the light of the disparate historical conditions under which the thinkers had been used to living, adds up to an intimidating array of problems.

xii

In *Political Theory and the Psychology of the Unconscious* I have a more modest endeavour in mind. When I started out studying political theory in the mid-1950s it was more or less a commonplace that political theory was in decline, if not simply dead. In fact Hannah Arendt once proclaimed: 'Our tradition of political thought had its definite beginning in the teachings of Plato and Aristotle. I believe it came to a no less definite end in the theories of Karl Marx.'[3] I think Arendt was demonstrably wrong on this point, and that Max Weber, for example, even though he might appear to be a sociologist, was also providing a central challenge to Marx which attempted to re-instate the centrality of politics as a vocation in a way which would be familiar to any student of Machiavelli. So part of the basis for the premature announcement of the death of political theory was caused by undue narrowness. Weber may have seemed centrally concerned with the sociology of religion, and its effects on economic life, but he had undertaken his writings out of a burning concern with the bases of national greatness, which was a familiar theme in the history of political thought.

My own special research has been on Freud, and how he too ranks, like Weber, as one of the most recent figures in the story of social philosophy. It is not hard to think of Freud in connection with Nietzsche and Schopenhauer, or Plato and Augustine for that matter. Whenever I have worked on the implications of Freud's thought, the main participants in the whole history of social thought have been present in my mind. In *Political Theory and the Psychology of the Unconscious* I have started off with John Stuart Mill as a pivotal figure in the development of modern liberalism; no one should contest his importance, even if hard-headed Marxists might not appreciate his tensions and spiritual inclinations. After dealing with Mill, in the context of his discontent with his Benthamite background, I move on to Nietzsche in order to demonstrate the philosophic and psychological analogies between Freud and this powerful leader in modern thought. Nietzsche was critical of British utilitarianism in a way which differed from Mill's own revisions of that tradition of thinking. And then finally I bring in Dostoevsky, so similar in some ways to Nietzsche, and yet writing from such a special perspective. Nietzsche actually read some of Dostoevsky, but only after Nietzsche had already developed his most distinctive ideas. Again Benthamism can be seen as a backdrop to Dostoevsky's reasoning.

Now the stage is set for Freud's ideas themselves. But having encountered Mill, Nietzsche, and Dostoevsky, I think what Freud had to say will seem more automatically a part of the main tradition of political thought. And yet perhaps the real case for Freud's standing within the history of political theory can only be established when one sees how some of the inheritors of his school of thought have proceeded to go about their business. He was reluctant to spell out the philosophical dimensions to his psychology, while some of his indirect pupils were more willing to link up with modern ideas about society and politics. And so I have separate chapters on Erich Fromm, Bruno Bettelheim, and Erik H. Erikson as a way of establishing how rich a contribution psychoanalysis can make to political theory. Even though both Berlin and Arendt would have, for different reasons, found this sort of psychoanalytic psychology an unwelcome guest within the world of political philosophy, I think Freud and his school deserve to belong as part of the great tradition of political theory.

The reader is being offered here a more informal gathering than that at which the greatest and most acknowledged philosophers can be present. By admitting Freud and the school of thought he started into the world of social philosophy I think that it will become more evident what political thought has been about all along. Freud was being as explicit as possible about the importance of having a theory of human nature, even if he was unusually reserved about drawing out the most general implications of his postulation of the significance of unconscious motivation. In my interpretations of Mill, Nietzsche, and Dostoevsky I will be trying to show how psychoanalytic matters can be considered central to understanding what they were interested in dealing with. Open-mindedness about who is relevant to the study of political theory should help keep the subject alive, and at the same time expand our appreciation of what earlier thinkers were dealing with.

Thirty years of university teaching underlies the conception of this book. For all that time I tried to introduce students to the study of political theory by means of a large lecture course on 'Psychology and Politics' which was organized essentially along the lines of *Political Theory and the Psychology of the Unconscious*. My objective was not to promote any particular ideological line; it has always been my conviction that radical and conservative, as well as liberal, conclusions can be drawn from the examination of the psychology of the depths which Freud first undertook. But I had hoped that by meeting up with these relatively recent writers, it might be easier to appreciate what the earlier thinkers had been preoccupied with. And so Freud leads back not just to Mill, Nietzsche, and Dostoevsky, but to Rousseau, Spinoza and Socrates as well as many others. To the extent that I have managed to get my interest in the historiography of psychoanalysis, where it is remarkably easy to be original, out of my system, I hope to have time left to return to studying the most widely acknowledged thinkers.

For reasons which I have continued to fail to understand, Freud remains largely outside the traditional canon of the study of political theory. To work on him has been for me to commit a kind of professional heresy, as I ignored various threats about what it would mean for my future. In the world I started out in, the creator of psychoanalysis was apt to be dismissed as the author of daffy ideas, and despite the fact that a wide range of social theorists during the last hundred years or so have been influenced by him, his work remains in a kind of limbo so that students of political theory are rarely expected to be knowledgeable about it. Serious political theorists will unashamedly admit to not having even read him. The problem cannot be just a question of how short a period has passed since his death in 1939, since a variety of lesser continental thinkers have attracted a good deal of the scholarship connected with twentieth-century political thought.

It is not necessary to propagandize on behalf of any part of psychoanalysis to see it as a doctrine in the history of ideas that demands scholarly scrutiny. The practice of psychoanalysis has recently encountered some especially heavy weather, but not in those places where philosophy and psychoanalytic thought have been kept together. I was sure forty years ago of the importance of Freud's writings, and little has shaken that early conviction of mine.

The last part of the *Political Theory and the Psychology of the Unconscious*, where I deal with Fromm, Bettelheim, and Erikson, becomes far more informal and personal than anything that comes before. For I try to describe my own encounters with these thinkers, including whatever my disappointments were with them. I have sometimes worried about whether my writings over the years have justified my youthful decision about what I chose to study. All the blinkers which clinicians of different ideological schools wear can be discouraging. But then sectarianism among traditional political theorists is no less marked.

In our culture as a whole Freud is generally acknowledged to have been the greatest psychologist of this past century, and whatever his many mistakes he will remain outstanding as a writer. I have been able to lecture on him in Russia, Argentina, Uruguay, Mexico, Japan, and Hong Kong, as well as Britain, Europe and North America. His volumes of correspondence will eventually dwarf in size the *Standard Edition of the Complete Psychological Works of Freud* which James Strachey edited. If somewhere around 25,000 of Freud's letters have survived the upheavals of two world wars, that is testimony to his capacities as a stylist which cannot be legitimately ignored.

Although an immense secondary literature surrounding Freud has grown up, professional legitimization among political theorists is still lacking. Hopefully *Political Theory and the Psychology of the Unconscious* will help demonstrate how central questions raised by psychoanalysis are to political theory. And perhaps in the future it will be easier for political philosophers to dare risk ridicule by taking Freud and his followers seriously. Without in any way reducing the scope of political theory by this proposed engagement with psychoanalysis, I believe that our understanding of past thinkers can only be enhanced by an examination of what the psychoanalysts have been concerned with. For example, notions of freedom, authority, aggression, and also selfhood, are central to the political theorists' world; yet too rarely have the strengths (as well as the limitations) of psychoanalysis been used to enlarge our knowledge of the history of ideas. A life spent in search of an education hopefully has to mean a process of broadening, even if a finite set of preoccupations must be characteristic of one's time and place. Perhaps the most rewarding aspect of studying political and social thought is how it draws one out, enabling one to question aspects of reality that are usually taken for granted. Genuine ethical enquiry starts, and I think should end, with a sense of enduring perplexity, which helps diminish the possibility of unthinking partisanship. I feel unusually lucky about the course my work has taken, and hope that *Political Theory and the Psychology of the Unconscious* may communicate some of the genuine excitement connected with the life of the mind.

NOTES

1. Paul Roazen, *Freud: Political and Social Thought*, 3rd edition, with new Introduction (New Brunswick, N.J., Transaction, 1999), p. 9.
2. Louis Hartz, *The Necessity of Choice: Nineteenth Century Political Thought*, edited, compiled, and prepared by Paul Roazen (New Brunswick, N.J., Transaction, 1990).
3. Hannah Arendt, *Between Past and Present: Eight Exercises in Political Thought* (New York, Penguin Books, 1977), p. 17.

Part One

Three Critics of
Utilitarianism

John Stuart Mill
and Liberalism

The history of political and social thought can be understood in terms of a series of epic intellectual confrontations. To take only some of the most famous controversial exchanges: Aristotle challenged Plato, Machiavelli reacted by subverting late medieval thinking, Locke specifically wrote to oppose Filmer, Rousseau implicitly crossed swords with Hobbes, Paine tangled with Burke, in addition to how, as I have suggested, Weber's whole sociological system can be seen as an extended answer to Marx. One good way of approaching the subject of political philosophy would be in terms of how each thinker has been dealing with a previous writer or school of thought whose works are held to be in need either of replacing or of radical revision.

So the tale of political theory as it has persisted over the centuries can hardly be understood in a social or historical vacuum. The work of each of these philosophers arose under concrete conditions, and often biographies can be helpful in providing the flesh-and-blood knowledge that helps make ideas vital and alive. Such thinkers have over the centuries been trying to relate human needs to the demands of social life, and one way of accomplishing such an objective has been to reflect on how we conceive of things. Examining the most basic premises of social thought has become one of the hallmarks by which we detect the characteristic activity we understand as political philosophy. And different psychological conceptions about people, as held by various major thinkers, have centrally affected their views on the role of human beings in society. Hugh Trevor-Roper long ago forcibly made the case on behalf of the significance of concepts of human nature for understanding politics:

1

> The study of history and politics is primarily the study of men, and ...
> all political theory and political science must begin with a clear view
> of the psychology of man, at least in certain aspects of his behaviour.
> All the great and effective political theorists have recognized this.
> Hobbes began his political theory with a psychological theory – his
> mechanical, despotic state was devised for a mechanical, fear-driven
> humanity. John Locke and his eighteenth century followers advocated
> political freedom – i.e. non-intervention by government – on the
> assumption that man was naturally good and self-improving and that
> his economic activities were naturally helpful to society; while the
> seventeenth century philosophers whom he challenged had proceeded
> from an opposite assumption. The same point can be made indefinitely.
> Political theory which does not start from a theory of man is in my
> view quite worthless.[1]

Most practising political theorists would have to agree with Trevor-
Roper, but almost none have concretely followed up on the implications of his argument.

For instance, John Stuart Mill (1806–73) was not one of history's
great system-builders, but his writings represent a turning point in
modern liberalism, and one which crucially hinged on his particular
psychological views. His involvement with Jeremy Bentham (1748–
1832), one of the great figures of the European Enlightenment, was
not just philosophic and political but intensely personal. John Stuart
Mill's father, James Mill, became one of Bentham's loyal followers
and most successful synthesizers. John Stuart Mill's upbringing went
along Benthamite lines, and has become legendary for how ration-
alistically a child can be educated. John Stuart Mill started to learn
Greek at three, Latin and arithmetic at eight, logic at twelve, and
political economy at thirteen. He later implied that this over-
stimulation of his intellect had left him emotionally starved. But his
father, described by one historian as 'a secular puritan',[2] had not just
helped expound the psychological principles implicit in Bentham's
outlook, but had also convinced Bentham to advocate the liberalization
of the electoral franchise in order to accomplish Bentham's utilitarian
reforms.[3] (Bentham had started out, like Voltaire, as an advocate of
enlightened despotism.)

After the deaths of Bentham in 1832 and James Mill in 1836, John
Stuart Mill published an 1838 essay about Bentham which joined the

growing clamour against the founder of the utilitarian school of thought. He singled out among Bentham's flaws as a philosopher 'the incompleteness of his own mind as a representative of universal human nature'. John Stuart Mill's indictment of Bentham became psychologically damning:

> In many of the most natural and strongest feelings of human nature he had no sympathy; from many of its graver experiences he was altogether cut off; and the faculty by which one mind understands a mind different from itself, and throws itself into the feelings of that other mind, was denied him, by his deficiency of Imagination.[4]

Mill was objecting to how Bentham's knowledge of human nature was too narrowly limited. He found it

> wholly empirical; and the empiricism of one who has had little experience. He had neither internal experience nor external; the quiet, even tenor of his life, and his healthiness of mind, conspired to exclude him from both. He never knew prosperity and adversity, passion nor satiety; he never had even the experiences which sickness gives, – he lived from childhood to the age of eighty-five in boyish health.[5]

Mill's assault on his father's great mentor moved from the intensely personal to the most general rejection of the heart of Bentham's abstractions:

> He knew no dejection, no heaviness of heart. He never felt life a sore and a weary burthen. He was a boy to the last . . . How much of human nature slumbered in him he knew not, neither can we know. He had never been made alive to the unseen influences which were acting on himself, nor consequently on his fellow creatures . . . Knowing so little of human feelings, he knew still less of the influences by which those feelings are formed. . . .[6]

Despite all this criticism John Stuart Mill could notably acknowledge the merits of Bentham's kind of tunnel vision:

> To reject his half of the truth because he overlooked the other half, would be to fall into his error without having his excuse. For our own part, we have a large tolerance for one-eyed men, provided that their

3

one eye is a penetrating one; if they saw more, they probably would not see so keenly, nor so eagerly pursue one course of inquiry. Almost all veins of original and striking speculation have been opened by systematic half-minds. . . .[7]

Still, John Stuart Mill's generosity toward Bentham's sort of single-mindedness was consistent with Mill's proposing that the inadequacies of Bentham's theory of human nature was a central flaw in his way of thinking.

At this point it may be well to remind ourselves, in the face of Mill's memorable onslaught, of the undoubted merits of Bentham's original point of view. Bentham's literary output, steadily maintained over so many years, was so vast that a large amount of what he wrote still remains unpublished. It is clear, though, that he was a great opponent of social hypocrisy, and by means of ridicule he denounced the traditionalistic defences of the *status quo* of any semblance of rationality. Bentham once amusingly debunked the concept of natural law by appealing to an optical image; he described two rays of light talking to one another as they approached a window pane, one warning the other of the punishment that would be meted out if they refracted at the wrong angle.[8] Bentham was deliberately anthropo-morphizing nature, to show how dubious the concept of 'natural law' could be. He was a dangerous controversialist, and once unforgettably characterized the notion of natural rights as being 'nonsense on stilts'. Bentham enjoyed pricking puffed-up balloons of pretentiousness.

Bentham's contempt for what he regarded as the prevalence of ancestor-worship led him to characterize lawyers in a way which has never been bettered in the literature of polemics. He described them as

a passive and enervate race, ready to swallow any thing, and to ac-quiesce in any thing: with intellects incapable of distinguishing right from wrong, and with affections alike indifferent to either: insensible, short-sighted, obstinate: lethargic, yet liable to be driven into con-vulsions of false terrors: deaf to the voice of reason and public utility: obsequious only to the whisper of interest, and to the beck of power.[9]

Bentham was so far ahead of his time as to have written over five hundred manuscript pages on the issue of homosexuality; he thought that before an act is criminalized it should be established that it does produce social harm. Madame de Staël went so far as to think 'that the era should be called not the age of Napoleon or the age of Byron but the age of Bentham'.[10]

When Mill criticized Bentham, he was not simply settling a personal score; Benthamism was a movement worth contending with. Throughout all the disputes that make up the history of political philosophy, scholars are agreed on the enduring importance of the central problem of obligation: why should anybody obey political authority? (This was at the heart of Socrates's final deliberations.) A variety of different answers have been offered: God, nature, history, the social contract, legitimacy and fear are only a few of the main responses to the single question of what justifies obedience. Bentham succeeded in offering an original principle of his own – utility. For he thought that one should always ask of social and political institutions: who stands to benefit by them? And so Bentham insisted on the central significance of the concept of interest, and he defined his utilitarian standard in terms of that which satisfied the greatest good of the greatest number.[11]

Now John Stuart Mill was hardly alone in his own assault on Bentham; Charles Dickens in his *Hard Times* (1854) relentlessly went after the implications of utilitarianism for the education of the young, and not surprisingly Marx loathed Bentham's thinking. In the face of these multiple criticisms of Bentham it is therefore worth remembering that in his long life Bentham had been a memorable critic and challenger of the English legal system. His 1776 *A Fragment of Government*, originally published anonymously, is still being studied today; the enemy of that tract, Sir William Blackstone, lost out in the long run among intellectuals.[12] Bentham could be a great stylist, and a relentless publicist, dispelling pompous nonsense through the acid effects of his use of rationality. He insisted that the goal of the state was to maximize human happiness, and the principle of utility was the banner of the school of thought he went on to found. Utilitarianism has gone on to retain a surprising vitality in late twentieth-century philosophy and social science.

Benthamism as a doctrine had arisen against a corrupt and inefficient political and legal system, and at the outset spoke on behalf of the needs of everyday people. At a later time Benthamite thinking may have served to reinforce some of the most mechanical tendencies of the modern world, but in the beginning Bentham was idealistically using self-interest in the service of a noble conception. The principle of utility meant that one should measure pains and pleasures in order to achieve the greatest happiness of the greatest number. But on behalf of this worthy purpose Bentham had deliberately to down-play the subjective, the inner dimension of experience, for otherwise the whole pleasure–pain calculus would not hold up. Utility was supposedly less subjective and capricious than the conservatively used standard of natural law which Blackstone had relied on. As H.L.A. Hart once explained how actual, or 'positive' law, could expect to escape conflicting with Blackstone's vacuous version of natural law:

> It is clear that very little could fail to pass the test that Blackstone proposes for the institution of positive law since for him the law of nature consists almost wholly of gaps: it is a net through which virtually everything must fall. I know of no other example of this indirect use of the doctrine of the law of nature to stifle criticism by applying to positive law an empty test and triumphantly drawing the conclusion that the institution under criticism has passed the test because it does not contradict any of its provisions. But it is perhaps plain why Bentham was so angry.[13]

Bentham stood for the rationalistic dissolution of society based on such insidiously traditionalist thinking. Reasons should have to be given for any law or a specific custom. History itself was held by Bentham (like Voltaire) to be merely the dusty record of the crimes and follies of mankind. The course of human progress, which he did not doubt was inevitable, could only be held back by the mistakes of the past, as well as the fraud and deceits which mankind's enemies had perpetrated. Bentham would not be alone among those who have been eager to accomplish external social reforms but neglected the significance of the subtle complexities of individual psychology.

In John Stuart Mill's posthumously published *Autobiography* (1873) he had given even more personal substance to his earlier indictment of Benthamism. He blamed his father for the Benthamite way in which he had been reared. 'For passionate emotions of all sorts, for everything which has been said and written in exaltation of them, he professed the greatest contempt. He regarded them as a form of madness.' John Stuart Mill went on: ' "The intense" was with him a byeword of scornful disapprobation.'

6

He regarded as an aberration of the moral standard of modern times, compared with that of the ancients, the great stress laid upon feeling. Feelings as such, he considered to be no proper subjects of praise or blame. Right and wrong, good and bad, he regarded as qualities solely of conduct – of acts and omissions; there being no feeling which may not lead, and does not frequently lead, either to good or to bad actions: conscience itself, the very desire to act rightly, often leading people to act wrong.

Mill was unremitting in his bleak account of his father as a man and a thinker:

Consistently carrying out the doctrine, that the object of praise and blame should be the discouragement of wrong conduct and the encouragement of right, he refused to let his praise or blame be influenced by the motive of the agent. He blamed as severely what he thought a bad action, when the motive was a feeling of duty, as if the agents had been consciously evil doers.

Mill's critique of Benthamism, as embodied in the character of James Mill, should send a chill to all subsequent fathers: 'The element which was chiefly deficient in his moral relation to his children was that of tenderness.' John Stuart Mill was contrasting his own reaction to his father with that of his siblings: 'They loved him tenderly; and if I cannot say so of myself, I was always loyally devoted to him.' It does seem to be remarkable that John Stuart Mill did not appear to realize just how dreadful he had made out his father to have been, nor how unintentionally revealing he may have been about his own restricted capacity for love.[14]

John Stuart Mill described how as a young man Benthamism had once been 'the keystone' of his beliefs: 'It gave unity to my conceptions of things. I now had opinions; a creed, a doctrine, a philosophy; in one among the best senses of the word, a religion; the inculcation and diffusion of which could be made the principal outward purpose of a life.' And then, at the age of twenty, he underwent a collapse of his early political faith; he had asked himself:

'Suppose that all your objects in life were realized; that all the changes in institutions and opinions which you are looking forward to, could be completely effected at this very instant: would this be a great joy and happiness to you?' And an irrepressible self consciousness distinctly answered, 'No!' At this my heart sank within me: the whole foundation on which my life was constructed fell down. All my happiness was to have been found in the continual pursuit of this end. The end had ceased to charm, and how could there ever again be any interest in the means? I seemed to have nothing left to live for.[15]

This account of his loss of his early utilitarian convictions, when his 'object in life' had been to be 'a reformer of the world', appeared in Chapter V of Mill's *Autobiography*; it was titled both 'A Crisis in My Mental History' and 'One Stage Onward'. Mill was telling his readers that he did undergo a major depression, but that it had had a long-term beneficial effect on his thinking. He had felt 'left stranded at the commencement' of his 'voyage, with a well-equipped ship and a rudder, but no sail . . . .' The period of 'the dry heavy dejection' lasted through 'the melancholy winter of 1826–27'.[16]

Then a turning point came in a way likely to make a traditional Freudian, believing in the enduring significance of the Oedipus complex, wryly smile.[17] For Mill 'accidentally' happened to read some memoirs in which the author related 'his father's death, the distressed position of the family, and the sudden inspiration by which he, then a mere boy, felt and made them feel that he would be everything to them – would supply the place of all that they had lost'. Mill reported that 'a vivid conception of the scene and its feelings came over me, and I was moved to tears. From this moment my burden grew lighter. The oppression of the thought that all feeling was dead within me, was gone. I was no longer hopeless; I was not a stock or a stone.'

Mill maintained that 'the cloud gradually drew off', and that he 'again enjoyed life: and though I had several relapses, some of which lasted many months, I never again was as miserable as I had been'. Mill was convinced that this 'mental crisis' had succeeded in enriching his thinking in the direction of psychological depth:

> I, for the first time, gave its proper place, among the prime necessities of human well-being, to the internal culture of the individual. I ceased to attach almost exclusive importance to the ordering of outward circumstances, and the training of the human being for speculation and for action. I had now learnt by experience that the passive susceptibilities needed to be cultivated as well as the active capacities, and required to be nourished and enriched as well as guided.

This new awareness on Mill's part of the importance of what he called 'the internal culture of the individual' helps explain his stinging indictments of Bentham, James Mill, and utilitarian psychology as a whole. 'The cultivation of the feelings,' Mill reported, 'became one of the cardinal points in my ethical and philosophical creed.'[18]

The intensity of his critique of Benthamite reasoning implies to me some persisting self-criticism on John Stuart Mill's part. For despite what he would elsewhere write about the value of diversity of spirit, and the glowing picture of the fully-realized individual that he would paint in his *On Liberty* (1859), Mill's own private life was tame if not dull. He was intensely bothered by the Victorian scandal of his relation with Mrs. Harriet Taylor, about which Thomas Carlyle notably gossiped. But Harriet's husband lived a long while, and the relation between Mill and her remained platonic; after John Taylor finally died, Mill and Harriet were able to get married, but by then they were both aging and in ill health; Harriet died shortly thereafter. Mill's letters to Harriet have seemed to me almost unreadably boring.[19] Nevertheless he did report a change in himself as a result of his early 'mental crisis'; he came to value not rationality and contentment, but versatility, variety, and fullness of life.

Mill spent his adult years working, like his father before him, at the India Office. He also was an accomplished journalist and man of letters, even entering the House of Commons late in life. Some of his best work was written when he was under the intellectual influence of Harriet Taylor; he attributed to her almost a hypnotic control over his mind. (It has been easy to think of her having played a role substituting for the inspiration he once got from his father.) Despite the effects of his 'mental crisis', he remained hesitant and solemn, a bit of a prig, painfully grave and lacking in gaiety of spirit. Mill was one of the most unpoetic and unromantic of men, who yet wrote on behalf of poetry, originality, and romance.[20]

Mill was also a major political philosopher, and the concept of human nature was as central to his thinking as to others in the history of social ideas; the insight he reported coming to about the significance of what he called 'the internal culture of the individual', and how it affected his thinking, can help demonstrate why he had to depart from the other principles of Bentham and James Mill. For Mill began to criticize some of the rationalistic assumptions of traditional liberal political and social thought, which others later, such as

Friedrich Nietzsche and Fyodor Dostoevsky, would carry much further. Still, liberalism after John Stuart Mill would never be the same as before.

I would like to illustrate how Mill's changed view of psychology helped lead him to alter his political and social thinking in ways which were necessarily different from how Bentham and James Mill had left liberal theory. John Stuart Mill had been brought up to be a staunch utilitarian, with a set of beliefs about the rational re-ordering of the political society of his time in accordance with the principle of the greatest happiness of the greatest number. He subsequently undertook to revise utilitarian thinking in three distinct areas – representation, individualism, and majoritarianism.[21] But the tensions in his thinking persisted throughout the various ways in which he implemented his own special insights.

Mill, it will be remembered, had argued against Bentham: 'knowing so little of human feelings, he knew still less of the influences by which those feelings are formed . . .' And Mill had also said of Bentham: 'How much of human nature slumbered in him he knew not, neither can we know. He had never been made alive to the unseen influences which were acting on himself, nor consequently on his fellow creatures.' The concept of the unconscious may have been put forward by Freud at the turn of the twentieth century, but that there were many great psychologists preceding him should go almost without saying. (One of the explanations for why psychoanalysts have been so combative with one another is that their alternative notions of the unconscious were to a large degree substitutes for earlier conceptions about God. Rival conceptions about how life might best be lived have helped fuel the many controversies within psychoanalysis.)

Especially among theologians have issues been traditionally raised which since Freud are usually associated with psychoanalytic thinking; what once were treated as religious problems later tended to be brought under the rubric of psychology. (The term 'psychology' originated in the sixteenth century, but had little success until the eighteenth century; today's general meaning of 'psychology' dates from about the middle of the nineteenth century.) Freud certainly saw religion as an enemy, and a rival to what he aimed to accomplish. He explicitly thought of his work as the secularization of religion, and making scientific what had earlier been literary insights. We shall see how the postulation of unconscious mental forces can help make

10

explicit the changes John Stuart Mill was trying to make in liberal social and political thinking.

Let us start by looking at the notion of representation. Jean-Jacques Rousseau had once memorably maintained that Englishmen are only free on election day; as he put it in his *Social Contract* (1762):

> The English people think that they are free, but in this belief they are profoundly wrong. They are free only when they are electing members of Parliament. Once the election has been completed, they revert to a condition of slavery: they are nothing. Making such use of it in the few short moments of their freedom, they deserve to lose it.[22]

Rousseau's idea, sceptical of all representative government, has had a long and vigorous life. (Marxist thinking, after all, implies that it is impossible for government, no matter how idealistically proclaimed, to become independent of the ruling class; for Marx politics is reflexive of class conflict.) Bentham as a reformer had started out, as we have said, no advocate of representation but in favour of en-lightened despotism; the reforms he wanted to accomplish could best, he initially believed, be put into place by the help of the crowned heads of state. After years of failing to convince these hereditary monarchs of the desirability of his suggestions, and under the in-fluence of James Mill, Bentham came to believe in the merits of democracy. One of the greatest contributions of nineteenth century English liberal political theory was to be the argument justifying democracy.

In James Mill's essay 'On Government' (1820), which appeared originally in the *Encyclopaedia Britannica*, he made the classic case for democracy.[23] He started off by assuming, in accordance with the utilitarian psychological assumption about the universality of egoism, that those who govern can be expected to be self-interested. In fact he thought that governors will exploit the people for their own advantage. He was, as John Stuart Mill had maintained, interested in conduct, not feelings. It followed then for James Mill that the only way to prevent those who have power from misusing it is to enable the potential victims to be able to unseat and displace the rulers. James Mill was proposing the principle of alternatives; politically, two evils are immensely better than one. Through the device of elections, the self-interest of the rulers can be fused with that of the ruled. For James Mill democracy was a system by means of which human badness can be converted into political goodness.

11

Some of the key assumptions in James Mill's proposal require critical reflection. For one thing his whole approach assumes the rationality of the voters to perceive their own advantage. An astonishing number of people seem at least sometimes to vote at odds with what experts might think of as their enlightened self-interest. It may still be an open question whether voters can be rational enough to fulfil the expectations of the kind of democratic theory that James Mill had faith in. (I am taking rationality to mean being able to pick the appropriate means to accomplish a given objective.) Just as the rationality of voters may be in doubt, so is that of the rulers themselves; James Mill's theory assumes that those who govern will bend to what is in their self-interest.

Furthermore, James Mill's approach takes for granted the rationality of the majority, namely that it will not be in its interest to tyrannize over a minority. If you are in a minority, it may make little difference whether it is a monarch who threatens to destroy you or a majority of the voters. Democracy has at least the potential for being worse for minorities, rendering elections a hollow form of leverage. Madame de Staël believed in fact that 'liberty is ancient', while 'despotism is modern', an aphorism which has too frequently proven true. Democracy makes possible a more monolithic impact of the majority on minorities than was ever possible before.

John Stuart Mill's reasoning saw that a functioning democracy requires much more than just formal checks on power. If rulers were as bad as James Mill supposed, as self-interested as he had thought, then the populace would never be able to get the system back once a set of governors had been established. Instead of elections making possible an alteration in elites, a permanent ruling class might arise. Self-interest is not as simple a concept as one might like to think. What is in the self-interest of a stockbroker, a salesman, or a manufacturer may be very different from self-interest as defined by a doctor, lawyer, teacher or professional writer. Advantage gets constructed out of one's values and beliefs. So in the case of political leaders, other social psychological forces – besides the strict fear of elections and the possibility of defeat – limit the power that democratic rulers can exercise.

National political cultures, provided that one does not invoke such notions mystically, become a very important political and social variable. People in any given society have characteristic consciences, which are made up of values, beliefs, and expectations which are typical for a particular political community. The police, for example, function differently in Britain as opposed to America, and this is at least partly a question of national character, and a different basic set of attitudes toward the state. Mill brought up phenomena like the sense of duty and feelings of philanthropy in the section on 'Logic of the Moral Sciences' in his *Logic*.

Customs, institutions, and moral traditions stemming from the past produce a sense of obligation that can be politically crucial. But these are just the sorts of intangible inner influences which Bentham so hated. Without taking them into account, however, it might be difficult to explain, for example, the timing of President Richard Nixon's resignation from the presidency. (Had he been impeached and convicted, he would have lost all sorts of perks that went with his having held office; but it was the 'smoking gun' found on the White House tapes that meant his political support evaporated, and he was reliably informed just how dire the situation had become.) Britain has been able to function democratically without a written constitution at all; convictions about 'what is done' as opposed to 'what is not done' are bound to be powerful in any successful democratic system. In addition to the Benthamite checks that James Mill had in mind, which do make up the formal rules of the game, there have to be more elusive psychological forces at play as well. And it was conscience as an element in human psychology which John Stuart Mill charged Bentham with having overlooked.

The power of history and tradition, basically a conservative rather than a liberal insight, amounted to a rejection of the Benthamite approach which saw them as the sum of errors and follies of past generations. Societies endure over time precisely because their members are socialized at relatively early ages; national character is made up of shared values and beliefs. And John Stuart Mill was prescient in thinking about the importance of what political scientists today know as 'political culture'. He was onto the whole issue of nationalism, and how seductive a force it can be. (Bentham and Marx together missed the significance of this powerful modern phenomenon; Freud too could not acknowledge its conceptual importance, and like them he universalized his insights.) A community is founded on emotions, as opposed to pure reason and self-interest. Symbols of national unity, the presence of heroes for example, help maintain deep historical ties.

John Stuart Mill was right in being unwilling to accept the Benthamite idea that societies are fictitious bodies created by people for the sake of promoting their self-interests.

John Stuart Mill also felt forced to go on to broaden the whole conception of individualism that he had inherited from his utilitarian predecessors. He wrote *On Liberty* in the great tradition of John Milton's *Areopagitica* (1644). John Stuart Mill wanted to expand the whole utilitarian conception of the self, so that freedom was understood as beyond just being a matter of civil and political liberties. He was proposing that human development be promoted in its richest diversity, as he appealed back to the ancient Greek ideal of the right and duty of self-development. Here again psychoanalysis, with its current notions of the 'true' as opposed to the 'false' self, would feel at home. But Mill was necessarily introducing a host of subjective considerations that the Benthamites had hoped to have definitively banished. He believed that people are improved by their capacity to make choices; and therefore they need to have the right to make their own mistakes. He had entered an area where neither Blackstone nor Bentham would have been comfortable following him.

John Stuart Mill defended intellectual freedom in a thoroughgoing way. To begin with, the truth may lie in unpopular opinions. Secondly, even if an idea that gets advanced be false, liberty of opinion gives strength to the truth through the criticism that falsehood provides. Mill also held that no opinion can ever be completely true, and that partial truths each contain valuable insights; Mill was advancing a kind of dialectical conception of liberty, one alien to the world of the Benthamites. Even if an opinion were wholly true, it requires the challenge of opposition if it is to retain its vigour and vitality.

Few societies have ever lived up to John Stuart Mill's libertarian ideals. Hitler's *Mein Kampf*, for example, is banned today as a book in France and Germany. And North American colleges have standards of political correctness which look with harsh disfavour on any thinking that smacks of racism; I am thinking, for instance, of the unpopularity of I.Q. studies which purport to relate intelligence to race or national origins. The whole notion of hate-crimes would seem to run contrary to the ideal principles that John Stuart Mill set forth. His notion that his mental crisis could be 'one stage onward' reflected a general complacency about progress. I doubt that many of us really believe in the value of free speech for neo-Nazis. The success of Hitler in gaining power democratically in Weimar Germany, essentially within the existing political rules of the game, ought to make us unsure whether the truth will in fact win out in the free market place of ideas.

But John Stuart Mill proposed the most stringent standards against the deprivation of liberty: 'the sole end for which mankind are warranted, individually or collectively, in interfering with the liberty of action of any of their number, is self-protection.' He tried to distinguish between actions which were other-regarding as opposed to those which are self-regarding: 'the only freedom which deserves the name, is that of pursuing our own good in our own way, so long as we do not attempt to deprive others of theirs, or impede their efforts to obtain it.' Mill had a radically negative conception of freedom, one which modern psychology might have trouble going along with. On what grounds is one entitled, for instance, to interfere with a suicidal act? John Stuart Mill maintained that 'the only purpose for which power can be rightly exercised over any member of a civilized community, against his will, is to prevent harm to others. His own good, either physical or moral, is not a sufficient warrant.'[24]

But our religious heritage, as well as modern psychiatry, sustain the tradition that to attempt suicide should continue to be illegal; and there are examples of people who decide to change their minds, but it proves too late to reverse an earlier decision. It is also hard to know how Mill's approach could square with much contemporary welfare or social security legislation, and even pension plans; such programmes usually rest on the assumption that individuals cannot be relied upon to take care of themselves, and could not work effectively if they were not compulsory. John Stuart Mill's apparent break with the utilitarian tradition proves more cautious than his indictments of its psychological principles might suggest. Strict Benthamism led to the ideal of a surprisingly circumscribed state, something like a night-watchman.

Whether or not one can go as far as Mill would like in his individualistic direction, he had learned something crucial from his own reaction against utilitarian education. Even in our own time rationalists like B.F. Skinner and others have been inclined to promote utopian, and ultimately authoritarian, forms of child-rearing. But Mill insisted instead that 'human nature is not a machine to be built after a model, and set to do exactly the work prescribed for it, but a tree, which requires to grow and develop itself on all sides, according to the tendency of the inward forces which make it a living thing.'[25] Such a

15

Romantic-sounding principle could find no place within Benthamite psychology.

In also warning that it might be rational for majorities to tyrannize over minorities, John Stuart Mill had touched on the basic problem of social conformism. Unlike the Benthamite kind of legislative calculations of pleasures and pains for the sake of promoting happiness, Mill saw threats to autonomy arising from within modern society. He was aware of the presence of insidiously conformist social pressures, and saw how they can undermine individualism as surely as any explicit legal regulations.

Mill was taking the issue of majoritarianism to a deeper level: it was not just a mathematical question of the majority dominating over a numerical minority. And James Madison's solution in *The Federalist* (1787–88), to expand the size of a country to help control separate minorities, was a practical gimmick that could not reach the extent of the problem as Mill saw it. He was worried about the impact of the majority being so great that the minority never even thinks of the possibility of defiance. Mill was raising the dangers of standardization, what he called the possibility of 'enslaving the soul itself'.[26] Alexis de Tocqueville was worrying about the same issue in France; John Stuart Mill publicly hailed Tocqueville's great study *Democracy in America* (1835–40), and the two men corresponded.

Mill believed that 'the greatest harm done is to those who are not heretics, and whose whole mental development is cramped, and their reason cowed, by their fear of heresy.' Mill's *On Liberty* can be read as a sermon on behalf of non-conformity, as he pleaded for the broadest possible diversity of opinion. 'If all mankind minus one, were of one opinion, and only one person were of the contrary opinion, mankind would be no more justified in silencing that one person, than he, if he had the power, would be justified in silencing mankind.'[27] He worried about the danger, not of the excess, but of the deficiency of personal impulses and preferences. Mass societies contain unique possibilities for the stifling of individuality; the rise of individualism, as Erich Fromm would argue in *Escape From Freedom*, can pave the way for the worst forms of collectivism. The old corporate societies of pre-Revolutionary Europe, as in France, had been rich in local diversity and variety.

Mill, however, was neither a great psychologist nor a profound system-builder; in fact he was not a particularly integrated thinker, which is one of the grounds for finding him so attractive. For he was an honest man struggling to express his various insights, even if with hindsight they appear contradictory. But it behoves us as students of intellectual history to be aware of what he could not always see.

Mill never acknowledged that a certain degree of psychological uniformity is essential to modern democracy. The psychological majoritarianism he feared was in fact one of the foundations for the political democracy that he wanted. Psychological and political individualism may be inherently at odds with each other. To have civil liberties at all, a certain degree of psychological conformity has to be essential. This is admittedly an unhappy thought, but realism demands that we appreciate it.

For when one gets real differences over the ultimate norms of society, there is likely to be a state of anarchy or civil war, which in turn can elicit politically despotic forces to settle the disputes. The history of the nineteenth and twentieth centuries did not fulfil the progress that John Stuart Mill had taken for granted. At various times democracies have collapsed in Spain, Italy, Germany, France, and elsewhere; Russia seems depressingly to have got nowhere over the last hundred years. And there may be more political prisoners in Algeria today than under French imperial rule. As a matter of fact, looking at the world today one would have to say that political democracy remains more the exception rather than the rule.

Such a proposition, about the relative rarity of successful democracy, has nothing to do with the mumbo-jumbo of hot-house academic thinking which supposes that totalitarianism and political liberalism are somehow inherently inter-connected. No worse form of totalitarian tyranny has ever existed than that under Stalin in the old Soviet Union; it does not require much argument to establish the extreme weakness of liberalism in Russia prior to the Bolshevik seizure of power. Stalin could flourish precisely because of the relative absence of liberal impediments to his authoritarian abuses of power. And in Germany, the only other place where it is generally agreed that totalitarianism has existed in its most full-fledged form, it took almost a revolution for the Nazis to succeed in establishing themselves. Once the Second World War was over, it can be considered a triumph of constitutional engineering, a sort of Benthamite planning, that democracy could be re-established. Far from its being an easily made transition from the Nazis to Adenauer's republic, it required an extraordinary combination of circumstances to succeed in re-intro-ducing parliamentary life. But the examples of Russia and Germany illustrate how dependent political forms can be on extra-political factors of a social, historical and often economic character to enable democracy to flourish. A constitutional political system rests on the existence of social variables that the original authors of democracy, including James Mill and his son John Stuart, never could have anticipated. In America James Madison was right about the new Constitution for the wrong reasons; his conception of a society torn by political conflict would in reality have imploded had it not been for the basic sorts of social unifying forces which he assumed or took for granted.

The truth is that some social coercions seem to be necessary, and an unspoken degree of moral consensus, which means silently agreed-upon values and beliefs, can be essential in order to make the toleration of opinion possible. Such a point of view is really a con-servative, or anti-liberal one, and proponents of human emancipation are unlikely to want to concede its truth. But the ability to com-promise, that essential constituent of any democracy, does not arise in a vacuum but rather flows from the presence of shared goals and commitments. In Britain Lord Balfour rather complacently maintained in 1927:

> Our alternating Cabinets, though belonging to different Parties, have never differed about the foundations of society. And it is evident that our whole political machinery pre-supposes a people so fundamentally at one that they can safely afford to bicker; and so sure of their own moderation that they are not dangerously disturbed by the never-ending din of political conflict. May it always be so.[28]

Dickens could amusingly contrast the doings of the 'outs' with the antics of the 'ins'. But Rousseau, writing in pre-Revolutionary France which was about to break apart, felt the essential value of a general will; that precarious social situation could not afford the luxuries of narrow political conflict. We are left with the dilemma that successful formal democracies may require a degree of informal authoritarianism. And despite the attractiveness of the ideals Mill expounded in *On Liberty*, regrettably we are bound to be less liberal and open-minded than we like to think.

Linking John Stuart Mill's liberalism to some modern ideas about unconscious motivation is not just a set of abstractions. For there was an intriguing set of personal circumstances bringing Freud and Mill together within intellectual history. Freud had in 1880 been asked to translate one of Mill's collections of essays into German; the editor of Mill's German works was a distinguished philosopher, Theodor Gomperz, who had been given Freud's name by one of Freud's teachers. As it happens Gomperz was in love with Harriet Taylor's daughter Helen, Mill's step-daughter. To illustrate just how small the intellectual world can be, Gomperz's wife Elise was in later years one of Freud's patients.

She was also involved in interceding on Freud's behalf with governmental officials when he finally was successful in applying for his Professorship at the turn of the twentieth century. And Heinrich Gomperz, a son of Theodor and Elise, in addition turned to Freud for help in understanding dream interpretations.

The links between Mill and Freud are not just these personal ones, but extend to the substance of their ideas. It is necessary to clear away a long-standing underbrush of confusion connected with the authorship of the four essays by Mill that Freud translated into German. According to Freud's biographer Ernest Jones: 'Three of Mill's essays were concerned with social problems: the labour question, the enfranchisement of women, and socialism. In the preface Mill said that the greatest part of these was the work of his wife. The fourth, by Mill himself, was on Grote's Plato.'[29] Jones was unreliable here, since only the piece on the enfranchisement of women (1851) should be attributed to Harriet Taylor; all the rest are by Mill, and were written after her death. The confusion surrounding the attribution of authorship has been further compounded by a tendency to mix up the 1851 essay on the enfranchisement of women with Mill's own more famous essay 'The Subjection of Women' (1869), which was not among those Freud translated.[30]

In 1883, during Freud's long engagement to be married, his wife-to-be seems to have read an essay by Georg Brandes on Mill which touched on his relations with Harriet. Freud indicated, in a letter to his fiancée which has now become famous, a serious difference between himself and Mill on the subject of women. Freud complained to his future wife about Mill's writing style in what Freud had translated. 'At the time I found fault with his lifeless style and the fact that in his work one could never find a sentence or a phrase that

19

would remain in one's memory.' But Freud was struck, in an almost uncanny sensitivity to style, by the contrast between the writing he had translated and what he read subsequently by Mill. 'But later on I read a philosophical work of his which was witty, epigrammatically apt and lively.' Freud had had a low opinion of what turned out to be a work by Harriet Taylor, not Mill. Freud wrote of Mill: 'Very possibly he was the man of the century most capable of freeing himself from the domination of the usual prejudices. As a result – and this always goes hand-in-hand – he lacked the sense of the absurd, on several points, for instance in the emancipation of women and the question of women altogether.' Freud objected to parts of the reasoning in Harriet's essay:

> I remember a main argument in the pamphlet I translated was that the married woman can earn as much as the husband. I dare say we agree that housekeeping and the care and education of children claim the whole person and practically rule out any profession; even if simplified conditions relieve the woman of housekeeping, dusting, cleaning, cooking etc. All this he simply forgot, just as he omitted all relations connected to sex.

At this point 'connected to sex' Freud's letter gets rather pointed about some of Mill's own human failings:

> This is altogether a topic on which one does not find Mill quite human. His autobiography is so prudish or so unearthy that one would never learn from it that humanity is divided between men and women, and that this difference is the most important one. His relationship to his own wife strikes one as inhuman, too. He marries her late in life, has no children from her, the question of love as we know it is never mentioned. Whether she was the wonderful person he revered is generally doubted. In all his writings it never appears that the woman is different from the man, which is not to say she is something less, if anything the opposite. For example he finds an analogy for the oppression of women in that of the Negro. Any girl, even without a vote and legal rights, whose hand is kissed by a man willing to risk his all for her love, could have put him right on this.

The intelligence of Freud's reaction to Mill's writings has been overwhelmed by two sentences of his which follow from the preceding: 'It seems a completely unrealistic notion to send women into the struggle for existence in the same way as men. Am I to think of my delicate sweet girl as a competitor?' Freud did entertain the possibility that different social conditions could radically alter the condition of women, but he feared it would mean suppressing 'all women's delicate qualities – which are so much in need of protection and yet so powerful – with the result that they could earn their living just like men.' Freud volunteered that 'it was possible' under such changed conditions that 'it would not be justifiable to deplore the disappearance of the most lovely thing the world has to offer us: our ideal of womanhood.'

> But I believe that all reforming activity, legislation and education, will founder on the fact that long before the age at which a profession can be established in our society, Nature will have appointed woman by her beauty, charm and goodness, to do something else.
>
> No, in this respect I adhere to the old ways, to my longing for my Martha as she is, and she herself will not want it different; legislation and custom have to grant to women many rights kept from them, but the position of woman cannot be other than what it is: to be an adored sweetheart in youth, and a beloved wife in maturity.[31]

Freud's wife and he were apparently in agreement, and the next published letter of his to her begins by addressing her as 'my dear princess'.[32] Freud, born in 1856, was inevitably a man of his time, yet he was – like Mill, although in different ways – pioneering in the emancipation of women. When before World War I some of Freud's younger followers wanted to exclude women from membership in the Vienna Psychoanalytic Society, he opposed them even though these anti-feminists had a sizable per cent of the vote. Whatever he said rhetorically about the need to respect their convictions, he ignored their objections, and went on to welcome women into the profession of psychoanalysis that he founded.[33] But I am not trying to weigh and assess here Freud's, or Mill's, standing in the history of the emancipation of women, so much as to isolate what Freud had to say specifically about Mill, since I am trying to elucidate what Mill's contribution to the psychology of modern liberalism amounts to.

Perhaps the closest link between Mill, liberalism, and Freud has to do with the development of a theory of individualism. Here Freud has to be put to one side, since he was so insistent in his mature years on not getting involved in what he somewhat disdainfully classified as philosophic matters. So he scarcely ever helped much on what it was that a so-called normal person was supposed to be like. But implicitly Freud was, by means of psychoanalytic therapy, trying to help people to become whole, even if he was not proposing to make people fit into any preconceived model of what a person should be like. He was not proposing that people crudely conform to outside social requirements; neurotics were in Freud's view admirable in that they were up against pre-existing societal restrictions. At the same time it was inevitable that Freud took for granted many of the social patterns which in hindsight stand out as conformist pressures that he did not challenge in trying to help his clients.

But critics of Freud have rightly seen that he gave encouragement to a special brand of modern egotism, in the form of the selfishness apt to be associated with the self-preoccupation linked to scrutinizing one's motives. The encouragement of the expression of feelings (also advocated by J.S. Mill) can make them seem inherently justified, and lead to a fresh form of self-indulgence. And I think that for all the differences Freud himself detected in his own thinking as opposed to Mill's, at least on the question of women, he and Mill both later attracted some of the same sorts of enemies. Freud has been assailed from the Left for being too reactionary about women, at the same time he has been criticized from the Right for having helped undermine traditional life, encouraging patients to choose narrowly for themselves apart from their obligations to the larger social situation. And there is truth in both sorts of accusations against Freud, as he would go to some lengths to undercut the possibilities of genuine altruism and service for others at the same time as he put himself in the category of the 'old' school about women.

John Stuart Mill has been attacked from the Left for having proposed a form of toleration of opinion which someone like Herbert Marcuse thought was inherently fraudulent if not ultimately repressive. Allowing the apparent free play of ideas gives people the illusion of free choice, reinforcing a social hierarchy which is inherently at odds with real human emancipation which Marxists inevitably see in terms of overcoming the constraints of class. But if the Left can disdain Mill for being namby-pamby, the Right has seen him as a notorious figure in having helped encourage some of the worst excesses of theories of self-development. Egotism acquired a new sort of life of its own thanks to Mill, or at least his conservative critics see it that way. If the promotion of the exquisite individuation of the self is the goal of Mill's theory, and after all some such tendency was implicit in his distancing himself from his father and Bentham, then naturally conservatives are right to see that people bent on justifying private egocentricity have been heralding Mill as a patron saint.

It seems to be the fate of liberalism to be caught between the extremes of the Left and the Right. Liberalism needs the Left's moral and ethical sensitivities just as much as the Right's empirical realism about what is ever going to be possible. Mill will always seem heroic to those who put a premium on the intrinsic value of the power of ideas. The fact that someone like Justice Oliver W. Holmes, Jr. put limits to the role of free speech does not make him any less a pioneer in the history of freedom. Yes, Holmes did say that 'the most stringent protection of free speech would not protect a man in falsely shouting fire in a theatre and causing a panic'.[34] Also, Milton's *Areopagitica*, written during the religious intolerances of the English Civil War, assumed that toleration would not be extended to Catholics. Political theory is not to be identified with sloganeering; having the socially 'correct' position is not the same as having thought through one's convictions. And few students of social philosophy would want to be identified with a Whig interpretation of history which assumes that our own time is the definitive definer of what should count toward so-called progress.

No intelligent political thinker has ever thought that freedom was without limits, and it seems to be bootless to try and tarnish Mill's liberal standing by assembling all the qualifications he made to his most central contentions in *On Liberty*. And once Holmes had got the full Supreme Court to agree unanimously in 1919 to his 'clear and present danger test' that words will bring about evils that Congress has a right to prevent, within a few years he would be dissenting (with the support of Louis D. Brandeis) from convictions on the grounds of so-called criminal anarchy. Holmes wrote: 'Every idea is an incitement.'

> It offers itself for belief and if believed it is acted on unless some other belief outweighs it or some failure of energy stifles the movement at its birth. The only difference between the expression of an opinion and an incitement in the narrower sense is the speaker's enthusiasm for the result. Eloquence may set fire to reason. But whatever may be thought of the redundant discourse before us it had no chance of starting a present conflagration.[35]

(To complicate the story-line of the history of liberal political thought, Holmes's jurisprudence was itself heavily indebted to Bentham. Toleration has to have a special standing within liberalism, and can make little comparable sense to either Marxist or conservative.)

Justice Louis D. Brandeis's liberalism was warmer, less sceptical than Holmes's (note Holmes's disdain for the 'redundant discourse' of the socialists). Still, Brandeis was in a real sense also following in the path Mill had set out; in an opinion that Holmes joined in, Brandeis wrote:

> Those who won our independence believed that the final end of the state was to make men free to develop their faculties. . . . They valued liberty both as an end and as a means. They believed liberty to be the secret of happiness and courage to be the secret of liberty. They believed that freedom to think as you will and to speak as you think are means indispensable to the discovery and spread of political truth. . . . [T]he greatest menace to freedom is an inert people. . . . [T]he fitting remedy for evil counsels is good ones.[36]

It is almost as tempting to quote every sentence here from Brandeis's whole opinion as from Abraham Lincoln at Gettysburg. Brandeis's objections to wire-tapping, in a different case, are also reminiscent of how John Stuart Mill had taken liberalism in a humane direction unanticipated by earlier utilitarian thinking. Brandeis wrote in terms of the concepts of 'happiness', 'pain', and 'pleasure', but expanded them along the lines of *On Liberty*:

> The makers of our Constitution undertook to secure conditions favourable to the pursuit of happiness. They recognized the significance of man's spiritual nature, of his feelings and of his intellect. They knew that only a part of the pain, pleasure and satisfactions of life are to be found in material things. They sought to protect Americans in their beliefs, their thoughts, their emotions and their sensations. They conferred, as against the Government, the right to be left alone – the most comprehensive of rights and the right most valued by civilized men.[37]

(It is ironic that both Bentham and Blackstone had been united in their hostility to the possibility of America's independence from England.)

24

One could write an essay comparing and contrasting the liberalism of the sceptic Holmes, who thought that people were entitled to go to blazes with their own new-fangled social convictions, as opposed to the liberalism of the more democratic Brandeis who was so much more positively-minded about social experimentation; their respective conceptions of human nature, which did not necessarily tally with how they behaved personally, inevitably coloured their political and social convictions. Admiring them does not mean that it is not necessary to acknowledge some of their central limitations. And the same point can, I think, be made about John Stuart Mill in relation to British liberal theory as he found it. For a variety of reasons, some which he understood and others which only stand out at a distance, he could not accept the psychologies promoted by his father and Bentham. Neither James Mill nor Bentham had made liberty in itself central in importance.

We are not led to any kind of determinism, involving the belief that one kind of theory of human nature inevitably leads to certain political and social conclusions. The history of ideas is not that simple; good theories are advanced by multiple means, and even bad psychology need not entail wicked politics. By the same token, however, attractive psychological premises do not necessarily yield compellingly appealing politics. Some of the most promising-seeming political recommendations may be based on premises which turn out to be fundamentally faulty. The connections between psychology and political thinking are more complicated than one might naively like to think.

Freud used to like to quote Dostoevsky's having maintained that psychology is a two-edged sword; and whatever the great Russian novelist might have meant by that aphorism, I want to use it for the sake of insisting that different political and social ideologies can make use of a wide variety of psychological premises. Conservatism and radicalism, as well as liberalism, have relied on various conceptions of human nature. By examining John Stuart Mill in relation to Benthamite thinking, and seeing how and why he became a critic of utilitarianism, as well as some of the limitations of what he accomplished, we get an insight into one of those famous confrontations in the history of ideas which makes the study of political theory so enduringly challenging.

NOTES

1. Hugh Trevor-Roper, 'Human Nature in Politics', *The Listener*, Vol. 50 (Dec. 10, 1953), pp. 993–94.
2. Shirley Letwin, *The Pursuit of Certainty* (Cambridge, Cambridge University Press, 1965), p. 195.
3. See Mary P. Mack, *Jeremy Bentham: An Odyssey of Ideas 1748–1792* (London, Heinemann, 1962), and Michael St. John Packe, *The Life of John Stuart Mill* (New York, Macmillan, 1954). Also see Isaiah Berlin, *John Stuart Mill and the Ends of Life* (London, The Council of Christians and Jews, 1959), reprinted in Isaiah Berlin, *Four Essays in Liberty* (N.Y., Oxford Univ. Press, 1969), Ch. 4; Crane Brinton, 'Bentham', in *English Political Thought in the Nineteenth Century* (Cambridge, Mass., Harvard University Press, 1949), pp. 14–30; Eli Halevy, *The Growth of Philosophic Radicalism* (Boston, Beacon Press, 1955); Joseph Hamburger, *How Liberal Was John Stuart Mill?* (Austin, The Harry Ransom Humanities Research Center, Univ. of Texas, 1991); Henry Hazlitt, 'Jeremy Bentham', in *The Spirit of the Age: Or Contemporary Portraits* (New York, Doubleday, n.d.), pp. 9–22; Gertrude Himmelfarb, 'Bentham Versus Blackstone' and 'Bentham's Utopia', in *Marriage and Morals Among the Victorians* (New York, Knopf, 1986), pp. 94–143; John Plamenatz, *The English Utilitarians* (Oxford, Blackwell, 1958); John Plamenatz, 'Bentham and His School', in *Man and Society*, Vol. II (London, Longmans, Green, 1963), pp. 1–36; George Sabine, *A History of Political Theory* (New York, Henry Holt, 1954), Chs. 31–32.
4. John Stuart Mill, 'Bentham', in *Essays on Politics and Culture*, ed. Gertrude Himmelfarb (New York, Anchor Books, 1963), p. 93.
5. *Ibid.*, p. 94.
6. *Ibid.*, p. 95.
7. *Ibid.*
8. Jeremy Bentham, *A Comment on the Commentaries*, ed. C. W. Everett (Oxford, The Clarendon Press, 1928), p. 41.
9. Jeremy Bentham, *A Fragment on Government*, ed. Wilfrid Harrison (Oxford, Blackwell, 1967), p. 12.
10. Louis Compton, *Byron and Greek Love: Homophobia in 19th Century England* (Berkeley, University of California Press, 1985), p. 19.
11. A. J. Ayer, 'The Principle of Utility', in *Philosophical Essays* (London, Macmillan, 1954), pp. 250–70.
12. But see Daniel J. Boorstin, *The Mysterious Science of the Law* (Boston, Beacon Press, 1958). See also William Blackstone, *Commentaries on the Laws of England* (Philadelphia, George W. Childs, 1863).
13. H. L. A. Hart, 'Blackstone's Uses of the Law of Nature', *Butterworths South African Law Review* (1956), p. 174. See also H. L. A. Hart, *Law, Liberty, and Morality* (Stanford, Stanford University Press, 1963).

14. John Stuart Mill, *Autobiography*, Preface by Harold J. Laski (London, Oxford University Press, 1958), pp. 41–43, 113.

15. *Ibid.*, p. 56.

16. *Ibid.*, pp. 117–18.

17. A. W. Levi, 'The "Mental Crisis" of J. S. Mill', *The Psychoanalytic Review*, Vol. 32 (1945), pp. 86-101; Bruce Mazlish, *James and John Stuart Mill: Father and Son in the Nineteenth Century* (New York, Basic Books, 1975). See Joseph Hamburger's review of Mazlish's book, *History and Theory*, Vol. 15, No. 3 (1976), pp. 328–41.

18. Mill, *Autobiography*, *op. cit.*, pp. 119–22.

19. F. A. Hayek, *John Stuart Mill and Harriet Taylor: Their Friendship and Subsequent Marriage* (Chicago, University of Chicago Press, 1951).

20. Packe, *The Life of John Stuart Mill*, *op. cit.*, pp. 109ff.

21. I am indebted to Louis Hartz's thinking; see Louis Hartz, *The Necessity of Choice: Nineteenth Century Political Thought*, *op. cit.*, Part III, pp. 137–55.

22. *Social Contract: Essays by Locke, Hume and Rousseau*, with an Introduction by Sir Ernest Barker (London, Oxford University Press, 1953), p. 373.

23. James Mill, *An Essay on Government*, ed. Currin V. Shields (New York, The Liberal Arts Press, 1955).

24. John Stuart Mill, 'On Liberty', in *The Philosophy of John Stuart Mill*, ed. Marshall Cohen (New York, The Modern Library, 1961), pp. 197, 200.

25. *Ibid.*, p. 253.

26. *Ibid.*, p. 191.

27. *Ibid.*, pp. 223, 204.

28. Walter Bagehot, *The English Constitution*, with an Introduction by Lord Balfour (London, Oxford University Press, 1928), p. xxiv.

29. Ernest Jones, *Sigmund Freud: Life and Work*, Vol. I, revised (London, The Hogarth Press, 1956), p. 62.

30. Carl Schorske mixed things up in his 'Freud's Egyptian Dig', *The New York Review of Books* (May 27, 1993), p. 35.

31. *Letters of Sigmund Freud 1873-1939*, ed. Ernst L. Freud, translated by Tania and James Stern (London, The Hogarth Press, 1961), p. 90.

32. *Ibid.*, p. 91.

33. See Paul Roazen, *Helene Deutsch: A Psychoanalyst's Life* (New York, Doubleday, 1975; with new Introduction, New Brunswick, N.J., Transaction, 1992).

34. Schenck v. United States (1919), in *American Constitutional Law*, Alpheus Thomas Mason and William M. Beaney (Englewood Cliffs, N.J., Prentice-Hall, 1954), p. 571.

35. Gitlow v. New York, in *American Constitutional Law*, *Ibid.*, pp. 578–79.

36. Whitney v. California, in *American Constitutional Law*, *Ibid.*, p. 583.

37. Olmstead v. United States, in *American Constitutional Law*, *Ibid.*, pp. 523–24.

Nietzsche and Freud: Two Voices from the Underground

The relationship between Nietzsche and Freud has been an obvious topic of interest for intellectual historians.[1] Yet the full implications of how disturbing a philosophy Nietzsche espoused, and the ways in which his spiritual subversiveness gets echoed throughout Freud's thinking, have rarely been spelled out. The relationship between Freud, Mill, and the utilitarian tradition may be an uncertain and fragile one, but Nietzsche himself brushed aside British liberalism with a sovereign-seeming contempt: 'Man does *not* strive for pleasure, only the Englishman does.'[2]

Nietzsche's sayings can be unforgettable, and it is easy simply to show how some of his aphorisms, such as those on the sources of conscience, strikingly anticipate classical psychoanalytic doctrine; the resemblances are in fact so close as to be almost eerie. 'Conscience is not,' Nietzsche once wrote, 'as is supposed, "the voice of God in man"; it is the instinct of cruelty, turning in upon itself after it can no longer release itself outwardly.'[3] Freud himself rarely wrote about positive self-esteem, although some psychoanalysts after him have proposed its key importance; but he did suppose, just like Nietzsche, that moral convictions rest on the internalization of aggression.

Freud went beyond simply discussing the clinical significance of aggressive urges and how they can be deployed, against the self for example; for in 1919 Freud postulated the existence of a death drive, as disturbing as anything Nietzsche wrote, for instance in praise of the inevitability of war.[4] In Freud's view the aggression that we fail to turn against ourselves must be directed outward. As Erich Fromm once pointed out, Freud left us with the 'tragic alternative' of destroying ourselves or destroying others; Freud could write: 'holding back aggressiveness is in general unhealthy and leads to illness.'[5] He went further: 'It really seems as though it is necessary for us to destroy some other thing or person in order not to destroy ourselves, in order to guard against the impulsion to self-destructiveness.'[6]

Freud's view came to be that the internalization of aggression was the instinctual source of ethics. In this connection Nietzsche's own account of the origins of morality and how we derive our values closely prefigure Freud's later notion of the nature of the superego. To quote Nietzsche again: 'the content of our conscience is that which was, without any given reason, regularly *demanded* of us in our childhood by people we honoured or feared.'[7] (Neither Nietzsche nor Freud could share Mill's reliance for ethics on the competition in the market-place of ideas.) Behind Nietzsche on the significance of early childhood can be found the thinking of Arthur Schopenhauer, but the curious collapse in our time of Schopenhauer's traditional standing means that a comparison of his ideas and those of Freud is bound to seem like an esoteric exercise.[8]

At the same time as Nietzsche criticized the prevalent moral beliefs of his era (especially Christianity), he was explicitly proposing a different ethical outlook. Nietzsche's preaching has had its different sorts of interpretations, partly based on strands in his thought which go off in multiple directions; it is somehow fitting that this should be true, since Nietzsche made so much of the significance of perspective and of how in the light of the present everyone is entitled to reconsider the past.

Freud, like Nietzsche, had a prophetic side to him; he was sometimes intent on relentlessly denouncing religion, as in his *The Future of An Illusion*. Unlike Nietzsche, however, Freud was capable of proposing the tyranny of reason over intellect; religion was in Freud's view, as in *The Future of An Illusion*, a wholly unnecessary institution, a collective superstition that should be abandoned. In that text Freud assaulted religion based on the model of how the individual could use rational intelligence to overcome primal impulses and fears. (For all the differences between Bentham and Freud, they also had something in common when it came to relying on reason.) Despite Freud's reformist purposes, as in his criticisms of unnecessary sexual taboos, Freud also wanted to go down in history as a scientist. He had in his view made certain 'discoveries' based on the perception of 'facts' which others found unpalatable; part of his moral fervour came from his conviction that he, unlike others, especially backsliding disciples, had been able to be strong enough to bear distasteful truths. Science involves disciplined self-correction, and Freud was in principle willing to take whatever the future might bring in terms of validating his 'findings'.

In keeping with the scientific cap Freud often liked to wear, he could utter a belief in the self-evidence of morality. He frequently expressed his dislike of philosophy. He once wrote in a 1937 letter: 'the moment a man questions the meaning and value of life, he is sick, since objectively neither has any existence; by asking this question one is merely admitting to a store of unsatisfied libido to which something else must have happened, a kind of fermentation leading to sadness and depression.'[9] Jean-Paul Sartre was fascinated by Freud, even though the current French wave of concern with psychoanalysis largely ignores Sartre's interesting points of view on the subject. But the central issues of modern existentialism, involving the agonies of choice in the absence of traditional religious directives, were clearly not those of Freud himself. Freud saw meaning everywhere. The death of God did not leave Freud with perplexing ethical uncertainties.

As Freud aged he talked about his 'indifference to the world'. But this detachment of his also meant that he could write with an air of sometimes shocking-seeming superiority: 'In the depth of my heart I can't help being convinced that my dear fellow men, with a few exceptions, are worthless.' He was so disappointed in what he had seen of mankind that he maintained: 'I have found little that is "good" about human beings on the whole. In my experience most of them are trash.' Freud thought of himself as a kind of superman: 'I have never done anything mean or malicious and cannot trace any temptation to do so. . . .' But 'other people are brutal and untrustworthy'.[10] (Freud was expressing himself more freely in his letters than he would have written for his publications, but these private sentiments are consistent with his articles and books; in any event even in his youth he had recommended a friend to save his letters, and surely in his mature years he knew that those he corresponded with were preserving what he wrote.[11]) As much as Freud and John Stuart Mill may have had in common in their reliance on the need for deference to leading public figures, one cannot imagine Mill sharing in the most savage of Freud's inhumane and anti-democratic-sounding views. As for the utilitarian goal of one-man-one-vote, which Mill tried to expand to include women, one can anticipate Nietzsche's contempt for any such egalitarian standard.

Freud was lucky enough, in contrast to Nietzsche's own extreme isolation, to be famous for much of his lifetime. Freud's fame added to that of Nietzsche's posthumous reputation and yet also derived strength from it. So that almost from the beginning of Freud's having a following, students of his were pointing out analogies in his work with that of Nietzsche. The lines between Nietzsche and Freud, those which separate them as well as the ones which form an important lineage, were fully apparent even while Freud was in the midstream of his psychoanalytic career. Of the 1911 meeting of psychoanalysts at the Congress in Weimar, Ernest Jones recorded: 'A few of us took the opportunity of paying our respects to Nietzsche's sister and biographer, who lived there, and she professed interest in various connections we had found between her famous brother's psychological insight and what psychoanalysts were now revealing in their daily work.'[12]

Freud's disciples Otto Rank and Heinz Hartmann, and perhaps others as well, brought some of Nietzsche's aphorisms to Freud's attention, and on one occasion Freud incorporated a bit of this material into one of his most famous case histories.[13] In 1908 two meetings of the Vienna Psychoanalytic Society were devoted to discussing aspects of Nietzsche's work. Freud more than once tried to deny Nietzsche's impact on him, and he also claimed that his fascination with Nietzsche was so overwhelming that it prevented him from reading this acknowledged philosophic master. Just before such a disclaimer of Freud's, one of his most loyal pupils had publicly commented:

Nietzsche had come so close to our views that we can ask only, 'where has he not come close?' He intuitively knew a number of Freud's discoveries; he was the first to discover the significance of abreaction, of repression, of flight into illness, of the instincts – the normal sexual ones as well as the sadistic instincts.

It was after this follower's presentation of his remarks that Freud chose to emphasize his independence. Freud was concerned with his autonomy for the sake of establishing his scientific right to priority; the proceedings record Freud remarking on his own peculiar relationship to philosophy; its abstract nature is so unpleasant to him, that he has renounced the study of philosophy. He does not know Nietzsche's work; occasional attempts at reading it were smothered by an excess of interest. In spite of the similarities which many people have pointed out, he can give the assurance that Nietzsche's ideas have had no influence whatsoever on his own work.

It must however have been based on some knowledge that Freud thought he was competent to have the right to be able to insist: 'Nietzsche failed to recognize infantilism as well as the mechanism of displacement.'[14]

A few months later we find Freud equally adamant about his alleged ignorance.

> Prof. Freud would like to mention that he has never been able to study Nietzsche, partly because of the resemblance of Nietzsche's intuitive insights to our laborious investigations, and partly because of the wealth of his ideas, which has always prevented Freud from getting beyond the first half page whenever he tried to read him.[15]

Walter Kaufmann, one of those Nietzsche experts who did the most to whitewash him of the charges of being a proto-fascist, comments credulously at this point about Freud: 'I have never found him to be dishonest about anything.'[16] (Kaufmann's view of the difficulties between Freud and people like Jung or Adler constitutes such a defence of the orthodox Freudian position as to read like an antique trade union manifesto; I can scarcely imagine many contemporary analysts, were they to examine for themselves the specific grounds for Freud's assault on Jung or Adler, being able to agree with the substance of Freud's points.) As one literary critic has observed of Freud, since the meetings of the Vienna Psychoanalytic Society had been specifically devoted to part of Nietzsche's *Genealogy of Morals* and his *Ecce Homo*, 'it would scarcely be possible to discuss these works without having read them'.[17]

Kaufmann's view of Nietzsche as a psychologist of artistic creativity and individualism became so influential that it was necessary for Conor Cruise O'Brien to remind us how ferocious Nietzsche could be, and how 'through the central thrust of his work' he advocated 'an authoritarian politics freed from the trammels of Christian, liberal, and democratic tradition. . . .'[18] A couple of examples of Nietzsche's *obiter dicta* can make the point:

Society, the great trustee of life, is responsible to life itself for every miscarried life – it also has to pay for such lives: consequently it ought to prevent them. In numerous cases, society ought to prevent pro-creation: to this end, it may hold in readiness, without regard to descent, rank or spirit, the most rigorous measures of constraint, deprivation of freedom, in certain circumstances castration.[19]

Or take this bit of Nietzschean ferociousness:

Multiplicities are invented in order to do things for which the individual lacks the courage. It is for just this reason that all communities and societies are a hundred times more upright and instructive about the nature of man than is the individual, who is too weak to have the courage of his own desires. . . . How does it happen that the state will do a host of things that the individual would never countenance? Through division of responsibility, of command and of execution. Through the interposition of the virtues of obedience, duty, patriotism and loyalty. Through upholding pride, severity, strength, revenge – in short, all typical characteristics that contradict the herd type. . . . None of you has the courage to kill a man, or even to whip him, or even to – but the tremendous machine of the state overpowers the individual, so he repudiates responsibility for what he does (obedience, oath, etc.).[20]

In some sense Mill's critique of the dangers of conformity can be compared to Nietzsche's indictment of 'the herd type', but Mill was never proposing the overpowering of the individual. In 1917 a field edition of 150,000 copies of Nietzsche's *Zarathustra* was published for the Austrian troops;[21] and the Nazis could disseminate to their military forces those of Nietzsche's sayings which fitted their own ideological purposes.

Whatever the noxious fruits of Nietzsche's politics, as a psycho-logist he can scarcely be matched. Freud considered himself the expert master on the phenomena of self-deception, a subject which Nietzsche prided himself on as well. So that Freud's special praise of Nietzsche could not have been more of a compliment: 'The degree of intro-spection achieved by Nietzsche has never been achieved by anyone, nor is it likely ever to be reached again.' But Freud also had his reservations: 'What disturbs us is that Nietzsche transformed "is" into "ought", which is alien to science. In this he has remained, after all,

33

the moralist; he could not free himself of the theologian.'[22] (Freud was clearly implying something about the superiority of his own more objective writings.)

We now know, thanks to two sets of relatively recently released Freud correspondences, that his indebtedness to Nietzsche was far more direct than one might have ever guessed. At least two of his close friends from young adulthood knew Nietzsche personally. One historian comments: 'Although Freud specifically denied reading Nietzsche until late in life, it seems quite probable that his philosophic friendships ... brought him at least a general knowledge of Nietzsche's outlook much earlier.'[23] Another observer notes: 'From the correspondence between Freud and his adolescence friend Eduard Silberstein, it is known that in 1873, during his first year at the University of Vienna, the seventeen-year-old Freud had read Nietzsche's published work, which at that date certainly included *The Birth of Tragedy* and probably also the first two *Untimely Meditations*.'[24]

In 1900 we can find Freud writing to his intimate friend Wilhelm Fliess: 'I have just acquired Nietzsche, in whom I hope to find words for much that remains mute in me, but have not opened him yet. Too lazy for the time being.'[25] It was no accident that when Otto Rank was separating off from Freud he sent in 1926 as a seventieth birthday gift to Freud the collected works of Nietzsche; nor should we be surprised to hear that Freud is reported not to have appreciated this gift, a reminder from a former student of his own about a spiritual teacher that Freud himself was dependent on.[26]

I am not bringing up the issue of Nietzsche and Freud, on which much more might be said, for the sake of tracing out any alleged influence. It is, however, worth noting that Lou Andreas-Salomé, Nietzsche's earliest popularizer and a woman to whom he supposedly once proposed marriage, was later a pre-World War I member of Freud's circle in Vienna and actually became a practising psychoanalyst. (The complexities of Nietzsche's letters to her seem to me almost paralysing; her own subtleties can be demonstrated in the diplomacy of her correspondence with Freud and the diary of her time in Vienna.[27]) But no more tricky problem exists in the history of ideas than trying to trace out the impact any one thinker has on another. (In Virginia Woolf's *To the Lighthouse* (1927) she makes fun, perhaps thinking of her father's work, of the general scholarly pursuit of hypothesized influence.)

My purpose in raising the Nietzsche–Freud problem is for the sake of contemporary political psychology. It is my conviction that theoretical inquiry in the field has been relatively neglected. Partly this is a consequence of the past arrogance of political theorists within political science; the subject of social thought was once considered to be an aristocratic preserve, above the hurly-burly of political life, and its study was pursued as the snob part of the academic discipline. When Harold Lasswell first proposed the significance of psychopathological thought for political science as a whole, he was understandably disdainful of the more traditional means of political knowledge and education. He was himself, of course, well-educated in social philosophy, and his private family letters display a degree of artistry which now seems remarkable.[28]

Being concerned with the implications of modern psychology should lead, in the long run, to a rapprochement with social philosophy. It will come as a disagreeable shock to many who think of themselves as mainline political theorists that Lasswell's *Psychopathology and Politics*, which is still in print after over half a century, must by their own standards count as a work of political theory.[29] For the survival of a text is traditionally the surest test for establishing whether a book deserves to be categorized as worthy of the political philosophy designation.

In addition to my general objective in bringing up the link between Nietzsche and Freud, I have a more specific one as well. And that is because the horrifying sides to Nietzsche, which were responsible for his reputation sinking to a low point after World War II, can also be matched by spooky aspects in Freud. (Jones's account of analysts going to visit Nietzsche's sister was dissociated from the information that Hitler too later paid his own courtesy call on her.) Nietzsche and Freud both emerged from the underground of Western thought, and they each sought to challenge some key aspects of traditional morality. The most frightening parts of psychoanalysis, which were accurately perceived as subversive by some of Freud's earliest adherents as well as his contemporary critics, may be harder to spot nowadays.

For a variety of reasons Freud's work since his death, especially in North America, has been tamed and conventionalized. Psychoanalysis is now a profession with its thousands of practitioners, and the field has had a powerful impact on how we think about ourselves; to be reminded of the most disquieting aspects to Freud's teachings is to invite a threat not only to the professional *status quo* of analysis, but to our sense of ourselves which has come in part to rest on acknowledging his creative contribution divorced from its more alarming components.

Each time one of Freud's undiscovered texts emerges, establishment figures can be found to deplore the jolt to preconceived contemporary thinking. One should not underestimate the extent to which intellectuals have played a part in prettifying the historical Freud. This was true, for example, in connection with the 1967 publication of the Freud-Bullitt study of Woodrow Wilson and also more recently with regard to the appearance in print of one of Freud's 'lost' metapsychological essays. In the case of the Freud-Bullitt manuscript, the idea of loyal partisans was to minimize Freud's hand in it; and with Freud's recently discovered World War I essay, which he himself had entitled 'Overview of the Transference Neuroses', this heading was in the published text demoted to the status of a subtitle, since the phylogenetic aspects of Freud's argument were so worrying that the publication came out as *A Phylogenetic Fantasy*.[30] The most speculative sides to Freud, however much we may not want to go along with them now, were an intrinsic part of his creative achievement.

Even a thoroughly sophisticated analyst was so appalled by some aspects of the Freud–Jung correspondence when it was finally released as publicly to wonder whether it should ever have been published.[31] (Jung himself found Nietzsche a favourite author, and two large volumes have recently come out based on his 1934–1939 seminar on *Zarathustra*.[32] It is a tribute to Jung that he took the philosophic implications of psychoanalysis more seriously than Freud himself did and therefore went further in exploring Nietzsche. On the other hand Jung's interest in Nietzsche reached its height precisely when Jung was engaged in collaborating with the then successful Nazi regime in Germany.)[33]

In the period since Freud's death many revisionists have sought to correct the harsh, negativistic imbalances in Freud's work; look at any current psychoanalytic periodical and one will not, unfortunately, find any concrete traces of reminders of Nietzsche, or of philosophic sophistication. (The French analytic tradition of thought would be a large exception to this generalization.) But from a clinical perspective the concept of a death drive, which almost none of Freud's followers endorsed and which seems a notion scarcely even remembered today, can by itself lead to therapeutic despair and nihilism. (Bettelheim, as

we shall see, invoked the death drive idea in connection with the behaviour of inmates in concentration camps.) A large block of disturbingly
pessimistic thinking lay behind Freud's death drive theory, and it is
this side of Freud which has been widely but imperceptibly influential,
an issue which Erich Fromm tried to bring up in the course of
defending himself against Herbert Marcuse's famous critique of neo-
Freudianism.[34]

Erik H. Erikson and others, notably Donald W. Winnicott, tried to
highlight the more positive, forward-looking aspects of psychotherapy,
all the time maintaining their respective ties of continuity within the
Freudian framework; no one who wants to influence how others think
can enjoy the perils of being excommunicated from the ranks of the
psychoanalytic faithful.[35] Still, it is not a simple question how to inject
healthy-mindedness in the heritage Freud bequeathed us. Unfortunately analysts who have been writing in Freud's school, as well
as those who have tried to set up alternative formulations, have not
often had Freud's own philosophic cultivation, and well-meaning
people have, with the best of intentions, committed themselves to
some rather simple-minded notions about health and emotional
'growth'.

Yet from the point of view of today's political thought the most
upsetting sides to Freud's thinking have something important to teach.
One could itemize, for example, all the occasions on which Freud
quoted with approval Goethe's Mephistopheles, or in which Freud
consciously identified himself with the devil. Freud wrote and said
some absolutely shocking things, even if contemporary psychiatrists
are apt for reasons of their own to downplay this side of things.

Freud flourished on controversy, and I would guess that he would
have relished the central standing which even radical feminists seem
to have accorded to his work. He has more often been attacked than
ignored, and he thought such 'resistances' were a sign of the secure
ultimate triumph of his message. For me at least, one of the chief
attractions in Freud's whole outlook is the challenge he continues to
pose to how we think about things today, and the threat psychoanalysis
poses for conventional political thought. Freud's concept of the unconscious does not readily suit the needs of North American social
science. There was a mystical side to him, a disdain for the provable,
that his New World practitioners have chosen to try to forget even as
they have often canonized his writings. Freud was memorably telling
us something about the limits of human rationality and what we cannot

expect ever to know. (He went much further in this direction than John Stuart Mill.) Despite Freud's occasional utopianism about the possibilities of scientific knowledge, on the whole he stood for the inevitability of suffering, the dark and tragic side of life.

One might go through the corpus of Freud's work and quote some of his letters and sayings in order to demonstrate the radical side of what he was like. For example, he did not mind speaking ill of the dead. Let me cite a sentence of his from a letter to Lou Andreas-Salomé written after the suicide of Victor Tausk. I got into trouble with many orthodox analysts, and especially Anna Freud, for daring to use this particular demonic passage, one which had originally been expurgated from Freud's published letters without even the benefit of the ellipses that should indicate an omission. (After my work was in print, the cuts in the letter were abandoned and the words restored in subsequent editions.) Tausk had been a devoted follower of Freud's for a decade; for a variety of reasons, professional and personal, Tausk sent him a touching suicide letter before tragically ending his own life. Freud then wrote a glowing, long obituary on Tausk's behalf. But Freud, who had privately come to view Tausk as a nuisance and a bother but also played his part in Tausk's undoing, wrote to Lou – who had once been Tausk's lover: 'I confess I do not really miss him; I had long taken him to be useless, indeed a threat to the future.'[36] (The concept of being 'useless' harks back to critiques of Benthamism like that we will encounter in Dostoevsky's *Crime and Punishment*.) In writing to Lou, Freud may have been competitively trying to out-Nietzsche Nietzsche. But Freud's comments to Arnold Zweig after Alfred Adler's death are equally arresting.[37]

We must take the savage side of Freud along with the rest of him. For it was in Nietzsche's own spirit that Freud was determined to defy traditional proprieties. When in 1930 his mother finally died in Vienna, an old woman of ninety-five, Freud chose not to attend the funeral and instead wrote that he had sent his daughter Anna to 'represent' him; it seems to me scary that he could stay home and instead write a letter to a newborn American relative: 'Welcome as a new output of life on the day great-grandmother was buried. Great uncle Sigmund.'[38]

To move from a biographical to a more theoretical level, Freud's assumption of the universality of bisexuality was intended to have a host of disturbing implications. Freud was proposing that human sexuality was at bottom incapable of gratification, and that mankind was destined to self-torture. At the same time Freud's convictions about bisexuality gave him a powerful interpretive handle, a means of control; Otto Rank thought that Freud's concept of 'unconscious homosexuality' was his way of tyrannizing over people in his circle of followers.

Freud thought up bold ideas but also was apt to faint at the sight of blood; his father had thought this trait boded ill for Sigmund's medical career. In his day-to-day life Freud was a conventional late-nineteenth-century physician; a barber came to his apartment every day to trim his beard, and he was surrounded by a large family – and six servants. The psychoanalytic movement became an extension of his own family. (It would be hard to think of a greater contrast to Nietzsche's own tortured, lonely existence.) Freud once said that he was so much 'a petit bourgeois' that he could not approve of one of his sons getting a divorce or a daughter having an affair.[39] (Curiously, one of Freud's sons had already been divorced, although Freud wrote as if it were not so.) However sexually conformist Freud made himself appear, in his thinking he dared to be outrageous, a side of him which too often gets underestimated today. He could be most arbitrary just when he was appearing the most cautious; it seems scarcely possible to untangle just what he was saying (besides being defiant) when he once wrote: 'I stand for an infinitely freer sexual life, although I myself have made very little use of such freedom. Only so far as I considered myself entitled to.'[40]

Freud saw himself, and those he cared most about, as exceptions. And the title to his *Beyond the Pleasure Principle* was clearly meant to echo a Nietzsche text, and themes important to critics of Bentham. Twice, in writing about his theory of dreams at the turn of the century, he put the phrase 'transvaluation of all psychical values' in quotation marks, without having explicitly to mention Nietzsche's name.[41] Freud silently invoked the Nietzsche image of a 'beast of prey'.[42] Freud's notion of a compulsion to repeat sounds like almost implicit mockery of Nietzsche's view of the perpetual recurrence of the same thing. Someone like Jacques Lacan may have been in effect expelled from the International Psychoanalytic Association with the approval of Freud's daughter Anna, but Lacan, like Wilhelm Reich and other so-called deviants before him, was building on a heretical streak within Freud himself.

When in *Civilization and Its Discontents* Freud takes apart a maxim like 'love thy neighbour as thyself', he is doing so in Nietzsche's own anti-Christian spirit. With all the ritualistic quoting that takes place in technical psychonanalytic journals (almost always the citations are taken out of any historical context), the following example of Freud as a Nietzsche-like warrior of the spirit usually goes unmentioned. Freud had chosen to pick apart 'one of the ideal demands' of 'civilized' society:

> It runs: 'Thou shalt love thy neighbour as thyself.' It is known through-out the world and is undoubtedly older than Christianity, which puts it forward as its proudest claim. Yet it is certainly not very old; even in historical times it was still strange to mankind.

Freud then proposes to think philosophically about the Golden Rule:

> Let us adopt a naïve attitude towards it, as though we were hearing it for the first time; we shall be unable then to suppress a feeling of surprise and bewilderment. Why should we do it? What good will it do us? But, above all, how shall we achieve it? How can it be possible? My love is something valuable to me which I ought not to throw away without reflection. It imposes duties on me for whose fulfilment I must be ready to make sacrifices. If I love someone, he must deserve it in some way. (I leave out of account the use he may be to me, and also his possible significance to me as a sexual object, for neither of these two kinds of relationship comes into question where the precept to love my neighbour is concerned.)

The egocentricity of Freud's argument has gone almost unnoticed; yet as early as before World War I Alfred Adler had pointed out the unacceptability of Freud's attack on altruistic love. (Adler came to believe that Freud's whole psychology, including the concept of the Oedipus complex, reflected the thinking characteristic of a spoiled child.) Freud, however, was unremitting in his dissection of the proposed ideal to love one's neighbour:

> He deserves it if he is so like me in important ways that I can love myself in him; and he deserves it if he is so much more perfect than myself that I can love my ideal of my own self in him. Again, I have to love him if he is my friend's son, since the pain my friend would

feel if any harm came to him would be my pain too – I should have to share it. But if he is a stranger to me and if he cannot attract me by any worth of his own or any significance that he may already have acquired for my emotional life, it will be hard for me to love him. Indeed, I should be wrong to do so, for my love is valued by all my own people as a sign of my preferring them, and it is an injustice to them if I put a stranger on a par with them.

Now Freud's voice seems to grow truly caustic; he was mordantly sceptical of the proposed universality of an ethics of love:

But if I am to love him (with this universal love) merely because he, too, is an inhabitant of this earth, like an insect, an earth-worm or a grass-snake, then I fear that only a small modicum of my love will fall to his share – not by any possibility as much as, by the judgment of my reason, I am entitled to retain for myself. What is the point of a precept enunciated with so much solemnity if its fulfilment cannot be recommended as reasonable?

I think Freud's hardness comes through as he illustrates inhabitants of 'this earth' with the crescendo 'like an insect, an earth-worm or a grass-snake . . .'.

Freud has only just got going in his denunciation; the suspicious way he viewed other people played its role throughout his theorizing:

On closer inspection, I find still further difficulties. Not merely is this stranger in general unworthy of my love; I must honestly confess that he has more claim to my hostility and even my hatred. He seems not to have the least trace of love for me and shows me not the slightest consideration. If it will do him any good he has no hesitation in injuring me, nor does he ask himself whether the amount of advantage he gains bears any proportion to the extent of the harm he does to me. Indeed, he need not even obtain an advantage; if he can satisfy any sort of desire by it, he thinks nothing of jeering at me, slandering me and showing his superior power; and the more secure he feels and the more helpless I am, the more certainly I can expect him to behave like this to me. If he behaves differently, if he shows me consideration and forbearance as a stranger, I am ready to treat him in the same way, in any case and quite apart from any precept.

At this point Freud moves in for the kill; he surely knew the moral significance of the ethical enterprise he was embarked upon:

> Indeed, if this grandiose commandment had run 'love thy neighbour as thy neighbour loves thee', I could not take exception to it. And there is a second commandment, which seems to me even more incomprehensible and arouses still stronger opposition in me. It is 'love thine enemies'. If I think it over, however, I see that I am wrong in treating it as a greater imposition. At bottom it is the same thing.

Having concluded that our neighbours are natural enemies, Freud put a footnote further illustrating the tough-minded meaning of his position:

> A great imaginative writer may permit himself to give expression – jokingly, at all events – to psychological truths that are severely proscribed. Thus Heine confesses: 'Mine is a most peaceable disposition. My wishes are: a humble cottage with a thatched roof, but a good bed, the freshest milk and butter, flowers before my window, and a few fine trees before my door; and if God wants to make my happiness complete, he will grant me the joy of seeing some six or seven of my enemies hanging from those trees. Before their death I shall, moved in my heart, forgive them all the wrong they did me in their lifetime. One must, it is true, forgive one's enemies – but not before they have been hanged.'[43]

Freud was repelled by the pieties of Christian moralizing. Readers of his writings can be misled by his tendency to make use of Viennese *schmaltz*, as for example when he addresses Romain Rolland in a 1926 letter:

> Unforgettable man, to have soared to such heights of humanity through so much hardship and suffering! I revered you as an artist and as an apostle of love for mankind many years before I saw you. I myself have always advocated the love of mankind . . . as indispensable for the preservation of the human species. . . .

A careless reader might overlook how implicitly carefully qualified ('for the preservation of the human species') was Freud's advocacy here of the 'love of mankind'. A sceptic might think that Freud was ingratiating himself to a Nobel-prize winning author; for in writing to Rolland, Freud approvingly refers to 'the most precious of beautiful illusions, that of love extended to all mankind'.[44]

Elsewhere Freud sounds more characteristically himself. To his way of thinking, 'most of our sentimentalists, friends of humanity, and protectors of animals have been evolved from little sadists and animal tormentors'. In accounting for his choice of medicine as a career, he noted that he lacked 'any craving in my early childhood to help suffering humanity'; he reasons by polar opposites, like Nietzsche: 'My innate sadistic disposition was not a very strong one, so I had no need to develop this one of its derivatives.' Dostoevsky gets termed by Freud a 'sadist', by which Freud says he means 'the mildest, kindliest, most helpful person possible'. It is no wonder that an astute commentator finds Freud 'capable of adopting a sardonic, levelling, almost Nietzschean tone'.[45] A 1924 *Time* magazine cover story about Freud quotes him as having said that he was 'the only rogue in a company of immaculate rascals'.

As much as Freud could perplex and debunk, at the same time he sought to replace traditional ethics with a higher morality. (It will be remembered though that he had criticized Nietzsche for transforming 'is' into 'ought', and for having remained therefore a 'moralist'.) It was one of Freud's hopes and expectations that within the psychoanalytic clinical situation lay the potential source of a new ethical approach. In Freud's daily work, despite all his many protestations about an analyst's scientific neutrality and his distancing himself from Nietzsche as a 'theologian', Freud took for granted a fundamental distinction between 'worthy' patients and those he deemed riff-raff, trash, or 'worthless'.

Psychoanalysis was intended by Freud as an ethic of self-overcoming; Nietzsche had likewise held that man had to conquer himself. Freud designed his treatment procedure for an elite; it was not suitable for everyone, even in theory. According to a well-established legend Freud once dismissed an American patient on the most devastating grounds – that 'he had no unconscious'. (Freud's theories, all of which have an autobiographical side to them, say that wit is a means for expressing hostility.)

If Freud had allowed himself to go further in Nietzsche's direction, he would have entertained more theoretical enquiry about the nature of human values. Freud would then have had to question the ideal character of the whole concept of psychological normality. Freud's maxim 'to love and to work' is a profound answer to the question of what a normal person can be expected to do. But a more philosophically minded observer would question the whole ethics of self-realization which is built into the psychoanalytic procedure. Nietzsche, too, tended to take for granted the morality of self-fulfilment.

Analysts who talk in terms of a 'higher' and 'lower' self, or a 'true' or 'false' being, have moved well beyond what Freud himself wanted to consider. Yet even they would be hard-pressed to explain on what grounds they justify that which they want to promote as 'authentic'. I am reminded of the convicted murderer who, on being released from prison, came for an analysis; the therapist tactfully explained to him that it had not been the 'real you' who killed. But the murderer protested that that was the worst of it, he had felt most like himself when he committed the crime. The analyst self-preservatively decided not to accept the patient for treatment.

As clear as Freud was about what constitutes a neurosis, he was shy indeed on the issue of what he might possibly mean by the concept of psychological health. Opponents of psychoanalytic thinking like Hannah Arendt scorned the whole notion of 'sanity'; she sounds almost exultant when the psychiatrists, half a dozen of them and who she derides as 'soul experts', certify Adolf Eichmann (at his trial in Jerusalem) as 'normal'.[46] Like Fromm, Arendt wanted to be able to denounce a whole culture; in this case she sought all the ammunition she could use against Germany and its multiple war crimes. Freud's own reticence about getting involved in the philosophic issue of what is meant by psychological normality entailed that his teachings could get used for conformist purposes that I am convinced he would in practice have disdained.

Even the standard of authenticity would have appeared to Freud, I believe, as too readily used as an excuse for human piggishness. Freud did sometimes think of his patients as swine if not ninnies. (Jung once accused Freud, in a final parting letter, of hating the neurotics he treated.) Freud like Nietzsche did in some sense glorify human instincts; but they both took for granted that they were writing for aristocrats of the spirit who could transmute and sublimate human conflicts. Both men had in mind the rare individual who stands apart from the 'herd'; and in Freud's case this could mean justifying all sorts of arbitrary conduct on his part. He did not even feel the need to defend his analysing his daughter Anna; yet what after all did he think he was doing in violating all his own technical rules which advised others against treating relatives or friends?[47] Like Nietzsche he proposed an ethic of transgression.

For Freud to have rejected so much of traditional Western ethical teachings does not mean, any more than with Nietzsche, that the result has to be a repudiation of all moral values. But when Freud got invited to testify at the Leopold and Loeb trial in Chicago, he ought to have been aware by then of the dangers of some of his teachings, and those of Nietzsche. Psychoanalysis was an implied invitation to normlessness, and the dangers of being a 'free spirit' were a legitimate concern to sceptics of this new psychology. Norman Mailer once argued that had he not attacked his wife with a knife he would have turned his aggression inward and got cancer.[48]

Whatever the implications of some of Freud's thinking, I am convinced that he was not personally advocating 'anything goes'. On the contrary, he took for granted a secure set of internalized controls. He criticized secondary schools, for example, because they fell 'short of their duty of providing a substitute for the family and of arousing interest in life in the world outside'. But he did not have in mind that schools become like life; he thought they could only succeed in their purpose by being a unique experience. 'The school must not take on itself the inexorable character of life; it must not seek to be more than a *game* of life.'[49]

Freud's inner security gave him the grounds for being suspicious of the ideal of altruism and for attacking the love of mankind; he saw humanitarianism as a sublimation of homosexuality, surely as debunking an insight as he ever proposed. (The notion that cooperation rests on a homosexual basis supposedly led a disaffected pupil of Freud's, Otto Rank, to declare: it is either psychoanalysis or humanity.) Like Nietzsche, Freud found in Christianity a corruption of human possibility. But by not doing enough philosophically to explore the implications of psychoanalysis for ethics, Freud left it for others after him to make the mistake of believing that the so-called science of psychology can automatically lead to moral values. Humanists like Fromm, Lasswell, and Erikson too readily thought that how we ought to behave could be simply derived from how we do in fact choose to live.

The figure of Nietzsche can not only remind us of a trend in psychoanalytic psychology that ought not to be forgotten and that can valuably complement social science today, but his example can alert us to the ancient Socratic goal: philosophers should ask the most basic kinds of questions. How we ought to live is a conundrum which both psychologists and philosophers need to keep posing. Reconsidering the bases for our reasoning, what I have referred to as thinking about how we think, does not get enough attention in our kind of society; it is the glory of that kind of speculative enterprise that I am trying to recall.

NOTES

1. See Lorin Anderson, 'Freud, Nietzsche', *Salmagundi*, Vol. 47–48 (1980), pp. 3–29; Jacob Golomb, 'Freudian Uses and Misuses of Nietzsche', *The American Imago*, Vol. 37, No. 4 (1980); Ronald Lehrer, *Nietzsche's Presence in Freud's Life and Thought* (Albany, State University of New York Press, 1995); Bruce Mazlish, 'Freud and Nietzsche', *Psychoanalytic Review*, Vol. 55, No. 3 (1968), pp. 360–75; Michael J. Scavio, Andrew Cooper, and Pamela Scavio Clift, 'Freud's Devaluation of Nietzsche', *Psychohistory Review*, Vol. 21, No. 3 (1993), pp. 295–318.
2. *The Portable Nietzsche*, ed. Walter Kaufmann (New York, The Viking Press, 1954), p. 15.
3. Nietzsche, *The Philosophy of Nietzsche* (New York, The Modern Library, 1927), p. 910.
4. Thomas Pangle, 'The "Warrior Spirit" As An Inlet to the Political Philosophy of Nietzsche's *Zarathustra*', *Nietzsche-Studien* (Berlin, Walter de Gruyter, 1986), p. 140; Tracy Strong, *Friedrich Nietzsche and the Politics of Transfiguration*, expanded edition (Berkeley, Univ. of California Press, 1988), p. ix; see Freud, 'Thoughts For the Times on War and Death', *Standard Edition*, Vol. 14, pp. 274–302; Freud, 'Beyond the Pleasure Principle', *Standard Edition*, Vol. 18, pp. 7–64.
5. Erich Fromm, *The Anatomy of Human Destructiveness* (New York, Holt, Rinehart & Winston, 1973), pp. 463–64.
6. Freud, 'New Introductory Lectures on Psychoanalysis', *Standard Edition*, Vol. 22, p. 105.
7. R. J. Hollingdale, *Nietzsche* (London, Routledge & Kegan Paul, 1973), p.150.
8. See Philip Rieff, *Freud: The Mind of the Moralist* (London, Gollancz, 1959), p. 295, and Christopher Young and Andrew Brook, 'Schopenhauer and Freud', *International Journal of Psychoanalysis*, Vol. 75 (1994), pp. 101–18.
9. *Letters of Sigmund Freud*, ed. Ernst L. Freud, translated by Tania and James Stern (New York, Basic Books, 1960), p. 436.
10. Paul Roazen, *Brother Animal: The Story of Freud and Tausk* (New York, Knopf, 1969; 2nd edition, with New Introduction, New Brunswick, N.J., Transaction, 1990), p. 182.
11. *Letters of Sigmund Freud, op. cit.*, p. 4.

12. Ernest Jones, *Free Associations: Memories of a Psychoanalyst* (New York, Basic Books, 1959; 2nd edition, with New Introduction by Mervyn Jones, New Brunswick, N.J., Transaction, 1990), p. 216; see also Ernest Jones, *The Life and Work of Sigmund Freud*, Vol. 2 (New York, Basic Books, 1955), p. 86.

13. Freud, 'Notes Upon A Case of Obsessional Neurosis', *Standard Edition*, Vol. 10, p. 184.

14. Herman Nunberg and Ernst Federn, editors, *Minutes of the Vienna Psychoanalytic Society*, Vol. 1, translated by M. Nunberg (New York, International Universities Press, 1962), pp. 359–60.

15. Herman Nunberg and Ernst Federn, editors, *Minutes of the Vienna Psychoanalytic Society*, Vol. 2, translated by M. Nunberg (New York, International Universities Press, 1967), p. 32.

16. Walter Kaufmann, *Discovering the Mind, Vol. III: Freud versus Adler & Jung* (New York, McGraw Hill, 1980), p. 268.

17. Peter L. Rudnytksy, *Freud and Oedipus* (New York, Columbia University Press, 1987), p. 199.

18. Conor Cruise O'Brien, *The Suspecting Glance* (London, Faber & Faber, 1972), p. 58.

19. *Ibid.*, p. 57.

20. *Ibid.*, pp. 57–58.

21. Edward Timms, *Karl Kraus, Apocalyptic Satirist* (New Haven, Yale University Press, 1986), p. 425.

22. Nunberg and Federn, eds., Vol. II, *op. cit.*, pp. 31–32.

23. William J. McGrath, *Freud's Discovery of Psychoanalysis: The Politics of Hysteria* (New York, Cornell University Press, 1986), p. 139.

24. Rudnytsky, *op.cit.*, p. 198.

25. *The Complete Letters of Sigmund Freud to Wilhelm Fliess 1887–1904*, translated and edited by Jeffrey M. Masson (Cambridge, Mass., Harvard University Press, 1985), p. 398.

26. Paul Roazen, *Freud and His Followers* (New York, Knopf, 1975; reprinted, New York, Da Capo, 1992), p. 412.

27. Sigmund Freud and Lou Andreas-Salomé, *Letters*, ed. Ernst Pfeiffer, translated by William and Elaine Robson-Scott (London, The Hogarth Press, 1972), and Andreas-Salomé, *The Freud Journal*, translated by Stanley Leavy (New York, Basic Books, 1964).

28. Douglas Torgerson, 'Political Vision and the Policy Orientation: Lasswell's early Letters', *Administrative and Policy Studies*, Working Papers (Trent University, 1987).

29. Paul Roazen, *Encountering Freud: The Politics and Histories of Psychoanalysis* (New Brunswick, N.J., Transaction, 1990), pp. 241–44.

30. Paul Roazen, *Freud: Political and Social Thought, op. cit.*, Epilogue; Paul Roazen, *Erik H. Erikson: The Power and Limits of a Vision* (New York, The

Free Press, 1976, reprinted, Northvale, N.J., Aronson, 1997), p. 13; Sigmund Freud, *A Phylogenetic Fantasy: Overview of the Transference Neuroses*, edited by Ilse Grubrich-Simitis, translated by Axel Hoffer and Peter T. Hoffer (Cambridge, Mass., Harvard University Press, 1987).

31. Charles Rycroft, 'Folie à deux', *The New York Review of Books*, April 18, 1974.

32. C. G. Jung, *Nietzsche's 'Zarathustra': Notes of the Seminar Given in 1934–39*, 2 volumes, ed. James J. Jarret (Princeton, Princeton University Press, 1988).

33. See Paul Roazen, 'Jung and Anti-Semitism', *Lingering Shadows*, ed. Aryeh Maidenbaum (Boston, Shambahla, 1991).

34. Erich Fromm, 'The Human Implications of Instinctivistic "Radicalism" ', in *Voices of Dissent*, ed. Irving Howe (New York, Grove Press, 1958).

35. Paul Roazen, *Erik H. Erikson: The Power and Limits of a Vision*, op. cit.

36. Roazen, *Brother Animal*, op. cit., p. 140.

37. Roazen, *Freud and His Followers*, op. cit., p. 209.

38. Paul Roazen, *Helene Deutsch: A Psychoanalyst's Life*, op. cit., p. 291.

39. Celia Bertin, *Marie Bonaparte: A Life* (New York, Harcourt Brace, 1982), p. 155.

40. *Letters of Sigmund Freud*, op. cit., p. 308.

41. Freud, 'The Interpretation of Dreams', *Standard Edition*, Vol. 4, p. 330; Freud, 'On Dreams', *Standard Edition*, Vol. 5, p. 655.

42. O'Brien, op. cit., pp. 55–56.

43. Freud, 'Civilization and Its Discontents', *Standard Edition*, Vol. 21, pp. 109–110.

44. Peter Homans, 'Disappointment and the Ability to Mourn', in *Freud: Appraisals and Reappraisals, Contributions to Freud Studies*, Vol. 2, ed. Paul E. Stepansky (New York, The Analytic Press, 1988), p. 78.

45. Edwin R. Wallace, 'Freud As Ethicist', in *Freud: Appraisals and Reappraisals*, Vol. 1, ed. Paul E. Stepansky (New York, The Analytic Press, 1986), p. 91.

46. Hannah Arendt, *Eichmann in Jerusalem: A Report On the Banality of Evil* (New York, The Viking Press, 1963), p. 22. See: Paul Roazen, 'Arendt and Goldhagen on the Holocaust', *Journal of the Psychoanalysis of Culture and Society*, Spring 1998; Paul Roazen, 'Review of *Between Friends: The Correspondence of Hannah Arendt and Mary McCarthy*; Ettinger, *Hannah Arendt/Martin Heidegger*', *Queen's Quarterly*, Winter 1995.

47. Paul Roazen, 'Freud's Analysis of Anna', in *The Death of Psychoanalysis: Murder?, Suicide?, or Rumor Greatly Exaggerated?*, ed. Robert Prince (Northvale, N.J., Aronson, 1999), pp. 141–51.

48. Wallace, 'Freud As Ethicist', op. cit, p. 130.

49. Freud, 'Contribution to a Discussion of Suicide', *Standard Edition*, Vol. 11, p. 232.

Dostoevsky:
The Politics of Suffering

The gratifications of studying political theory are similar to those associated with working on all great literature. The best books acquire a life of their own, and the passage of time and the perspective of different social circumstances enhance our appreciation of the challenging quality of those texts which have acquired the stature of classics. Circular reasoning necessarily gets involved here, since one of the ways of determining whether a book deserves the standing of greatness is whether future generations continue to argue about it. Some exceptional works do disappear for a time, only to be later rediscovered and then acknowledged as works deserving of lasting attention. On the whole, though, books that are going to last become noteworthy closer to the date of their publication. Any sort of best-sellerdom is, though, an unlikely guide to selecting works that are destined to matter in the future; Hannah Arendt's *Eichmann in Jerusalem* or George Orwell's *1984* may be the exceptions that prove the rule.

The question whether fiction rightly belongs as a secure part of social philosophy is at least as controversial as how psychologists should rely on literature. From time to time political theorists have talked about the relevance, for example, of novels or plays. And Irving Howe once wrote an outstanding collection of essays *Politics and the Novel*.[1] Yet despite how much respect Howe may have earned among political theorists, few professional students in the field have followed his example. It is far more likely for literary people to make observations about political life than it is for students of political theory

49

to pay attention to literature by writing about the works of novelists or playwrights. (Ever since Plato, poetry has had a poor reputation for political soundness.) Yet throughout the twentieth century claims were made bemoaning the fact that political theory seemed to be disappearing, without adequate awareness that one source of such a falling-off might have been an unnecessary degree of trade-unionism which attempted to exclude from the field those works without the more standard credentials for qualifying as political thought.[2]

A good education in political theory would be unthinkable, I believe, without taking for granted everything by Shakespeare, not to mention other giants in the history of ideas. And just within twentieth century politics, I cannot imagine anyone serious being unaware of the novels by Orwell, Albert Camus or Arthur Koestler. Arthur Miller's *The Crucible* has been performed all over the world, and appreciated by victims of many sorts of inquisitions. To follow up on only the more recent works of novelists, it would be inconceivable to think about race without the fiction of Richard Wright or Ralph Ellison. And Robert Penn Warren's *All The King's Men* should be a classic in reflecting about a certain kind of political leadership and the opposition it arouses. At least for me, Boris Pasternak's *Dr. Zhivago* will endure as a unique testimony to a critical human side of the old Soviet Union, and the capacity of precious values to survive even the worst forms of tyranny. Graham Greene's *The Quiet American* is, in my judgment, the best single examination of the American involvement in Southeast Asia. To continue a brief survey of recent political novels, an unforgettable side of the problem of Whittaker Chambers and Alger Hiss comes through in Lionel Trilling's *The Middle of the Journey*. And an essential aspect of the Rosenberg case was expressed in E.L. Doctorow's *The Book of Daniel*. B.F. Skinner's *Walden Two* may not by any stretch of the imagination be a great novel; still it has striking political implications that are worthy of careful consideration. To turn to a writer of unquestioned literary genius, almost everything by Joseph Conrad has political and moral aspects that deserve scrutiny.

Of all modern figures, however, probably no creative artist appears more relevant to a political theorist than Fyodor Dostoevsky. Partly this is a question of how uniquely literature and politics have been entwined throughout the course of modern Russian history. In a society where all political expression was suspect, and the various regimes have looked askance at any dissidence, literature has been an avenue for expressing political ideas that might otherwise have evoked outright censorship if not imprisonment. In our own time Alexander Solzhenitsyn is an outstanding example of a novelist who has made his political mark; Russian poets have also been deeply political. Whatever may have been the case elsewhere, imaginative writers in Russia have characteristically been thoroughly concerned with questions that bear on political theory.

In Dostoevsky's case it is fairly well-known that as a young man he had been arrested for subversive political activities, sentenced to death and then finally exiled in punishment to Siberia. Afterwards Dostoevsky's politics changed drastically, and he became a great national figure whose works of literature were widely sold and appreciated throughout Russia. It is not hard to find traces of political commentary throughout his writings which rise to the level of philosophic (and psychological) importance. His *Notes From the Underground* are sometimes assigned to introductory political science students, since they have an immediacy of appeal to those beginning to examine the great issues of social philosophy.

Dostoevsky had, in his youthful phase of political activism, been influenced by Western reformist thought, yet I doubt that anyone ever delivered a more powerful indictment of rationalist utilitarian thinking inspired by Jeremy Bentham than Dostoevsky's underground man. Dostoevsky administered his assault on Benthamite liberalism in the course of a soliloquy which reminds me of those in Shakespeare, or in Melville's *Moby Dick*. For the man from the underground asks rhetorically:

> Oh, tell me, who was it first announced, who was it first proclaimed, that man only does nasty things because he does not know his own interests: and that if he were enlightened, if his eyes were opened to his real normal interests, man would at once cease to do nasty things, would at once become good and noble because, being enlightened and understanding his real advantage, he would see his own advantage in the good and nothing else, and we all know that not one man can, consciously, act against his own interests, consequently, so to say, through necessity, he would begin doing good?[3]

Dostoevsky was attacking a radical Russian essayist and novelist Nikolay Chernyshevsky, author of the novel *What Is To Be Done?*

51

Dostoevsky thought that Chernyshevsky had embodied 'soulless materialism', and at least one literary critic has held that 'the Bolshevik mentality ... steps right out of the pages of *What Is To Be Done?* It is no accident that Lenin should have taken over the title of Chernyshevsky's novel for one of his most famous pamphlets'.[4]

But Dostoevsky's own early politics had also been utilitarian; and in *Notes from the Underground* he went after the concept of self-interest as a motive with all the bitterness of a disappointed apostate:

> Oh, the babe! Oh, the pure, innocent child! Why, in the first place, when in all these thousands of years has there been a time when man has acted only from his own interest? What is to be done with the millions of facts that bear witness that men, *consciously*, that is fully understanding their real interests, have left them in the background and have rushed headlong on another path, to meet peril and danger, compelled to this course by nobody and by nothing, but, as it were, simply disliking the beaten track, and have obstinately, wilfully, struck out another difficult, absurd way, seeking it almost in the darkness. So, I suppose, this obstinacy and perversity were pleasanter to them than any advantage. . . .

Dostoevsky was assailing the bases for utilitarian psychology, and prefiguring Freud's concepts of neurosis and self-division. Self-interest became a central part of modern social scientific thinking, but advantage can be harder to imagine than one might think. No one has ever made this point more forcibly than Dostoevsky in his *Notes from the Underground*:

> Advantage! What is advantage? And will you take it upon yourself to define with perfect accuracy in what the advantage of man consists? And what if it so happens that a man's advantage, *sometimes*, not only may, but even must, consist in his desiring in certain cases what is harmful to himself and not advantageous? And if so, if there can be such a case, the whole principle falls into dust.[5]

(Freud too, as we have seen, relied on appealing to the irrelevance of advantage, but in the course of denouncing the Golden Rule, which was hardly on Dostoevsky's own agenda, since to him Christian ethics were centrally valuable.)

Bentham's reliance on the ability to calculate pleasures and pains, in the reforming pursuit of the greatest happiness of the greatest number, seemed to Dostoevsky (like Nietzsche) a rationalist illusion, one that defied what Dostoevsky felt he understood about the complexities of human motives, the way people can seek their own suffering. Dostoevsky thought he was, in the face of utilitarian reasoning, trying to rescue an intrinsic part of mankind's humanity. In *Notes from the Underground* he went on further to criticize utilitarian forms of reasoning.

> And why are you so firmly, so triumphantly, convinced that only the normal and the positive – in other words, only what is conducive to welfare is for the advantage of man? Is not reason in error as regards advantage? Does not man, perhaps, love something besides well-being? Perhaps he is just as fond of suffering? Perhaps suffering is just as a great a benefit to him as well-being? Man is sometimes extraordinarily, passionately, in love with suffering, and that is a fact. There is no need to appeal to universal history to prove that: only ask yourself, if you are a man and have lived at all.

Thomas Hobbes (ironically one of Bentham's forefathers) had made an important appeal to such self-knowledge at the outset of *The Leviathan* (1651), although the central concept that Hobbes was trying to explore was fear, not suffering. Dostoevsky's critique of Bentham's utilitarianism went in the same general direction as those of John Stuart Mill and Nietzsche, although each of these writers expressed themselves in characteristically different ways. John Stuart Mill and Nietzsche repudiated Bentham's central premises. And Dostoevsky's own suggestions about the nature of human psychology would have just as effectively wiped out the classical underpinnings to British liberalism:

> As far as my personal opinion is concerned, to care only for well-being seems to me positively ill-bred. Whether it's good or bad, it is sometimes very pleasant, too, to smash things. I hold no brief for suffering nor for well-being either. I am standing for . . . my caprice, and for its being guaranteed to me when necessary. Suffering would be out of place in vaudevilles, for instance; I know that. In the 'Palace of Crystal' it is unthinkable; suffering means doubt, negation, and what would be the good of a 'palace of crystal' if there could be any doubt about it?

And yet I think man will never renounce real suffering, that is destruction and chaos. Why, suffering is the sole origin of consciousness.[6]

These passages from Dostoevsky prefigured much of twentieth century literature; it is no wonder that he has been considered one of the main sources of existentialist philosophizing. He had in 1862 visited the Crystal Palace at the second London World's Fair, which opened in 1851 as a monument to the latest triumphs of science and technology. This 'huge cast-iron and glass building, covering nineteen acres' had become for Dostoevsky 'an image of the unholy spirit of modernity . . .'.[7] Dostoevsky heralded twentieth century authors who dwelt on the multiple irrational sides of human motivation. André Gide's concept of the gratuitous act was straight out of Dostoevsky (Gide wrote a book about Dostoevsky[8]). And Thomas Mann's approach to artistic creativity fitted Dostoevsky's notion of the unique role of suffering. Freud even argued that the psychoanalyst should not hasten to alleviate the problems of neurotic patients on the grounds that without adequate suffering there would be no incentive to overcome difficulties through rational insight. Freud, however, was trying to be a scientist who claimed to believe in the principle of predictability, and he could denounce religion as a collective neurosis which was hindering mankind's capacities to be ideally rational. Dostoevsky would reject the whole idea of mechanistic causality as an offence to the essential mystery of personality; his defence of religion, and Christianity in particular, would be a core part of his belief system.

Dostoevsky's novels and short stories developed and illustrated his core convictions about man's nature; perhaps partly because of a speech in *The Brothers Karamazov* about the central significance of parricidal impulses, Freud singled it out as his favourite novel. In 1928 Freud in fact published a now-famous essay 'Dostoevsky and Parricide'. Out of the various 'facets' that could be 'distinguished in the rich personality of Dostoevsky', Freud thought that that of

the creative artist is the least doubtful: Dostoevsky's place is not far behind Shakespeare. *The Brothers Karamazov* is the most magnificent novel ever written; the episode of the Grand Inquisitor, one of the peaks in the literature of the world, can hardly be valued too highly. Before the problem of the creative artist, analysis must, alas, lay down its arms.[9]

But Freud had serious doubts about Dostoevsky's credentials as a moralist. To Freud 'the essence of morality' was 'renunciation': 'A moral man is one who reacts to temptation as soon as he feels it in his heart, without yielding to it.' Anyone 'who alternately sins and then in his remorse erects high moral standards lays himself open to the reproach that he has made things too easy for himself'. Nor did Freud think that the final outcome of Dostoevsky's conflicts with himself was 'anything very glorious':

> After the most violent struggles to reconcile the instinctual demands of the individual with the claims of the community he landed in the retrograde position of submission both to temporal and spiritual authority, of veneration both for the Tsar and for the God of the Christians, and of a narrow Russian nationalism – a position which lesser minds have reached with smaller effort. This is the weak point in that great personality. Dostoevsky threw away the chance of becoming a teacher and liberator of humanity and made himself one with their gaolers.

Freud even thought that Dostoevsky had been condemned to this 'failure' by his 'neurosis'.[10]

Freud also proposed that Dostoevsky's epilepsy was a form of 'severe hysteria' rather than an organic affliction. And Freud traced its beginning in 'the shattering experience of his eighteenth year – the murder of his father'. Freud brushed aside the evidence that the epilepsy first occurred during Dostoevsky's Siberian exile, although that now seems to be the established view. One of Dostoevsky's small children died of epilepsy, which would point in the direction of an inherited illness in the family. Recent evidence has also thrown doubt on the idea that Dostoevsky's father had been murdered by his serfs.[11] And since it can no longer be argued that 'Dostoevsky's condemnation as a political prisoner was unjust and he must have known it', in that he had participated in a real political conspiracy, it becomes less clear that his political convictions can be attributed to guilt feelings related to supposed murderous intentions toward his father. Freud could only understand Dostoevsky's debt to 'the Christ ideal' as part of his irrational guilt-ridden psychology. And Freud found it 'impossible' to understand Father Zosima's bowing down to Dmitri Karamazov 'as an expression of admiration' for the suffering in store for Dmitri; he thought instead that 'the holy man' was 'rejecting the temptation to despise or detest the murderer and for that reason humbles himself before him.' No matter what flaws we can find in Freud's reasoning, in a way he was leaning over backwards in attributing Dostoevsky's political and religious views to 'an intellectual inhibition due to neurosis'. An alternative reading, which Freud considered a 'conservative' one, would be to 'take the side of the Grand Inquisitor' and condemn Dostoevsky differently.[12]

In a letter about Freud's essay to Theodor Reik Freud admitted a further aspect of his view of Dostoevsky, which like much of what he wrote about the great novelist can be taken to be a form of Freud's own self-criticism; for Freud, who was so concerned with psychopathology himself, claimed to regret that Dostoevsky's 'insight was so much restricted to abnormal mental life'.

> Consider his astonishing helplessness in face of the phenomena of love. All he really knew were crude, instinctual desire, masochistic subjection and loving out of pity ... [I]n spite of all my admiration for Dostoevsky's intensity and pre-eminence, I do not really like him. That is because my patience with pathological natures is exhausted in analysis. In art and life I am intolerant of them.[13]

Freud was more deeply identified with Dostoevsky than a naïve reader might suspect. For he himself also suffered from fainting fits, even though not epileptic ones; and these seizures can be understood along the exact lines that Freud used to understand Dostoevsky's own 'deathlike attacks':

> They signify an identification with a dead person, either with someone who is really dead or with someone who is still alive and whom the subject wishes dead. The latter case is the more significant. The attack then has the value of a punishment. One has wished another person dead, and now one *is* this other person and is dead oneself.[14]

Dostoevsky's understanding of the psychology of such self-punishments remains unmatched, and his outlook on suffering can lead to a re-evaluation of the whole liberal theory of punishment, which was originally put forward by Bentham.

But first let us look at the episode of the Grand Inquisitor, which appeared within *The Brothers Karamazov*. For this is an exchange in which Dostoevsky puts a powerful argument on behalf of 'miracle, mystery, and authority' into the mouth of an aged sixteenth century Spanish cardinal; he addresses his eloquent speech to Christ, who 'in

His infinite mercy' (Dostoevsky's characteristic irony is frequently missed) has come again on earth. Like Milton in *Paradise Lost*, who gave such wonderful words to Satan, it would not be sound to find the author necessarily behind even the most eloquent sentiments allotted to the Grand Inquisitor.

The dialogue in 'The Grand Inquisitor', which Dostoevsky called a 'poem in prose', is almost completely taken up with the Grand Inquisitor's own words at the time of the burning of heretics. He is a prince of the Roman Church, while Dostoevsky's allegiances were not to Catholicism of the West but to the Russian Orthodox Church. 'Is it You? You?' the inquisitor begins his examination, and receiving no answer 'he adds at once': 'Don't answer, be silent. Indeed, what can You say? I know too well what You would say. And You have no right to add anything to what You had said of old. Why, then, have You come to hinder us?' The Grand Inquisitor promises to burn Christ the next day as a heretic:

> You may not add to what has been said of old, and may not take from men the freedom You exalted when You were on earth. Whatsoever You reveal anew will encroach on men's freedom of faith . . . But now you have seen these 'free' men ... Yes, we've paid dearly for it . . . but at last we have completed that work in Your name . . . now, today, people are more persuaded than ever that they are completely free, yet they have brought their freedom to us and laid it humbly at our feet . . . For only now . . . for the first time it has become possible to think of the happiness of men.[15]

One of the central paradoxes of the Grand Inquisitor's reasoning is that he justifies his labours, which entail reducing mankind to slavery, in the terminology of liberalism's ideal of happiness, an absence of suffering.[16] And he maintains that most people are 'weak, sinful, worthless and rebellious', unable to live up to the high ideals of the few:

> And if for the sake of the bread of Heaven thousands and tens of thousands shall follow You, what is to become of the millions and tens of thousands of millions of creatures who will not have the strength to forego the earthly bread for the sake of the heavenly? Or do You care only for the tens of thousands of the great and strong dear to You while the millions, numerous as the sands of the sea, who are weak but love You, must exist only for the sake of the great and strong?[17]

The Grand Inquisitor claims to be the real humanitarian and democrat: 'We will tell them that we are Your servants and rule them in Your name. We will deceive them again, for we will not let You come to us again. That deception will be our suffering, for we will be forced to lie.' In that way the Grand Inquisitor will have 'satisfied the universal and everlasting craving of human beings and of the individual to find someone to worship':

> Man is tormented by no greater anxiety than to find someone to whom he can hand over quickly that gift of freedom with which the unhappy creature is born . . . For the secret of man's being is not only to live but to have something to live for . . . Did You forget that man prefers peace, and even death, to freedom of choice in the knowledge of good and evil? . . . You chose what is utterly beyond the strength of men, acting as though You did not love them at all – You who came to give Your life for them! Instead of taking possession of men's freedom, You increased it, and burdened the spiritual kingdom of mankind forever with its sufferings.[18]

The Grand Inquisitor and the Church (who alone will be unhappy) have corrected Christ's work:

> You judged men too highly, for they are slaves, of course, though rebellious by nature. Look round and judge; fifteen centuries have passed, look upon them. Whom have you raised up to Yourself? I swear, man is weaker and baser by nature than You believed him to be. Can he, can he do what You did? By showing him so much respect, You acted as though You had ceased to have compassion for him, because You asked too much from him. . . .[19]

The power of the Grand Inquisitor's reasoning, which is wholly antithetical to the liberal hopes of John Stuart Mill, gets only one response from Christ, who 'suddenly approaches the old man in silence and softly kisses him on his bloodless aged lips. That was His whole answer'.[20] Through that kiss there was a genuine dialectic in exchange between the Grand Inquisitor and Christ. (To complicate Dostoevsky's meaning, and lest we be tempted to see Dostoevsky only standing behind Christ, Judas had kissed Christ to identify him to the Romans, whereas Christ had remained silent when questioned by Pilate.) Dostoevsky had been able to express his thinking precisely through the duality of both positions, that of the Grand Inquisitor and Christ, and such artistry has to remain beyond the kind of tidy consistency that traditional social philosophy aims at.

Dostoevsky's whole life was as tortured as any of the most tormented characters in his fiction, and as divided as his argument in 'The Grand Inquisitor'. Unlike either Bentham or someone like John Stuart Mill, Dostoevsky was always poor and his sickliness could match that of Nietzsche. While Dostoevsky was imprisoned in Siberia he accumulated material for *The House of the Dead*, which was as powerful as any of the twentieth century accounts of concentration camps; Dostoevsky saw the perpetrators of suffering as also Christians, which lent his characterization of even the most depraved of human beings a special poignancy. Gradually he grew more and more conservative, although the emancipation of the serfs remained a central objective. His life was harrowed by conflict; for Dostoevsky happiness seems to have meant 'entrancement', and suffering amounted to 'annihilation'.[21] Everything for him seemed to be a question of all or nothing, as opposed to the Benthamite sorts of calculations of pleasures and pains. In Dostoevsky's fiction his characters yearn for degradation at the same time as they desire sainthood. Dostoevsky achieved a tremendously moving conception of human dignity, and for all his collectivist enthusiasms he developed, in the context of his Christian convictions, one of the most touching views of individualism imaginable.

Dostoevsky's novels and short stories all had a political and social side to them. And as an artist he believed in stretching emotions to their greatest intensity, 'in order to attain the maximum degree of feeling'.[22] Like Freud and Nietzsche, Dostoevsky was preoccupied with the undersides of human possibility, and the three of them steered clear of what William Dean Howells once called 'the smiling' aspects of life. Dostoevsky expressed some of his literary intentions in his correspondence. As he wrote in 1869–70 letters,

> What most people regard as fantastic and lacking in universality, *I* hold to be the inmost essence of truth … I mean to utter certain thoughts, whether all the artistic side of it goes to the dogs or not. The thoughts that have gathered themselves together in my head and my heart are pressing me on; even if it turns into a mere pamphlet, I shall say all that I have in my heart.[23]

One cannot imagine either Turgenev or Tolstoy, Dostoevsky's great contemporaries, taking such a stand. Not long after Dostoevsky's death he was being considered a saintly prophet, but Tolstoy protested: 'One simply cannot set up on a pedestal for the edification of posterity a man who was all struggle.'[24] Further, Dostoevsky's proclamation about his artistic intentions was a universe away from the world of a liberal like John Stuart Mill who claimed to have sat at Mrs. Taylor's feet, trying to embody her ideas into his publications. It is touchingly familiar to find the great Russian liberal Alexander Herzen writing to a contemporary: 'Dostoevsky was here yesterday – he is a naïve, not entirely lucid, but very nice person. He believes with enthusiasm in the Russian people.'[25]

Well might Herzen have doubted Dostoevsky's lucidity, and been impressed with his 'enthusiasm'. (His faith in the people was almost mystical, and not like John Stuart Mill's confidence in an enlightened electorate.) The exceptional fascinated Dostoevsky – the fantastic, the tragic. The reader will remember Freud's complaint about John Stuart Mill's inadequate sense of the absurd. Freud too had started off with a special interest in the abnormal; he thought that through examining mental distress, one could see the everyday in exaggeration. Through-out Dostoevsky's fiction one can find characters exhibiting what Freud thought of as conversion symptoms, or what more commonly are described as psychosomatic illnesses.

To Dostoevsky an apparently 'sane' writer like Turgenev seemed to skate on the surfaces, and was a mere painter of the superficial or the typical. Dostoevsky would savagely portray Turgenev's literary vanity in *The Devils*.[26] Unlike Bentham's harmonizing principle of utility, or John Stuart Mill's conviction that the market place of ideas could resolve the clash of incompatible beliefs, for Dostoevsky people are afflicted with unfulfillable longings and disharmonies, what one recent writer has called 'life's tragic dissonances'.[27] Dostoevsky's characters are tormented by the conflicts between values – they are yearning and restless, self-torturing and aspiring. Dostoevsky became known as the Russian Shakespeare because of the drama of his tales and the way he could isolate the human soul.

For Dostoevsky, any calculations of the greatest happiness of the greatest number had to reduce mankind's most precious individuality. Dostoevsky was great enough to engage in self-irony, and therefore he portrayed how an idea like that of purification through suffering, as with the underground man, could become a rationalization for viciousness. Dostoevsky was suspicious of liberalism for promoting, as in John Stuart Mill (and later in Freud), egotism. But he might have appreciated the psychoanalytic proposal that the capacity for suffering with others may lie behind the development of the talent for empathy.[28] Yet, unlike Freud who thought in terms of the values of survival and attaining human decency, Dostoevsky was obsessed with the key issue of salvation. He would have hated Freud's kind of scientism, and anyway Dostoevsky could be outspokenly anti-Semitic; awareness, which to Freud was so all important therapeutically, got translated in Dostoevsky's thinking into the dangers of self-consciousness. In order to attain the highest forms of humanity Dostoevsky thought one had to be vulnerable, exposed 'to sufferings and crises of conscience', which compelled one to face 'unequivocably the dilemma of God'.[29] Dostoevsky was a secular preacher who, like Nietzsche, might have well seen Freud as too small-minded in his objectives for mankind.

For Dostoevsky the purpose of suffering was to batter down pride, egoism, and wounded self-esteem. As Joseph Frank has so well put it,

> The highest aim of Dostoevsky's Christianity . . . is not personal salvation but the fusion of the individual ego with the community in a symbiosis of love; and the only sin that Dostoevsky appears to recognize is the failure to fulfil this law of love. Suffering arises from a consciousness of this failure. . . . Only that suffering is valuable which by testifying to an awareness of insufficiency in responding to the example of Christ, also proclaims the moral autonomy of the human personality.[30]

To Dostoevsky the model of Christ had the function of awakening and quickening mankind: 'Suffering is no more an end in itself than madness or chaos, and remains subordinate to the supreme value of the assertion of moral autonomy; but it serves as a prod to keep alive this sense of moral autonomy in a world deprived of human significance by determinism. . . .'[31] Dostoevsky, although he is such a precursor to so much in Freud, could not have accepted his objective of being a scientist, since he thought that any such scientific pretensions undermined the capacity for human choices. In this sense Jean-Paul Sartre is more directly Dostoevsky's heir than Freud. It should be said that Freud did try, at least in private, to distinguish between worth and health, thereby acknowledging a difference between morality and empirical psychology. But to Dostoevsky both Freud and Sartre would have seemed too secular in their atheism. It would have been unacceptable to Dostoevsky for Freud, echoing the Grand Inquisitor, ever to have considered certain patients 'worthless', and therefore outside the bounds of psychoanalytic treatment.[32] Dostoevsky was asserting the Christian value of the dignity of every human soul, and the all-importance of the ideal of human brotherhood. Freud could appreciate neurotics in line with John Stuart Mill's value of non-conformity, but both these writers fell far short of the aims of Dostoevsky's version of Christian faith. (For all Nietzsche's approval of Dostoevsky, he drew the line when it came to Christianity, which he considered a slave morality.)

Although Freud does not seem to have appreciated why Dostoevsky has Father Zosima bowing down to Dmitri Karamazov, the old man was paying 'prophetic homage to the sacredness of evil, to infernal temptations so destructive that in them the power of God's challenge and the infinity of His forgiveness are doubly manifest'.[33] Unlike John Stuart Mill's confidence in the flowering of human freedom, it was the burden of freedom which impressed Dostoevsky; man must bow down, relieving himself of the weight of his pride. That was an essential part, I think, of the many lessons built into the legend of the Grand Inquisitor. (One of Goethe's maxims had been that 'Man is not born to be free'.[34])

None of Dostoevsky's reasoning would have suited the premises of Bentham or John Stuart Mill. The Grand Inquisitor had revived the ancient idea of Plato's about the necessity of the 'royal lie'. Dostoevsky was describing human beings in an essentially Fallen state. The Grand Inquisitor's whole line of thought was in a way too rationalistic to be readily identifiable with that of Dostoevsky himself. But he was intending to highlight the craving for submission and the fear of political freedom which strikes us now as so clairvoyantly contemporaneous.

Dostoevsky, though no liberal, was not in favour of suppressing opinion; he valued what came out of the dissonance of the clash between points of view. Nihilism could not be fought without freedom of speech.[35] Suffering therefore was a key to salvation, and though this may sound abstractly theological, in his novels his people were vibrantly alive. He mentioned the Japanese custom that when one is humiliated, one humiliates oneself even further – through disembowelment. Although that seems extreme, Dostoevsky was convinced that moral freedom, 'being open to the choice between good and evil, is unthinkable without suffering'.[36] Freedom should not be confounded, Dostoevsky held, with either goodness or happiness. But all of this has to be a world away from either the rationalism of Bentham or the romanticism of John Stuart Mill. And it was of course out-of-kilter with Nietzsche's anti-Christian program.

With all Dostoevsky's pessimism, anti-Westernism, and hostility to reformism, he wanted nothing less than to transform the world. Like Dickens and Tolstoy too, Dostoevsky thought that what would be necessary had to be a fundamental change of heart; if everyone became everyone's brother, then out of that would come the brotherhood of man. And Dostoevsky was ironic about himself, as he knew that this concept of purity of heart could be used to excuse a great deal of wrong-doing. Dostoevsky was capable of brutal self-parody when it came to this notion of greatness of soul, rising to heights of scepticism that were unknown to John Stuart Mill.

For Dostoevsky it was the unique mission of Holy Russia to redeem the world through her suffering and her faith. Modest Mussorgsky would express the same theme in his *Boris Gudonov*. In contrast to the secularism in British liberalism (and later in Freud), Dostoevsky thought religion was a critical form of social cement. Here Dostoevsky had a true insight in political theory. He proposed that a great moral idea can unite people into the strongest possible union. Jean-Jacques Rousseau had proposed something of the same sort with his concept of the civic religion; but for Rousseau it was to be a 'civil' religion, whereas for Dostoevsky Christianity was itself capable of reconciling national and spiritual oppositions. Here perhaps Carl Jung would have had more in common with Dostoevsky than Freud. Dostoevsky thought that psychic tensions were an inevitable part of human experience, which puts him far apart from Bentham's form of utopianism.

The question 'Do you believe in God?' became transformed for Dostoevsky into the proposition that he believed in Russia. In contrast to the Benthamite lack of understanding of nationalism, for Dostoevsky Russia was to be the redeemer, since for him Europeans were the heathen. The hyper-consciousness of the West needed to be combated with a revival of purified Christian faith. On the other hand, it would be characteristic of many Central Europeans like Freud to look on Russians as barbarians. And it was almost a cliché of late nineteenth century to think of Russia and America as the two threatening dual powers for the coming century – Alexis de Tocqueville,

Henry Adams, and Matthew Arnold would be united on this one point. Freud's own sour view of America became notorious partly because of how it got temporarily suppressed by his disciples for the sake of the politics of the psychoanalytic movement.

For all the differences between Dostoevsky and earlier liberal thinking, the one political concept that they shared which could never be discussed the same way again was that of punishment. Dostoevsky had demonstrated how people can need punishment and self-suffering. In *The Brothers Karamazov*, for example, Ivan creates his own accusatory double to handle his guilt over death wishes toward his father. (The clash between fathers and sons, as in John Stuart Mill, was a standard nineteenth century theme; there would be little talk then of mothers, and this generalization would hold true for Freud as well.) Raskolnikov in *Crime and Punishment* acts out his irrational guilt by attaching it to the external deed of murder of killing a 'useless' old woman, and then proceeds to give himself away slowly to the public prosecutor. Raskolnikov blunders in his crime, and then gradually undermines himself as he confesses.[37] (Camus's *The Stranger* would put this in twentieth century terms by dramatizing the lack of feeling after the death of a mother.) Dostoevsky's superb sense of human dignity, obviously stemming from Christianity, meant that when Raskolnikov confesses his crime to Sonia, she cries out: 'What have you done to yourself!' The self, unlike in Bentham or even John Stuart Mill, was for Dostoevsky inherently at odds with itself.

The whole utilitarian notion of punishment would be transformed after Dostoevsky. He thought there was an inherently degrading aspect to punishment; and that if you humiliate someone, they are likely to respond by humiliating themselves further. The utilitarian tradition had started out by looking on punishment, and the infliction of suffering, from the point of view of a rational group of legislators fixing sanctions of appropriate hardship in order to deter rational people from breaking the law. We might now think that only the failures, or the stupid ones, get caught. But the utilitarian liberals thought that pleasure and pains could be carefully balanced; they reasoned that it was barbaric to cut off limbs, for example, because of minor offences. The Benthamite idea was that potential offenders could be deterred; the threat of inflicting suffering on law-breakers should work by itself. And also, the utilitarians thought that the law could serve purposes of reform, in addition to deterrence. (But Nietzsche had protested: 'The object of punishment is to improve him *who punishes. . . .*'[38]) The reforming liberals in Britain were sensitive to the degrading aspects of imprisonment, the idleness and self-hatred promoted by the traditional penal system, as a consequence of the barbarism implicit in vengeance.

The Benthamite approach was at odds with the old Kantian tradition of retribution. This older tradition had emphasized the social fictitiousness of trying to trace criminality motivationally to rational miscalculations about the risks and costs of certain acts. For this other way of looking at punishment, only legally defined crime demands punishment. The problem with the utilitarians was that their orientation was so in terms of consequences that it might justify a new sort of injustice. The principle of deterrence could be used to justify the punishment of an innocent man, provided only that he were believed to be guilty. Pragmatism in law could backfire on humanitarians, as the link between genuine guilt and crime gets snapped; the Soviet show trials of the 1930s might be defended on grounds of their political usefulness. And just as the standard of deterrence could become a loose cannon, the idea of reforming people might mean that even if someone were bad, though not criminal, they might benefit from imprisonment. The old-fashioned notion of the talionic code, or an eye for an eye and a tooth for a tooth, might not be after all so primitive. At least it meant that the grounds for punishing a grave crime had to be greater than a trivial one. And talionic reasoning also meant that the criminal has so much coming to him and no more, administered in specified ways and under set conditions.

On utilitarian grounds one was entitled to question how effective any system of law was. If, as Dostoevsky suggested, suffering can become pleasurable, and relieve guilt feelings, then the utilitarian program had a central psychological problem. In Bentham's way of thinking suffering was the result of miscalculation, a mistake, or an error of history. John Stuart Mill had tried to challenge this approach in his indictment of Bentham's own lack of familiarity with adversity and ill health. But Dostoevsky's approach to suffering was far more thoroughgoing an indictment of utilitarian psychology. Freud would propose, along Dostoevsky's lines, that there could be such a phenomena as 'criminality from a sense of guilt', meaning that there were deeds which a criminal does principally because they were forbidden, and because their execution was accompanied by mental relief for their doer. He was suffering from an oppressive feeling of guilt, of which he did not know the origin, and after he had committed a misdeed this oppression was mitigated. His sense of guilt was at least attached to something . . . With children it is easy to observe that they are often 'naughty' on purpose to provoke punishment, and are quiet and contented after they have been punished.[39]

Such an outlook on Freud's part was consistent with Dostoevsky's reasoning, and Freud acknowledged that Nietzsche knew of the sort of psychology he was proposing. As much as Freud might have agreed with the psychologies of his predecessors like Dostoevsky and Nietzsche, in a way he was also taking his stand alongside Bentham in that Freud was after all aiming in therapy to proceed in a meliorist spirit to relieve suffering.

Psychoanalysis would go on to elaborate the intricacies of criminality from a sense of guilt. Unconscious guilt could, when attached to something external, act as a relief; and to the extent that this is so, then suffering can be a positive lure rather than a deterrent. Punishment can become an outlet for internalized aggression; in exchange for suffering instinctual relief is possible. In this way conscience might be bribed and made corruptible. The notion of criminality from a sense of guilt may be statistically an exceptional problem, but the idea points to the universal issue of how one regulates one's self-esteem. Criminality takes place as a result not just of rational miscalculation, but to get attention, to achieve notoriety, to reassure one's own or someone else's contact with reality, and also to express a social grievance. The psychology of the great Spanish Inquisitions was based on such modern sounding reasoning; the inquisitors were determined to save the souls of those they persecuted, even if it meant the destruction of their earthly existence. And to bring this whole argument back to our starting point in John Stuart Mill's essay *On Liberty*, he had been trying to prevent political authority from being used on behalf of people's own so-called good.

Morals are concerned with internal states of mind, what people intend. And Dostoevsky in *The Brothers Karamazov* delivered a powerful speech about the parricidal guilt all men share, in desiring the deaths of their fathers. But liberalism, and this includes Bentham, had sought to try to keep law distinct from morality. Americans, for example, because of their constitutional heritage find it exceptionally difficult to keep straight law and ethics; it is hard for America, one of whose founding documents includes the idealistic opening paragraph in Jefferson's Declaration of Independence, to remember that what is bad need not also be unconstitutional. Liberalism has characteristically relied on procedures and insisted that such formal niceties are an essential means for preserving human freedom. As Justice Felix Frankfurter once put it in a Supreme Court opinion: 'This is a court of review, not a tribunal unbounded by rules. We do not sit like a kadi under a tree dispensing justice according to considerations of individual expediency.'[40]

It has been political reactionaries and revolutionaries – not liberals – who have been willing to sit in judgment on people's hearts. Freud's legacy would cut in different ways, since modern psychiatric knowledge can get used not just to promote autonomy but to encourage conformism or even tyranny.

Liberalism had maintained, in Lord Acton's famous words, that all power tends to corrupt, and that absolute power corrupts absolutely. Liberal thinking, as exemplified by John Stuart Mill, broadened this proposal so that opinion, and not just legislation, would be affected; in that spirit we are supposed to listen even to opinions that we hate. An ancient maxim from English common law had maintained that 'the thought of man is not tryable; the Devil alone knows the thought of man'. To attempt to judge the human soul, instead of actions, seemed to open the way to inquisitorial tyranny. And an essential division between inner and outer states had played its part in the whole history of the rise of religious toleration. The 'render unto Caesar' as opposed to 'unto God' line of reasoning in someone like John Locke had meant that certain subjects were questions relevant to political authority, while others, such as religious belief, were matters of conscience which should not be subjected to outside regulation. To concentrate on inner sinfulness could lead to political authoritarianism.

Justice is supposed to be blind, unaware of the individuals involved in one side or another in a particular case. Liberalism has tried to uphold the norm of confining the state's interest to external behaviour rather than inner feelings. One of Bracton's maxim's from the Middle Ages had held that we should be governed 'not under man, but under God and the law'. (Those words are inscribed in Latin over the entrance to Langdell Hall at Harvard Law School.) Neutrality is an essential value and goal of all liberal thought.

It is in this context that Dostoevsky's thinking proves so perplexing. Granted that we must reject the rationalism implicit in Benthamite thinking, and revise our psychological expectations in accord with what we have learned from John Stuart Mill, Nietzsche, and Dostoevsky, still it has to be worrying how many of the values of liberalism need to be undermined in this process. For most of us want to hold on to some of the central tenets of liberal thinking even in the face of the psychological realism that we are forced to contend with.[41]

Does Dostoevsky's psychology, for example, need to lead to Dostoevsky's politics? If we acknowledge the validity of the fresh insights that John Stuart Mill, Nietzsche, and Dostoevsky have held out to us, and if we realize how much they anticipated someone like Freud, how do we go about salvaging the central liberal tenets that most of us cherish? Liberalism may have helped blind us to many forms of human expressiveness, which may be one reason why so much of contemporary social science and philosophy is still able to be utilitarian-sounding.

Bentham may have had his central flaws, and even John Stuart Mill seems to have been naïve in his implicit faith in progress. The utilitarian liberals had optimistically hoped that by extending the suffrage democracies would come to flourish. It has to be a permanently sobering aspect of our thinking to remember how Adolf Hitler came to power in Germany, as we have said; he did not seize office illegally, but was voted into office as many other governments have become established in a parliamentary regime.

The history of the past century has warned us that liberalism is far more fragile than its original promoters had believed. The core values of individualism, rationality, and self-government that make up liberalism are by no means guaranteed to find themselves historically implemented. Those ideals of liberty, equality, and fraternity which the French Revolution brought forward have run into serious trouble over this past century. And someone like Dostoevsky defied everything the French Revolution had held to be so valuable; he was resolutely a nationalist in the face of European cosmopolitanism.

We now have been forced to acknowledge many of the realities of whose existence classical liberalism was unaware. As John Stuart Mill realized, there are threats to individualism that liberal ideals neglected – internal coercions, psychological barriers, that could even lead to what he called the 'enslavement of the soul' itself. The nature of the self, including introspection and repression, is of key significance to political theory, and gets explored by Freud's disciples. What once might have been commonly discussed in a theological context, has now become commonly talked about within a psychological framework. And Nietzsche, as well as Dostoevsky, has helped bring to our attention certain psychological processes that traditional liberal theory ignored. If one sometimes wonders how people got along before Freud and his psychology, we should remember how traditional concepts about God, as we have mentioned, were one way of dealing with the phenomenon that Freud discussed under the rubric of the unconscious.

To put the matter in another way, if we want to reject Dostoevsky's authoritarian politics, can we still hold onto his psychological insights nonetheless? Assuming we want to promote anything like the autonomy that John Stuart Mill had in mind, one has first to be aware of all the obstacles to fulfilling it. And Nietzsche and Dostoevsky went further than Mill did himself in acknowledging the difficulties to realizing any ideals connected with notions about 'fully developed' human beings. No longer can we believe simplistically in a device like proportional representation on a national level, which seems to have helped encourage the legitimacy of the political extremes in the last days before the pre-Hitlerite Weimar democratic German system collapsed into tyranny. America's Al Smith had once announced that the 'cure for democracy' was 'more democracy', but after Hitler, who was preceded by stalemated politics, one has to be respectful of the legitimate tensions between the needs of government as opposed to the demands of representativeness.

The history of ideas deals with parallels, analogies, and discrepancies. It cannot hope to solve all our intellectual dilemmas at once. Studying political theory should make us more sensitive to the alternatives at issue. Psychological enquiry, using the ideas of John Stuart Mill, Nietzsche, Dostoevsky, as well as Freud, should help us to broaden our understanding of what some of the central difficulties are in the face of keeping alive a liberal society. It is easy to see how all liberal thinking, and not just that of John Stuart Mill, is incapable of any neat final reconciliation with itself. By the end of his life Mill had moved in a distinctly socialist direction.

But a system of thought like liberalism is not necessarily fatally deficient because it acknowledges some of its own internal weaknesses. Spell-binders who offer us more consistent-looking simplicities are sometimes held to be more attractive than liberalism with all its hesitations. Thanks to what we can learn from some of those like

Nietzsche and Dostoevsky who were declared enemies of liberal theory, we can be better armoured to defend those precious core values that we are nonetheless determined to retain. Psychology, whether it comes from the literature of Dostoevsky or the so-called science of Freud, has an immense amount to teach us socially and politically. Political theory will thrive best when it is least restricted by conventional boundaries of knowledge. The problem of what is the good life, and how the state and society can enhance it, constitutes a large enough set of questions so that we can afford to draw on as rich a body of sources as we can lay our hands on. The aims of political theory can be fulfilled if we have asked as many of the key questions that exist; and the raising of issues, rather than the settling of particular conclusions, is as I understand it the main objective of the social philosopher.

NOTES

1. Irving Howe, *Politics and the Novel* (New York, Meridian Books, 1957).
2. Judith Shklar, *After Utopia: The Decline of Political Faith* (Princeton, Princeton University Press, 1957).
3. 'Notes from the Underground', in *Three Short Novels of Dostoevsky*, edited by Avrahm Yarmolinksy, translated by Constance Garnett (New York, Doubleday Anchor, 1960), p. 196.
4. Joseph Frank, *Through the Russian Prism: Essays on Literature and Culture* (Princeton, Princeton University Press, 1990), p. 199.
5. 'Notes From the Underground', *op. cit.*, p. 196.
6. *Ibid.*, p. 209.
7. Joseph Frank, *Dostoevsky: The Stir of Liberation, 1860–1865* (Princeton, Princeton University Press, 1986, p. 239
8. André Gide, *Dostoevsky* (New York, New Directions, 1961).
9. 'Dostoevsky and Parricide', *The Standard Edition*, Vol. 21, p. 177.
10. *Ibid.*, p. 177.
11. Joseph Frank, *Dostoevsky: The Seeds of Revolt, 1821–1849* (Princeton, Princeton Univ. Press, 1976), pp. 86–87.
12. 'Dostoevsky and Parricide', *op. cit.*, pp. 179, 181, 186, 187, 189. See Joseph Frank, 'Freud's Case-History of Dostoevsky', Appendix, *Dostoevsky: The Seeds of Revolt, op. cit.*, pp. 379–91.
13. 'Dostoevsky and Parricide', *op. cit.*, p. 196.
14. *Ibid.*, pp.182–83. See Paul Roazen, *Freud and His Followers, op. cit.*, pp.246–50.
15. Dostoevsky, *Notes from the Underground and The Grand Inquisitor* (New York, Dutton, 1960), p. 123–25.

16. Edward Wasiolek, *Dostoevsky: The Major Fiction* (Cambridge, Mass., MIT Press, 1964), p. 171.

17. Dostoevsky, *Notes from the Underground and the Grand Inquisitor, op. cit*, p. 127.

18. *Ibid.*, pp. 128–29.

19. *Ibid.*, p. 131.

20. *Ibid.*, p. 139. Cf. also Vasily Rozanov, *Dostoevsky and the Legend of the Grand Inquisitor*, edited and translated by Spencer E. Roberts (Ithaca, Cornell University Press, 1972).

21. Stefan Zweig, *Three Masters*, translated by Edan and Cedar Paul (New York, The Viking Press, 1930), p. 133.

22. *Ibid.*, p. 141.

23. *Letters of Fyodor M. Dostoevsky to his Family and Friends*, translated by Ethel Colburn Mayne, with an Introduction by Avrahm Yarmolinsky (London, Peter Owen, 1961), pp. 167, 187.

24. Aileen M. Kelly, *Toward Another Shore: Russian Thinkers Between Necessity and Chance* (New Haven, Yale University Press, 1998), p. 79.

25. Joseph Frank, *Dostoevsky: The Stir of Liberation, op. cit.*, p. 191.

26. Joseph Frank, *Dostoevsky: The Miraculous Years, 1865–1871* (Princeton, Princeton University Press, 1995), p. 463.

27. Kelley, *op. cit.*, p. 97.

28. Helene Deutsch, 'Absence of Grief', in *Neuroses and Character Types: Clinical Psychoanalytic Studies* (New York, International Universities Press, 1965), p. 234.

29. George Steiner, *Tolstoy Or Dostoevsky: An Essay in the Old Criticism* (New York, Vintage, 1961), p. 289.

30. Joseph Frank, *Dostoevsky: The Stir of Liberation, op. cit.*, p. 307.

31. *Ibid.*, p. 328.

32. Paul Roazen, *Brother Animal: The Story of Freud and Tausk, op. cit.*, p. 182.

33. Steiner, *op. cit.*, p. 299.

34. Kelly, *op. cit.*, p. 94.

35. Joseph Frank, *Dostoevsky: The Miraculous Years, op. cit.*, p. 53.

36. Philip Rahv, *The Myth and the Powerhouse* (New York, Farrar, Straus & Giroux), p. 172.

37. W. D. Snodgrass, 'Crime For Punishment: The Terrror of Part One', *The Hudson Review*, Vol. 13, No. 2 (Summer 1960), pp. 202–53.

38. Friedrich Nietzsche, *Joyful Wisdom* (New York, Ungar, 1960), p. 199.

39. 'Some Character-Types Met With in Psychoanalytic Work', *Standard Edition*, Vol. 14, pp. 332–33.

40. Terminiello v. Chicago, in *American Constitutional Law*, Alpheus Thomas Mason and William M. Beaney (Englewood Cliffs, N.J., Prentice-Hall, 1954), p. 618.

41. I am indebted once again to the work of Louis Hartz. See Louis Hartz, 'Democracy: Image and Reality', in *Democracy Today: Problems and Prospects*, ed. William N. Chambers and Robert H. Salisbury (New York, Collier Books, 1962), pp. 25–44.

Part Two:

Psychoanalysis

Freud's Power

It was during the late 1890s, while Nietzsche was still alive but no longer functioning as a philosopher, that Freud, who had been trained as a Viennese neurologist, created his new field of psychoanalysis which was designed to understand and treat neurotic afflictions. An essential key to Freud's thinking about psychopathology lies in the character of the last days of the Habsburg Empire, although psycho-analysis's claims as a science have discouraged attention to the social origins of Freud's ideas. An unusual gulf then between reality and official ideology stimulated a search for the actualities beneath the pious formulas of public truth. This general intellectual revolt was led by the educated Jews who were ideally placed to see the discrepancy because they had nothing to gain from accepting the official view. Mordant irony was one weapon for piercing the veil of the structure of formal beliefs. The cultural conflict between East and West that had its vortex in Vienna's cosmopolitan intellectual life, and the sense that liberal culture was on the verge of being undermined, would be reflected throughout Freud's mature thought. Stefan Zweig's *The World of Yesterday*[1] (1943) remains, I think, the best single account of that lost era.

Freud's starting point as a therapist was the existence of inner conflicts which interfered with the lives of suffering patients. He proposed that symptoms be looked upon as substitute satisfactions, the result of failure adequately to deal with early childhood patterns. Freud highlighted persistent infantilism as the ultimate source of adult neurotic problems. In this way he was led to an explicit theory of human nature which was to inspire multiple social and political im-plications.

It is memorable how Freud held that neuroses are psychologically meaningful, and he interpreted them as compromise formations between repressed impulses and censoring parts of the mind. One portion of every symptom was understood as the expression of wish-fulfilment, and another side represented the mental structure that reacted against the primal wish. Initially Freud thought that neurotic anxiety arose from sexual sources; specifically, he indicted dammed-up sexuality as the physical basis for neurosis, and he stood for modifying pre-existing social norms about sex.

But Freud conceived sexuality so broadly as to include virtually all aspects of childish pleasure-seeking. Fantasies of sexual grati-fication stemming from early childhood were allegedly the source of adult neurotic dilemmas. Freud proposed that a person's emotional attitude toward parents encapsulated the core problems of neurosis, and he coined the term Oedipus complex to describe a boy's first childish desires for his mother and a girl's earliest affection for her father. Freud understood that someone's emotional attitude towards a family consisted of conflicting emotions involving rivalry as well as guilt, not just desire. And he believed that the most troublesome feelings stemmed from emotional problems about which the individual remains unconscious.

Freud was insisting that people have motives which can be opera-tive without their knowing anything about them. His special viewpoint was that of a psychologist, and he sought to pierce the mysteries of memory and false recollections. Freud thought that the compromise formations in constructing our image of the past were just like those in dreaming, everyday slips of the tongue and pen, as well as the ones underlying neurotic symptomatology. He thought that the past lives on in the present, and psychoanalytic treatment consisted in the exploration of each patient's early history.

Freud was ambitious as a theorist, and his notion of neurosis became part of a full-fledged system of thought. A central implication of his approach amounted to an assault on liberal confidence in our ability to think rationally. Freud was saying that people are funda-mentally self-deceptive, and prisoners of their infantile past. Neurosis was a form of ignorance, and Freud saw it as his task to propose to utilize the power that came from enlightenment.

As much as Freud's work can be understood as a critique of the capacity for self-understanding, he could be superlatively rationalistic about psychoanalysis itself. He thought he had discovered a science of the mind, and that he had uncovered a realm of meaning which could be objectively verified. The technique of free association, which he relied on during treatment, was one that others could be trained to use. Once patients submitted to the analytic situation, involving daily meetings each lasting fifty minutes six times a week, such commitment could be used by the analyst to promote personal autonomy. Freud was relying on a structured situation in order, like Rousseau's proposed aim in *The Social Contract*, to force people to be free.

One of the chief defects in Freud's approach was his unwillingness to concede the philosophical underpinnings to his approach, as illustrated by his comments about Nietzsche. He was convinced that psychoanalysis was capable of transforming thought and undermining previous moral positions, yet he fancied that he had been able to do so without importing any ethical baggage inside his teachings. Still, Freud was clearly expressing a morality of his own; he once explained to a patient that the moral self was the conscious, the evil self being the unconscious. Freud qualified this distinction by maintaining that his approach emphasized not only evil wishes but the moral censorship that makes them unrecognizable. He was insistent that morality was 'self-evident',[2] at the same time he himself supposedly adhered to a higher standard of ethics than humanity as a whole.

Since Freud wrote so much about abnormality, it might seem that he would have been obliged to discuss his picture of mental health. But whatever Freud had in mind has to be teased out of his system of thought, since he remained loath to deal frontally with a concept like normality. It is clear that he did not envisage a utopian version of personal happiness; anxiety and despair were to him inevitable parts of the human condition. Freud sought not to eradicate human conflicts, but to teach how one can come to terms with them.

Even as Freud claimed to be intent on steering away from speculative theorizing, repeatedly he allowed himself to become engaged in social philosophy. In each of the last three decades of his life he wrote a book centering on different aspects of the psychology of religion. Early on he had made the analogy between religion and obsessional neurosis,[3] and pointed out how often outer forms have obliterated the inner religious intention, as with any other self-defeating neurotic structure. The one social coercion Freud felt to be humanly unnecessary was religion. In *The Future of An Illusion*[4] (1927) he stressed the inner instinctual core that strains beyond culture's reach; he was differing from the classical liberal tradition to the extent that he saw man not as a unit, but as an opposed self – in line with both Nietzsche and Dostoevsky. Yet it is also the case that Freud proposed that there was deep within mankind a central portion of the self that had to remain in opposition to society.

It was Freud's Enlightenment heritage that led him to denounce religious belief in so bold a manner. As of 1927 Freud insisted that human helplessness was at the origin of religious convictions; people need religion because of the failure to outgrow the dependency of childhood. Religion is an illusion in the sense that it is the product of wish-fulfilment. Freud sceptically saw religion as a pack of lies, fairy-tales which were a product of emotional insecurities. Because religion was based on irrational fears, its unreality may undermine the civilization it currently supports. Illusions are dangerous, no matter how comfortable. Freud ignored his earlier comments on religion, relating it to fears of death and guilt, as he concluded that superstition is intolerable. He was so intolerant of the infantile and the regressive that he had difficulty understanding their constructive functions.

Freud saw the family as the prototype for all authority relationships. As he had argued that God the father was needed to allay the deepest fears, so he thought that the Oedipus complex also illuminated the social cohesion of political groups. He elaborated these ideas in his *Group Psychology and the Analysis of the Ego*[5] (1921). Freud was suspicious of the masses and disdainful of the lower classes; his elitism lay behind a good deal of his social thinking. Religion always seemed to Freud a more intolerable irrationality than political authority. Politically he was impressed (like Dostoevsky) by the extent of human inner instability and the craving for authority. Although Freud's whole form of therapy aimed at liberation and independence, central objectives of Mill's liberalism, politically he remained a pessimist.

In *Civilization and Its Discontents*[6] (1930) Freud eloquently expressed his full sense of the conflictedness of life. He stressed the inevitable pervasiveness of suffering in civilized society. Although he could, as in *The Future of An Illusion*, write like an eighteenth century libertarian, here his sense of the inevitable cruelties of life was uppermost in the argument.

For civilization to be powerful enough to protect people from each other and against nature, it must, according to Freud, have at its disposal an equally intense energy. Throughout Freud's thought there is a sense of the necessary limits in life, the truth behind the maxim that one cannot have one's cake and eat it too.[7] Social unity can only be achieved on the ruins of human desires. People need the security of civilized life so deeply that they renounce the gratification of instincts in exchange for society. Freud concluded that the frustration of sexual and aggressive drives is entailed by their very character. Only if society can successfully internalize human instinctuality can civilization be maintained.

A long tradition of left-wing thinkers have dismissed psychoanalysis as a decadent form of soul-searching. At least starting with Lenin Marxists have been unhappy about what to do with Freud. Yet within socialism there has been a history of theorists eager to unite Marxist concepts with those of Freud. Trotsky, for example, was open-mindedly receptive to the significance of Freud's teachings and in personal contact in Vienna with Alfred Adler (1870–1937), one of the earliest members of Freud's circle which was first founded in 1902. Adler, although one of Freud's initial students, was also a socialist who went on to found a school of 'individual psychology', apart from Freud's own. Adler had a special concern with the social and environmental factors in disease, and emphasized the role of compensations for early defects in his study of organ inferiority; he was proposing that under the best circumstances defects in a child could create a disposition toward better performance. He was not as exclusively concerned with infantile sexuality as Freud, but was instead preoccupied with ego mechanisms and aggressive drives. In contrast to Freud's own relative lack of interest in politics, Adler sought to improve the world through education and psychotherapy.

In 1911 Freud decided to bring his differences with Adler to a head, and the result was Adler's resignation, along with about half the membership of the young Vienna Psychoanalytic Society. Adler was stressing the extent to which emotional problems stemmed from current conflicts and cultural disharmonies rather than from the patient's childhood past. he interpreted symptoms as a weapon of self-assertion, often arising from deep-seated feelings of inferiority. But he looked on the patient's wholeness as the key to neurosis; Adler was therefore concerned with what are now known as character problems.

Adler proposed to help patients with their feelings of inferiority, by leading them out of their self-preoccupied isolation into participation in the community. Through the cultivation of social feeling and by means of service to society one could subdue egotism. (This line of thought was diametrically opposed by Freud's reasoning in his *Civilization and Its Discontents*.) Adler was pioneering with his interest in the ego as an agency of the mind, and thought he could thereby help to bridge the gap between the pathological and the normal.

By 1920 Adler had directed his efforts to setting up consultations with schoolteachers; he had been intrigued all along with the psychology of the family group. He was especially compassionate toward victims of social injustice, and thought it of primary importance to help promote human dignity. Women in particular were suffering, he thought, from socially patterned oppression. Adler understood how people, out of their own inadequacies and lack of self-esteem, can bolster themselves by degrading others. Once a group or class has been treated as inferior, these feelings can be self-sustaining and lead to compensatory manoeuvres to make up for self-doubts. Chronic neurotic suffering stems from psychological over-sensitivity, and feelings of inferiority are often compensated for through protest and fantasies of greatness. Adler understood some of the key social bases for destructiveness, and those concerned with race as a psychological force in the modern world – including Frantz Fanon and Kenneth Clark – have acknowledged themselves in Adler's debt.[8]

Wilhelm Reich (1897–1957) was a Viennese psychiatrist who was also one of Freud's most talented pupils. Freud had conceived of neurosis primarily as a memory problem, a failure to recapture early childhood, while Reich tried to show that the real issue to be studied was not isolated symptomatology but the whole personality. In his work on character analysis in the 1920s Reich broadened the earlier conception of what was suitable for analytic concern.

While Reich helped to shift the focus of attention to nonverbal means of expression, he failed to convince analysts of the diagnostic significance of orgastic sexual satisfaction. Reich thought that mental health depended on orgastic potency, and he was in favour of full and free sexual expression. (Freud sharply disagreed with these ideas.) As a practical reformer Reich held that many adult problems would never develop if sexual expression were not prematurely stifled.

What orthodox analysis called sublimation, the transmutation of instinctual drives into cultural expression, was deemed by Reich to be the rationalized product of bourgeois sexual inhibitions. He started to argue in the late 1920s that Freud was betraying, out of conformist pressures, his original revolutionary stand on behalf of the rights of libido. Freud in turn objected that Reich was trying to limit the concept of sexuality to what it had been before psychoanalysis.

Reich was not only a Marxist but a Communist, and he became one of the few analysts to start building bridges between psychoanalysis and social thought. He proposed to prevent the rise of oedipal problems rather than simply study and cure them after the fact. The key, he thought, was to ameliorate human suffering through changes in the traditional Western family structure. He believed that only the dissolution of the middle-class family would lead to the disappearance of the Oedipus complex. Freud viewed neurosis as an outgrowth of the biological necessity of the family, and composed his *Civilization and Its Discontents* as an answer to Reich's position.

Reich's *The Mass Psychology of Fascism*[9] first appeared in Germany in 1935, and was written at the high point of Reich's involvement with Freudian and Marxist concepts. The central interpretive thesis was that modern man is torn by contradictory impulses toward conservatism and revolution. He craves authority, fears freedom, but is simultaneously rebellious. The authoritarian patriarchal family, Reich held, distorted some of man's most generous and cooperative instincts. Fascism represents not so much any one political party as the organized expression of the average man's enslaved character. Reich's main sociological point was that society is capable of transforming man's inner nature, producing a character structure that then reproduces society in the form of ideologies. In Reich's time the distressed German middle class became members of the Nazi radical right, and he chose to explain modern nationalism as an outgrowth of suppressed genital sexuality.[10]

Erich Fromm (1900–1980), another Marxist psychoanalyst, published *Escape From Freedom*[11] in 1941, and it immediately became a notable event in intellectual history. He won the enmity of the orthodox analysts of his day for daring to discuss factors such as the role of the environment in personality development, and the creation of social character. Societies do tend to produce and reproduce the character types they need to survive and perpetuate themselves; social character gets shaped by the economic structure of society through processes of psychological internalization. In turn, the dominant personality traits become forces in their own right in moulding the social process itself. As external necessity becomes part of the psyche, human energy gets harnessed for a given economic or social system. In this way we become what we are expected to be.

Fromm was concerned with the pathology of normality and considered it legitimate to speak of an 'insane' society and what happens to people in it. Fromm's earliest papers in the 1930s had focused on the alleged defects of the middle-class liberalism implicit in Freud. As Fromm turned away from the pessimism of Freud's instinct theory, he insisted on the potential significance of changes in the social environment as a means of altering the human condition. (Fromm acknowledged the impact of Reich's general influence on him.) Freud had not been much interested, aside from criticizing sexual mores, in the social sources of suffering and exploitation. Fromm, on the other hand, was intrigued with the way our culture fosters conformist tendencies by suppressing spontaneous feelings and thereby crippling the development of genuine individuality. Although he considered himself a socialist, these central themes of his fit John Stuart Mill's liberalism too.

Instead of seeing the unconscious as something frightening, a seething cauldron according to Freud, Fromm held that truth is repressed by an unconscious that is basically socially determined. He also thought that too often we fear our superior potentialities and, in particular, the ability to develop as autonomous and free individuals. He traced destructiveness to 'unlived life' rather than to Freud's mythical death drive. If cruelty is one of the ways of making sense of existence, it only illustrates Fromm's theory that character-rooted passions should be considered psychosocial phenomena.

For Fromm selfishness was not, as in Freud, the same as self-love. Fromm thought these traits were diametrically opposite, and therefore the possibility of altruism as an aspect of self-expression becomes a real one. Whereas Freud liked to debunk the legitimacy of altruism, Fromm – like Adler – tried to combat egocentricity. To often we hold our ego as a possession, the basis for identity, a thing.

In addition to assailing egotism, Fromm set out to combat greed and human passivity, bewailing the prevalence in the modern world of competition, antagonism, and fear. He distinguished between subjectively felt needs and objectively valid ones. He had in mind the aim of self-realization; for him self-affirmation was a process of exercising human reason in a productive activity.

Fromm believed that reason properly exercised will lead to an ethic of love, which for him was a process of self-renewing and self-increasing. Society has aimed not, as Freud thought, to repress sex, but to vilify sex for the sake of breaking the human will. Social conformism succeeds to the extent that it breaks independence without our even being aware of it.[12]

In 1955 Herbert Marcuse (1898–1979) published *Eros and Civilization*,[13] an important critique of so-called revisionist Freudian psychology like that promoted by Fromm. With great polemical skill Marcuse punctured the inspirationalist pretensions of writers who had tried to update psychoanalytic thought in a culturalist direction. Marcuse had first turned to a serious examination of Freud during the late 1930s, when he felt forced to reformulate Marxist premises. Bourgeois society had survived terrible economic crises, the proletariat was proving susceptible to fascist appeals, and the Soviet Union, both domestically and internationally, had not fulfilled revolutionary hopes. Marcuse disclaimed an interest in the clinical side of psychoanalysis, but selectively picked those concepts from within orthodox Freudian writing that might support his purposes. Relying on what he called a 'hidden trend' in psychoanalysis, Marcuse tried to demonstrate the feasibility of a non-repressive society. He maintained that Freud was the true revolutionary and that his cause had been betrayed by those who had diluted his message for purposes which turned out on inspection to be socially conservative.

Marcuse had launched a fundamentalist Freudian attack on revisionists like Fromm. By drawing on the reasoning in *The Future of An Illusion*, and through building on the Marxist concern with alienation, Marcuse was able to make use of classical psychoanalytic theory for socially utopian purposes. It seemed to Marcuse that to abandon, or minimize, the instinctivistic side of Freud's theories was to give up those concepts that underlined the opposition between man and contemporary society. Marcuse relied on Freud's instinct theory in order to ensure an energic basis within individuals for the hope of challenging the *status quo*.

It had also been Fromm's intention to alter psychoanalytic thinking in the direction of socialism. Fromm and Marcuse, former colleagues in the Frankfurt school of critical sociology, represent (adapting a distinction of William James's) the tender-minded and the tough-minded union of Freud and Marx. But although he was accurate in pointing out the somewhat Pollyannaish-sounding flavour to much of the psychoanalytic writing since Freud's death, Marcuse did not sufficiently appreciate the pragmatic and moral grounds on which these writers set out to alter their earlier commitments to certain doctrines. They had, for instance, abandoned Freud's instinct theory for the sake of avoiding what they saw as Freud's unnecessary pessimism which could seem to border on therapeutic nihilism.

Marcuse relentlessly pursued what he considered the banalities of the revisionists. In addition to attacking Fromm, he went after the ideas of Karen Horney and Harry Stack Sullivan. Despite the injustices of Marcuse's attacks, it is hard not to admire the conceptual power of his mind as he criticized the way analysts can belabour the obvious. A kind of potential social conformism can be seen as implicit in the sort of mental massage advocated by such revisionist theorists. For Marcuse there was no possibility of free personality development in the context of a fundamentally unfree society, in which basic human impulses have been made aggressive and destructive.[14]

If psychoanalysis has been used by Marcuse and others for radical social purposes, Freud has proved no less useful for conservative aims. Carl Gustav Jung (1875–1961) led the most painful of the 'secessions' from psychoanalysis; of all the pupils in Freud's life, Jung played the most substantial intellectual role. His contact in the 1930s with the Nazis only put the final seal of disapproval on a man Freud's pupils had already learned to detest.

There were long-standing sources of difference between Freud and Jung, even during their period of cooperation from 1906 until 1913; but Freud had come to depend on Jung as his 'crown prince' destined to lead the psychoanalytic movement in the future. Nevertheless, Jung had hesitated to extend the concept of sexuality as broadly as Freud wished, and came to interpret much of so-called infantile clinical phenomena as of secondary rather than primary causal importance; current difficulties, he held, could reactivate past conflicts. Further, Jung insisted that the past can be used defensively to evade the present, a clinical point which would command widespread later agreement; but at the time they split apart Freud saw Jung as merely retreating from the boldness of psychoanalysis's so-called findings.

Less rationalistic and suspicious of the unconscious than Freud, Jung began to formulate his own views on the compensatory functions of symptoms. No better critique of Freud's excessive rationalism can be found than in Jung's collected works. He proposed that symptoms are always justified and serve a purpose. (Many years later R.D. Laing and others would forward this same point.) Also, Jung was interested in further stages of the life cycle than the oedipal one. It is still not widely known how early he emphasized the central importance of the personal rapport between patient and analyst if therapy is to be successful, as he warned against the dangers of authoritarianism implicit in the neutral-seeming analytic technique. And Jung also, as the son of a pastor, took religion as a far more deep-rooted and legitimate set of human aspirations than Freud would acknowledge.

At the time of their falling out before World War I, Freud publicly accused Jung of anti-Semitism. After Hitler came to power, Jung accepted the leadership of a German psychiatric association, in what he described as an attempt to protect psychotherapy there. Continuing to live in Switzerland during this time, he helped numerous Jewish therapists to escape to England and elsewhere. But Jung had described some of the characteristics of Freud's psychoanalysis as Jewish, and he allowed his comments on the supposed differences between Jewish and 'Aryan' psychology to appear in a 1934 article published in Nazi Germany. The closeness of Jung's distinction to the Nazi one between 'Jewish science' and 'German science' has to be arresting. Despite the opportunistic collaboration with the Nazis, which has damaged Jung's historical standing, his genuine psychological contributions deserve to be acknowledged.

Freud's seeing creativity as the result of the denial of other human capacities was, to Jung (as also to Reich), an expression of Freud's sexual inhibitions. While Freud was consistently suspicious of the human capacity for regression, Jung saw the non-rational as a profound component of human vision. He had appreciation for the creative potentials of the unconscious, and saw in the unknown as much of the life forces as of death drives. Jung held that the therapist must be prepared to meet the patient at all levels, including the moral. Jung tried to deal with the philosophical dimensions of depth psychology, and was willing to discuss the implications of these ideas for a modern conception of individualism. Further, he used his notion of the collective unconscious to stress that an individual always exists in the context of a social environment.[15]

The issue of the rise of Hitler serves as a reminder of how easily psychology can be misused for the worst kinds of conformist purposes. Dr. Matthias Göring, a cousin of Hitler's deputy, headed an Institute which claimed to be housing psychotherapists. To a remarkable extent in Nazi Germany so-called psychotherapists were able to achieve the support of professional institutionalization. The success of the Göring Institute, its links to the notorious S.S. and its part in helping the Luftwaffe promote the war effort, has to besmirch the whole tradition of German 'psychotherapy'. We should be wary of the implications of any ideas which aim to harmonize the individual and the social order, a point which stands out when the society is Hitlerian. Since the practice of psychoanalysis could only be preserved in Germany by means of the departure of Jewish analysts, and the cover of the Göring name, a fatal flaw had to mar the pursuit of the psychotherapeutic profession in Hitler's Germany.

Matthias Göring's organization had solid links to pre-Hitlerian practitioners, as well as to those in post-World War II Germany. Göring had joined the Nazi party as a matter of conviction and national loyalty, and he also condemned the Jewish influence in his occupation. As early as 1933–34 he made *Mein Kampf* required reading for all his therapists. He was sufficiently partisan that his relationship with his own deputy ruptured in early 1945, over Göring's insistence that those in charge of the Institute serve as advisers to the last German units defending Berlin against the Russians. Göring maintained, in the face of the argument that such actions were futile, that it would be defeatist to do otherwise.

For reasons that are worrying in terms of intellectual history, earlier philosophical ideas, and in particular a Romantic tradition in German psychology (including Nietzsche), could be made use of by the Nazis. A special irony can be found in the Nazi conviction that in principle mental disorder within the 'master race' could not be considered essentially an organic matter, which was why Göring's applied depth psychology had its special role to play under the Third Reich. Such Nazi racism promoted the practice of Göring's form of 'psychotherapy'.

It might almost go without saying that therapists at the Göring Institute were not permitted to treat Jews. To protest against the Nazi reign would have risked not only personal destruction but also damaged the whole profession of 'psychotherapy' itself, which amounts to a damning indictment of what Göring's Institute accomplished. No one has ever been able to understand how patient confidentiality can be maintained under totalitarian political circumstances. So the Nazi regime had succeeded in destroying psychotherapy as it should be known. The German practitioners of their craft betrayed an obligation they owed to patients, humanity at large, and to the people in countries that the Nazis assaulted.[16]

Although I hesitate to bring it up after discussing Hitler's Germany, the full-scale development of ego psychology, one of the main currents in psychoanalytic theory since the late 1930s, had its own special conservative implications.[17] And it was Freud himself who set this theoretical change in motion. In the 1920s he maintained that the ego functions as a protective barrier against stimulation, whether coming from the drives in the psyche or from external reality. The ego's main task is to keep the individual on an even keel of psychological excitation. Anxiety is a danger-signal against the threat of helplessness in the face of overwhelming stimulation. Analysts, following Freud, increasingly discussed the ego as a coherent organization of psychic forces.

One does not have to look far within early psychoanalytic theory to find how Freud's negativism had been reflected in his earlier work, and why ego psychology later proved so attractive. His whole system was designed to explain motivation when a person is in conflict, and the ego has relatively failed at its integrative task. As a therapist Freud was preoccupied with pulling problems apart and tearing fixations asunder, on the assumption that the patient's ego would be able to put the pieces back together again. For Freud analysis was automatically synthesis; constructive processes had originally been taken for granted by him, an issue on which Jung had challenged him. All sorts of philosophical traditions, not just the one starting with J.S. Mill, would after Freud's death start to get brought back into psychoanalysis.

Freud had been a master at understanding the means of self-deception, but he ignored many processes of self-healing. Therefore a main trend since he stopped working has been to correct this imbalance, and to focus on the ego as an agency integrating inner needs and outer realities. The ego has a unifying function, ensuring coherent behaviour and conduct. The job of the ego is not just the negative one of avoiding anxiety, but also the positive purpose of maintaining effective performance. The ego's defences may be adaptive as well as maladaptive. Adaptation is itself bedevilled by anxieties and guilts; but the ego's strength is not measured by the earlier psychoanalytic standard of what in a personality is denied or cut off, but rather by all the extremes that an individual's ego is able to unify.

A defective ego identity can be responsible for pathology which once would have been traced by Freud to instinctual drives. Rage, for example, can result from an individual's blocked sense of mastery. Aggression can stem from an inability to tolerate passivity. Because of ego psychology's explicit attention to the interaction of internal and external realities, it opened up possibilities for interdisciplinary co-operation in the social sciences.

At the same time that ego psychology shifted from the more traditional concern with the defensive ego to the problems of growth and adaptation, it looked for the collective sources of ego develop-ment. For instance, there can be a need for a sense of identity to be confirmed by social institutions, as Erik H. Erikson (1902–94) pointed out; and here organized religion and ritual can play a positive role. But there are those who have wondered whether the upshot of ego psychology must not be inherently conservative. (We have already encountered the disturbing question of whether Dostoevsky's psy-chology has to lead to his politics, and touched on the possible connections between Nietzsche and fascism.) Society can either stimu-late or cripple the development of the individual self, and also offer a pseudo-identity in place of the authentic self.

It is possible for ego psychology to give an undue weight to conformist values. The role of work was often neglected in earlier Freudian thinking. Yet it would be misleading to look at work just individualistically and not also socially; the spirit in which work gets done may matter little if its social purpose is questionable. It may even turn out to be an advantage not to have a secure sense of self. A peripheral standing can be a source of creativity, and alienation may be meritorious. Ego psychology can fail to distinguish between genuine and artificial continuities, in keeping with its tolerance for myth and legend.

Erikson could accordingly take one-sided views of his biographical subjects. In studying Martin Luther Erikson concentrated on the young man, isolating the ethical preacher from his career as an active political leader with mixed results for human betterment. And he saw Mahatma Gandhi as primarily a reconciler of religious and political propensities. In each case Erikson sanctified a hero, leaving the impression of advocating bold change while ignoring the reactionary implications of the life under scrutiny.

Erikson's concepts always specified respect for the inner dimension of experience. But the 'sense' of identity can be different from genuine identity, and illusory feelings do not equal social reality. Ego psy-chology can communicate too much of what we want to hear, and hopefulness should not be only linked to social conservatism. Ego psychology needs to confront the possibility that there may be few social groups worth being 'integrated' with.[18] On the other hand

Freud's own kind of hostility to illusions does not guarantee that psychology will not be used complacently to justify the *status quo*. (His own politics in the 1930s led him to justify a reactionary Austrian regime, and he wrote more warmly about Mussolini than one would have liked.[19])

Walter Lippmann (1889–1974), probably the foremost American political thinker of the twentieth century, was one of the first in the English-speaking world before World War I to recognize the significance of Freud's contribution to moral thought. When the British Fabian socialist Graham Wallas was teaching at Harvard while Lippmann was still an undergraduate, Lippmann became his course assistant; and Wallas, already the author of a famous text on *Human Nature in Politics*[20] (1908), had a lasting influence on Lippmann's orientation. Lippmann seems to have first picked up on the significance of Freud through a friend who was translating Freud's *The Interpretation of Dreams*[21] (1900). World War I had a central impact on Lippmann's political thought, and starting with his *Public Opinion*[22] (1922) he grew increasingly critical of liberalism's naïve hopes for public participation in decision-making. That book was centrally concerned with the political role of the irrational. Lippmann introduced an unforgettable contrast between the complexities of the outside world and the distortions inherent in our need for simplifications in our heads. This antithesis between the immense social environment in which we live and our ability to perceive it only indirectly has continued to haunt democratic thinkers. Not only do our leaders acquire fictitious personalities, but symbols can govern political behaviour.

Between each of us and the environment there arises what Lippmann considered a pseudo-environment. He thought that political behaviour is a response not to the real world but to those pseudo-realities that we construct about phenomena that are beyond our direct knowledge. (Lippmann was relying on Plato's conception of human beings living in a cave.) The implications he drew went beyond the importance of propaganda. Along with other critics of utilitarian psychology, he held that social life cannot be explained in terms of pleasure-pain calculus. Despite all the criticisms of Benthamism that so many writers have advanced, self-interest still dominates the motives social science is apt to attribute to people; yet advantage, Lippmann believed, is itself not an irreducible concept.

In the light of the psychological insights he was emphasizing it is no wonder that Lippmann questioned idyllic conceptions of democracy, all of which have a lineage to British liberal thought. It is still hard for many people to accept the degree to which democracy, designed for harmony and tranquillity, rests on symbols of unity, the manufacture of consent, and the manipulation of the masses. Yet Lippmann offered reasons enough for permanent scepticism about dogmas of popular sovereignty.

Perhaps the peak of Lippmann's conservatism came during the Eisenhower presidential years, when the place of businessmen in high public office helped to evoke his most elitist proclivities. His *The Public Philosophy*[23] (1955) was a natural law critique of democratic government, and yet his writing continued to belie his own most reactionary principles; in seeking to be a public educator, he never lost the rationalist faith that clear-headedness on public matters can be communicated to the people effectively. He did not relinquish the democratic ideal that the voters can be rallied in defence of the public interest. Although Lippmann became doubtful about the capacity of democracy to survive under the complicated conditions of post-World War I life, he devoted his journalistic talents to the democratic ideal of purifying the news for the public's consumption. He remained troubled by the inability of a modern electorate to secure the needed information on which to act rationally.[24]

In his respect for the dignity of his patients which made his innovations possible, by means of his conviction that despite appearances all people are psychologically one, and through his individualism, Freud ranks as a great heir of the Enlightenment. He was among those who are ever demanding more freedom. At the same time, however, in the development of psychoanalysis the open-ended quality of liberalism led to a revision of some of its most cherished premises. For Freud represents an aspect of liberalism's self-examination. While at bottom it was an Enlightenment ideal to coordinate political impulses with the aim to achieve the best in us, movements of thought that ran counter to the Enlightenment also got absorbed into Freud's system.

The central trouble with the liberal tradition was its narrowness of understanding, as both Nietzsche and Dostoevsky had argued. It is frequently maintained for instance that *The Federalist*[25] exhibits a realism about human motives, as well as a lack of utopianism toward history, that might well benefit contemporary political thinking. Yet in comparison to Freud *The Federalist* seems as shallow on human nature as much of the rest of liberalism. For while Madison, Jay, and Hamilton had a shrewd eye for human motivation, they lacked a sense of the limitlessness of human lusts and ambitions. Madison tells us that ambition can be made to counteract ambition; human drives can supposedly be rearranged and engineered until a clocklike mechanism of checks and balances emerges to ensure constitutionalism. This smacks more of a utilitarian gimmick than of modern psychological depth.

In Freud's quest for an understanding of human feelings he transcended liberalism and joined hands with thinkers usually associated with traditions alien to it. Along with Edmund Burke he recognized the intensity of destructive urges and the sense in which societal coercions can be psychologically necessary. With Karl Marx he extended our appreciation of the extent of self-deception, self-alienation, and bad faith.

Freud also challenged traditional liberal democratic theory. He demonstrated the degree to which the child lives on within the adult, the way psychological uncertainties prevent people from ruling themselves. Liberalism in the spirit of John Stuart Mill has long sought for an elaboration of what a fully developed person would be like, and psychoanalytic conceptions of normality, including notions like Jung's individuation and Erikson's life cycle, are at least two such models of humanity.

In some sense Freud does fit into the liberal tradition's quest for a theory of individualism; his whole therapeutic approach did encourage a kind of self-expression that was congenial to the aims of thinkers like Mill. Whatever the excesses to which psychoanalytic ideas were sometimes put, the historical Freud did not advocate self-indulgence; he might romantically posture in defiance of Western traditions, sounding like Nietzsche in repudiating Christian ethics for example, yet Freud implicitly stood for order and civility.

Freud might be appalled at how the public now craves personal knowledge about historical figures and all public people, so that privacy today gets used in a manipulative way, and this state of intimacy is a political and social reality of contemporary life. Freud himself used his disguised autobiography, in his *The Interpretation of Dreams* and *The Psychopathology of Everyday Life*[26] (1901), to establish his principles. By daring to treat dreams and symptoms as meaningful, Freud had marked the end of an era that considered such material legitimately personal and outside the bounds of historical enquiry. Although he worked on behalf of autonomy, the implications of his ideas may have helped undermine certain features of the ideal of individualism.

Freud was ready to call feelings and acts neurotic, yet he was cautious about describing what health might consist in. Normality is one of those ideas which can be discussed endlessly, not because it is an unreal question but precisely on the grounds that psychological health remains such a challenging idea. When one thinks what it might mean to treat patients in the context of a social environment of varying degrees of cruelty or social injustice, the significance of having some broad views of normality – as opposed to proposing a conformist adaptation to whatever the *status quo* might be – should be apparent.

The humanistically oriented revisionists of Freud's views, like Fromm or Erikson, were trying to inject genuine humanitarianism into a psychoanalytic world view that appeared to end in therapeutic despair and ethical nihilism. In Fromm's neglected retorts to Marcuse's famous dissection of neo-Freudianism he accused Marcuse of ultimately advocating a nihilistic position.[27]

There may be less danger of psychoanalysis being a devastating threat to Western culture than of its lending undercover support to objectionable conformist practices. As an aspect of the success of Freudian ideas psychodynamic notions of normality have become part of the prevailing social structure around us. One need only think about how Anna Freud (1895–1982) and her collaborators at Yale Law School came up with defending the idea of psychological parenthood and used it to support the notion that continuity in child custody cases should prevail over what these 'experts' considered mere biological parenthood. The value of continuity can be as unthinkingly enshrined as a part of middle class morality as the alleged dangers of traumas were once used to frighten people into conformity.[28]

In correspondence and conversation Freud acknowledged that health was only one value among others, and that it could not exhaust morality as a whole. If he was wary about this whole subject of normality it was because he realized what kind of potential quagmire he was in danger of entering. He touched on the subject of normalcy only on the rarest occasion. Once, in an essay designed to refute Jung's views on psychological types, Freud said that an ideally normal person would have hysterical, obsessional, and narcissistic layers in harmony; his idea communicated one of his characteristic demands about how high a standard he expected of people, for to be able to bear that much conflict and still function effectively presupposes a considerable degree of self-control and capacity to endure stress. Freud typically took for granted that the people he liked best to work with were creative and self-disciplined.

Freud feared that the more original and disturbing aspects of his ideas would be destroyed by the widespread acceptance of his work in the New World. But I wonder whether he did enough to prevent precisely this outcome. By not providing more hints about normality and not owning up publicly to the wide variety of psychological solutions he found both therapeutically tolerable and humanly desirable, Freud helped contribute to what he most sought to prevent. He had set out, in the spirit of Nietzsche, to transform Western values; he was eager to go beyond accepted good and evil. When he assaulted 'love thy neighbour as thyself' as both unrealistic and undesirable, he was explicitly trying to overturn Christian ethics. For all Freud's appreciation of Dostoevsky's psychological insights, he could not go along with his conclusions about religion. Yet Freud kept his cards close to his chest when it came to what he thought about the nature of human values.

It is logically impossible to talk about neurosis without at the same time implying a standard of maturity as well, and yet despite how powerful psychology can be in outlining human defects and weak-nessses, it has not been nearly as successful in coming to terms with the positive sides of human strength and coherence. In the end the issue of the significance of normality and its relationship to nihilism has to be left an open question. Freud's psychology did contribute to our understanding of what it can mean to be human, and in that sense his ideas will be permanently interesting to political theorists. But it is impossible to attempt to spell out in a definitive way the ideological implications of psychoanalysis. The writers who have been influenced by Freud constitute a wide range of people.

It was an old analyst and loyal disciple of Freud, Helene Deutsch[29] (1884–1982), who had the most appropriately philosophic attitude towards the perplexing issue of normality. In her earlier years, when she had been one of the most prominent teachers in the history of psychoanalysis, she used to make it a practice to ask prospective analysts in the course of interviewing them for acceptance into training what they thought a normal person would be like. It is of course an ultimately unanswerable conundrum, and yet one that as civilized people we too are obliged to raise repeatedly. Like all genuine questions in political philosophy, the problem of normality can never be solved; it remains a real issue, nonetheless, to the extent we choose to find it intolerable to contemplate a universe lacking in moral values.

NOTES

1. Stefan Zweig, *The World of Yesterday* (London, Cassell, 1953).
2. *Letters of Sigmund Freud 1873–1939*, ed. Ernst L. Freud, translated by Tania and James Stern (London, The Hogarth Press, 1961), p. 314.
3. 'Obsessive Actions and Religious Practices', *Standard Edition*, Vol. 9, pp. 117–19.
4. 'The Future of An Illusion', *Standard Edition*, Vol. 21, pp. 5–56.
5. 'Group Psychology and the Analysis of the Ego', *Standard Edition*, Vol. 18, pp. 69–143.
6. 'Civilization and Its Discontents', *Standard Edition*, Vol. 21, pp. 64–145.
7. Paul Roazen, 'Tragedy in America', *Clinical Studies*, Vol. 4 (1999), pp.1–13.
8. Roazen, *Freud and His Followers*, op. cit., Part V.
9. Wilhelm Reich, *The Mass Psychology of Fascism*, translated by Vincent R. Carfagno (New York, Farrar, Strauss and Giroux, 1970).
10. Roazen, *Freud and His Followers*, op. cit., pp. 503–06.
11. Erich Fromm, *Escape From Freedom* (New York, Holt, Rinehart and Winston, 1941).
12. Paul Roazen, *Encountering Freud: The Politics and Histories of Psychoanalysis* (New Brunswick, N.J., Transaction Books, 1990), pp. 128–33.
13. Herbert Marcuse, *Eros and Civilization: A Philosophical Inquiry Into Freud* (Boston, The Beacon Press, 1955).
14. *Sigmund Freud*, ed. Paul Roazen (Englewood Cliffs, N.J., Prentice Hall, 1973; reprinted, New York, Da Capo, 1987), pp. 15–16.
15. Roazen, *Freud and His Followers*, op. cit., Part VI.
16. Roazen, *Encountering Freud*, op. cit., pp. 34–37.
17. *Ibid.*, pp. 152–60.
18. Paul Roazen, *Erik H. Erikson: The Power and Limits of a Vision* (New York, The Free Press, 1976, reprinted Northvale, N.J., Aronson, 1997).
19. Paul Roazen, 'Psychoanalytic Ethics: Freud, Mussolini, and Edoardo Weiss', *Journal of the History of the Behavioral Sciences*, Oct. 1991.
20. Graham Wallas, *Human Nature in Politics* (London, Constable & Co., 1948).
21. 'The Interpretation of Dreams', *Standard Edition*, Vols. 4–5.
22. Walter Lippmann, *Public Opinion* (New York, The Macmillan Company, 1922).
23. Walter Lippmann, *The Public Philosophy*, with an Introduction by Paul Roazen (New Brunswick, N.J., Transaction, 1989).

24. Roazen, *Encountering Freud, op. cit.*, pp. 245–51, 283–88.
25. Alexander Hamilton, James Madison, John Jay, *The Federalist*, ed. Benjamin F. Wright (Cambridge, Mass., Harvard Univ. Press, 1961).
26. 'The Psychopathology of Everyday Life', *Standard Edition*, Vol. 6.
27. Erich Fromm, 'The Human Implications of Instinctivistic "Radicalism" ', in *Voices of Dissent*, ed. Irving Howe (New York, Grove Press, 1958), pp. 313–20. See also John Richert, 'The Fromm–Marcuse Debate Revisited', *Theory and Society*, Vol. 15 (1986), pp. 351–400.
28. Joseph Goldstein, Albert J. Solnit, Sonja Goldstein, and Anna Freud, *The Best Interests of the Child* (New York, The Free Press, 1996).
29. Paul Roazen, *Helene Deutsch: A Psychoanalyst's Life, op. cit.*

Part Three:

Responses to Three
Post-Freudian Thinkers

Erich Fromm's Courage

The duty of an intellectual, as I understand it, entails a commitment to resisting power. This principle amounts to the proposition that it behoves freethinkers to oppose, as a matter of principle, whatever current fashions might dictate. It has always appalled me how, both in academic life as well as in the outside world, most people seem so apt to worship blindly that which is currently established. This sort of enslavement may make some sort of sense for those who stand to gain, in terms of self-interest, by following the dominant trends in society. But for individuals who are supposed to be devoted to the life of the mind, uncritically endorsing any aspects of the *status quo* amounts to a special sort of degradation. Intellectual life, as I see it, is a secularized priestly calling. And therefore I treasure such program-matic statements as can be found in books like Julien Benda's *The Betrayal of the Intellectuals*,[1] or Raymond Aron's *The Opium of the Intellectuals*.[2] And while I think that Fromm would doubtless have been unhappy, on political grounds, for me to link him with Aron's work, since Aron directed his polemic at the way Marxism could attract so many otherwise cultivated French thinkers, what I have to say would seem to me in keeping with the dominant thrust of what I take to be the essential spirit of Fromm's teachings.

Although many of my writings have been about Freud and those thinkers who considered themselves loyal to the movement he started, I have also been especially concerned with the fate of the analysts who were stigmatized as so-called deviants. Freud made no bones about calling both Alfred Adler and Carl Jung, for example, heretics.

In light-hearted moments Freud found no difficulty, despite all his proclamations as a scientist, in likening himself to the Pope, even if he surely knew that his was a new Church, one that was explicitly opposed to traditional religions.[3] Fromm makes an interesting exception to most generalizations connected with alleged dissidents from the 'mainstream' of psychoanalysis. For on the one hand, like others who have caused trouble for the prevailing powers-that-be in psychoanalysis, Fromm insisted that he was singularly faithful to the true meaning of Freud's message; he thought he was genuinely psychoanalytic while he believed those who invoked Freud's legacy, within the International Psychoanalytic Association and its affiliates for example, were actually false to the truest implications of Freud's heritage. At the same time Fromm took some pains to distance himself, for instance, from Jung, Freud's most notorious enemy, who founded an early break-away school of analysis. And yet Fromm became, in his own lifetime, one of those underdogs to whom I think it should be the job of intellectuals to accord special credit for the kind of accomplishments he was able to achieve. I am singling out Fromm now among Freud's many other heirs because the merits of what Fromm accomplished have become matched by how he has been so relatively forgotten.[4]

Even within my own adulthood Fromm's reputation has undergone a dramatic change. It was while I was taking a government department honours tutorial at Harvard College in my sophomore year, 1955–56, that I first read his *Escape From Freedom*. At the time nobody could be considered well educated in the social sciences without having absorbed Fromm's argument in that text, and I think that *Escape From Freedom* remains a momentous contribution in twentieth century intellectual life. Anyone educated in political theory was likely to spot familiar-sounding ideas. Fromm was centrally concerned with the fate of spontaneity in the modern world; like J.S. Mill (and also Henry D. Thoreau), he thought that 'the right to express our thoughts means something only if we are able to have thoughts of our own . . .'.[5] Fromm was moving as an analyst far from Freud's own narrower precepts, and into territory of social philosophy which should be familiar to us. For he was worried about the way our culture may foster tendencies to conform, and suppress spontaneous feelings, thereby crippling the development of genuine individuality.

Fromm had many merits as a social thinker, and was one of the earliest psychoanalysts to criticize the effects of modern mass society.

He touched on themes which are congenial to the spirit of J.S. Mill, at the same time that he was pointing to the inner unconscious sources of coercion. In a sense Fromm was drawing out the implications of Freud's concern with oppression. At the same time he was also raising Dostoevsky's problem of the fear of freedom; for he too doubted whether mankind in fact desires anything like the choices which liberal theory assumes and takes for granted.

Fromm had early on been heavily influenced by Marxist thought, and perhaps his most powerful concept was what he called 'social character'. Whereas Freud had started out from the presence of symptoms, and only later talked about individual character structure, Fromm wanted from the outset to discuss centrally how social forces interact with individual psychology. Societies do, he maintained, tend to create and duplicate the personality types that they need to sustain themselves. Peasant culture or capitalism thrive by implanting the characterology in people that leads to the maintenance of the social system as a whole. '[T]he social character internalizes external necessities and thus harnesses human energy for the task of a given economic and social system.'[6] These 'external necessities' include the economic structure of society. Social character is moulded by the economic modes of existence of a society, and in their turn the dominant character traits become productive forces shaping the social process. Fromm was expanding Mill's insights into the role of broad political culture, even if the question of which comes first, the individual or society, has to be left as a chicken-and-egg matter.

Fromm was writing on behalf of what he called a productive as opposed to a non-productive mode of being. For him it was not too much to hold that a whole society can be neurotic. Often we are 'well adapted only at the expense of having given up' the 'self in order to become more or less the person' we believe we are 'expected to be'.[7] (It is likely that Fromm had never read much Jung, or else he would have found a similar-sounding line of reasoning in that pioneering analyst; Fromm was substantially put off by Jung's politics.) Fromm was providing new arguments on behalf of J.S. Mill's own fears of the growth of conformism. He talked about what he called 'automaton conformity' in which 'the individual ceases to be himself; he adapts entirely the kind of personality offered to him by cultural patterns; and he therefore becomes exactly as all others are and as they expect him to be'.[8]

Freud had only once in print briefly touched on the issue of freedom, in a footnote: 'after all, analysis does not set out to make pathological reactions impossible, but to give the patient's ego *freedom* to decide one way or the other.'[9] Fromm was outspokenly eager, as the years passed, to confront the classic problems of moral philosophy. He complained that 'modern man . . . has not gained freedom in the positive sense of the realization of his individual self; that is, the expression of his intellectual, emotional and sensuous potentialities.'[10] (Fromm remained less wary than he might have been about the dangers of 'positive' freedom as emphasized by Sir Isaiah Berlin; Berlin partly was relying on Mill's authority to uphold what Berlin called 'negative' freedom.[11]) Fromm, like Bentham, thought it was possible to derive objective standards of how we ought to live, but Fromm was relying on the science of psychology to yield normative standards. Traditional philosophy had too often ignored the inner sources of blockage: 'although man has rid himself from one enemy of freedom, new enemies of a different nature have arisen; enemies which are not essentially external restraints, but internal factors blocking the full realization of the freedom of personality.'[11] Such self-betrayal would be characterized by someone like Jean-Paul Sartre as 'bad faith', while Fromm tried to handle the same subject by extending the kinds of concepts Freud had put forward. Fromm might have turned away from Freud's instinct theory, because of its pessimistic conclusions, but he was still concerned, as we have mentioned, with destructiveness not as a consequence of human drives but as the outcome of what he chose to call 'unlived life'.

Fromm had taken a different outlook on the social environment from what can be found in Freud, and he interpreted the Oedipus complex, for example, as an aspect of traditional patriarchal culture. The problem of female psychology was also understood by Fromm within social terms as well as Freud's more strictly individualistic drive theory.[13] Fromm went on to write other important books of interest to all social scientists and political theorists, such as *Man For Himself* (1947), *The Sane Society* (1956), and *The Anatomy of Human Destructiveness* (1973),[14] but it was *Escape From Freedom* in 1941 which brought down on his head the wrath of orthodox analysts who felt he had betrayed the purity of Freud's psychological message. The commercial success the book had must also have done much, I suppose, to have offended some of Fromm's former allies at the Frankfurt school of critical sociology, which had moved to New York City temporarily during World War II, since they were less successful than

Fromm in being able to articulate an argument that could appeal to the broad reading public. So from among the Freudian as well as Marxist camps Fromm had his ideological enemies.

Like others, such as today's most resolutely systematic popularizing defender of Freudian orthodoxy, Peter Gay, I was initially attracted to psychoanalysis by Fromm's writings.[15] As far as I can recall, I was reading Fromm's many books long before I studiously set out to read Freud himself, although I had been assigned Freud's *Civilization and Its Discontents* in my first year as an undergraduate in an introductory course in political philosophy. At one time I could be certain that I had read everything by Fromm, at least all that had been translated into English. I whisked through his book *Sigmund Freud's Mission* when it first came out in 1959, although I am afraid at the time I did not believe some of his critique of Freud.[16] My scepticism about Fromm's argument, I hope, can be traced to the way in which, as the years passed, he was increasingly tempted to make Marx into a hero, while I had always been dubious about Marx's standing in Western thought.[17] Max Weber, and in particular his *Protestant Ethic and the Spirit of Capitalism*, had an early appeal to me because of his insistence on the independent force of religious ideas, and in general the power of the mind to affect the course of history.[18] Marx's insistence on the inevitability of class struggle, and the dependence of thought on class as a part of social structure, seemed to me alien to the world as I (and for that matter, Marx himself) had experienced it, and then Fromm appeared bent on humanizing some of Marxism's most revolutionary features.

Although I was dubious about parts of the thesis in *Sigmund Freud's Mission*, it was not long before I began reading for myself Ernest Jones's three volume biography of Freud.[19] At the time, the early 1960s, Jones's detailed account of Freud's life and ideas seemed enormously seductive, and hard to challenge. Jones constructed an edifice that has attracted many besides myself, and as an expert in power-seeking, he knew the force that historical legend could exert.[20] I later found out that some famous orthodox analysts, in New York City for instance, were grateful for the successful political act that Jones had accomplished through his biography.

It took me some time to appreciate the central weaknesses in Jones's approach. An orthodox analyst like Robert Waelder had known enough to wade in and write an article against Fromm's *Sigmund*

Freud's Mission.[21] Jones's saga, in the meantime, appeared incontrovertible. It was only when I undertook to do my own interviewing, in the mid-1960s, of those people still living who had had personal contact with Freud, that the blinders I had once shared started to dissipate, and I could absorb the full merits of Fromm's position about Freud. By the time Fromm sent me a personally inscribed copy of *Sigmund Freud's Mission*, with an acknowledgement of what I had accomplished with my 1969 *Brother Animal: The Story of Freud and Tausk*, I understood how successful Fromm had been so early on in pulling the rug out from under Jones's version of Freud.

When I met Fromm in 1966, he was a relatively isolated figure within the world of psychoanalysis. It was paradoxical that it was in the radical days of the late 1960s that his reputation among North American intellectuals began its serious slump. The more successful Fromm became in running rings around official psychoanalysis and the better he was able to appeal to general readers, the easier it became to write him off as a popular preacher, a psychoanalytic Norman Vincent Peale.

In the hindsight appropriate to the history of ideas, Fromm deserves full acknowledgment for being one of the earliest to have raised some of the key, even if elementary-seeming, questions about Freud's work. Fromm undertook a psychoanalytic exploration of Freud's life, in the course of his short text on Freud's 'mission'; Jones, with all his invaluable documentary material, had been able to evade attempting anything like an objective appraisal of Freud's psyche. Fromm, for example, asked some deep questions about Freud's relation to his mother, a subject which has still received an inadequate amount of attention in the vast literature about the creator of psychoanalysis.[22] I doubt that Fromm knew some of the minutiae about Freud's life, for example his failure to attend his mother's funeral in Vienna that we have already mentioned. (Despite the case to be made against committing the naturalistic fallacy in ethics, it does seem to me that in our culture certain acts and feelings are required as part of what I think of as natural piety.) Freud was also late for his father's funeral, another detail I suspect Fromm may have ignored; but Fromm had the brains to detect that Freud's complex tie to his mother was something that Jones neglected to explore, even though that key relationship necessarily had to be an essential constituent of Freud's whole psychology.

Fromm's courage seems to me the most obvious attribute of his contribution. The large number of his works that are in print around the world indicates that his independence has paid off. In contrast, Erik H. Erikson, an analyst who was terribly fearful of being excommunicated from the movement and temperamentally given to having only the most elusive confrontations with Freud, had not fared nearly as well with the general population. Erikson was enormously talented as a psychologist.[23] And yet the cautious way he expressed himself, with the exquisite care he took in distinguishing his own work from Freud's, has meant that Erikson has been in a slump of his own in recent times. He was determined not to have his own work associated with that of Fromm, despite the similarities in their using social science as a corrective to Freud's framework, and Erikson would have been unhappy to have been mentioned in association with Fromm. But Fromm's outspokenness, and the bravery he showed in constructing his own theoretical system, has meant that his writings are today readily accessible in Spanish, Italian, German, French, English, and other languages too, in a way that Erikson's books are not as likely to be.

By the time I interviewed Fromm he was seemingly detached from the outside world. When I travelled to see him, he was not even available in Mexico City, and I went to visit him in Cuernavaca. Yet millions of people are still reading his works today; no other psychoanalyst's writings, around the world, are still as available to airport bookstore browsers. And yet these books are not studied as class assignments in schools or most training institutes; nor does Fromm's audience depend on whatever prestige may be associated with lining office bookshelves with 'official' authors – which explains why many psychoanalytic texts are bought even if they remain unread. Furthermore, Fromm's capacity to achieve his success, such that it has been outside of most official psychoanalytic circles, is all the more remarkable in that he was for the most part not writing in his native language.

At the time I met Fromm, vicious stories were circulating about him in North America. One famous neo-Freudian analyst in New York City said that Fromm was then inhabiting a palace carved from stone outside Mexico City. In fact Fromm lived in circumstances that were modest, certainly as compared with the lavish Park Avenue apartment my informant enjoyed. One relatively emancipated Toronto analyst, who at the time was probably earning about 300,000 Canadian dollars a years thanks to a lavish provincial insurance system that subsidized analysis for an unlimited amount of time, not only thought of Fromm as immensely rich, but also maintained that Fromm was 'quietly going mad' in Mexico.

Today psychoanalysis in North America has long since been eclipsed by the many advances that have taken place in so-called biological psychiatry. If I were a young man now, instead of being as concerned about the abuses of power within psychoanalysis as I was then, I would probably be making a study of contemporary psychiatrists, for, with a naïve commitment to the possibility of making exact-sounding diagnoses, they are capable of perpetuating the kinds of misuse of scientistic authority that took place around the turn of the century before Freud's revolution in ideas got under way.

Fromm's interest in asking the most fundamental questions, and his conviction that Freud had not been radical enough, meant that he was able, starting in the 1930s, to tease out some of the central moral and philosophic bases of Freud's outlook. Fromm was shrewd as a Marxist in spotting the bourgeois premises Freud took for granted. At the same time he shared Freud's belief, especially as expressed in Freud's post-1923 cancer-ridden phase, that psychoanalysis had succeeded in attaining the status of being a neutral scientific body of knowledge. We now know that despite Freud's protests about being compared with traditional philosophers, even as a young man he was far better acquainted with philosophy and more widely-read than one might have imagined. I am told that in Freud's library in London there is a book of Kant's with Freud's marginalia in it, despite the fact that there is scarcely even now, with all that has been written about Freud, anything to speak of about his links with someone like Kant.

Fromm's special contribution as a psychologist was to be concerned with understanding the social forces that both stabilize as well as undermine society. Freud had looked on society chiefly as the individual's enemy. But Fromm was interested in the problem of social change, and how such sociological issues can be understood in the light of depth psychology. Fromm's concern here was not just a theoretical one, although his abstract contributions as a thinker were remarkable. For in his last years he helped co-author a fascinating study of Mexican peasantry, *Social Character in A Mexican Village*, which shows how he was able to think through concrete problems

106

afresh.[24] His posthumously published *The Working Class in Weimar Germany*, which only appeared in English in 1984, illustrates how he had always possessed an empirical dimension to his thinking, even though he has so often been accused of merely being a moralist.[25] Freud too had a rabbi's voice in him, but had a way of camouflaging it so that at least for a time in North America the intelligentsia swallowed the line that he was primarily a scientist.

Fromm naturally had his predecessors within psychoanalysis, and as we have seen, Wilhelm Reich may be perhaps the most notable among those who tried to unite Marxist and Freudian thinking. Reich has, however, because of his unfortunate last years, tended to be almost eliminated from the orthodox history of the development of Freud's thinking. As in Stalinist historiography, which rewrote the past to exclude the contributions of someone like Trotsky, so Reich's key role within the Vienna Psychoanalytic Society has been obscured by simply omitting to mention his work or even his name.[26] Reich's attack on the role of patriarchal family structure in mobilizing oedipal reactions, and his yearnings for a utopian society in which the worst constraints of middle class family life would be lifted, so that a new and non-neurotic humanity might arise, seemed serious enough to arouse Freud to have warned against Reich's sort of thinking.

Fromm's reputation has suffered from different sources than those that have undermined Reich's contributions (which included notable works by Reich on negative transferences, the role of nonverbal communications, and the problem of so-called technique in psychoanalytic therapy.) Orthodox Freudians not only succeeded in wiping Reich off the map of the history of modern psychology, but they nearly managed to efface Fromm's work as well. Once Fromm was dead, it no longer seemed necessary to carry on diatribes against him; but I was amazed, for instance, when my collection *Sigmund Freud* first appeared in 1973, containing an article by Fromm, how much of the review in the *International Journal of Psychoanalysis* was taken up with an assault on Fromm.[27]

After Fromm's death in 1980 he necessarily became less menacing to orthodoxy. Certain psychoanalytic journals, which have been known to reject advertisements for books by 'deviants', now began to accept money from publishers of Fromm's books. Thanks to the feminist movement, and a reconsideration of Freud's alleged ideas about female psychology, Karen Horney's works have notably crept back into the bibliographies of papers that appear in official psychoanalytic quarterlies. It may still be the case that it would be unwise, if one is to get a paper accepted by an orthodox psychoanalytic journal, to list too many citations to the works of someone like Jacques Lacan, but then he is a current-day danger, and his followers still a threat to the International Psychoanalytic Association, whereas Horney is no longer deemed such a terrible problem.

Fromm's standing has suffered not just from the most fanatical Freudians, but there are other modern ayatollahs as well in his case, and die-hard Marxist hard-liners have been determined to dismiss Fromm as a so-called social democrat. In certain circles such a designation is as damning as it would be for someone to be called a Jungian in the New York Psychoanalytic Society, or to acknowledge an indebtedness to Franz Alexander in Chicago. The school of self psychology, initiated by Heinz Kohut in Chicago, came to be deemed by Anna Freud as 'anti-psychoanalytic'; but Kohut, one of the leaders in trying to thaw out the rigidities of classical analysis, would have shied away from being linked with the 'dissidence' of either Jung or Alexander. Fromm had to deal with the same sort of sectarianism not only within psychoanalysis, but from embattled Marxists as well. It is still true in Canada, for example, that the standing of Theodor Adorno, who disapproved of his former ally Fromm, rides high; and Adorno's friend Herbert Marcuse published that famous critique of Fromm.[28] Despite Fromm's telling 1958 response to Marcuse's failure to understand the therapeutic side of Freudian thinking, his rebuttal of Marcuse's indictment has still not attained the currency it deserves.[29] It is hard for outsiders to over-estimate the degree of sectarianism among Marxists: but it is certainly telling that in 1936 Adorno could think that for the sake of correcting Fromm's critique of orthodox psychoanalysis Fromm needed 'to read Lenin'.[30]

Fromm, when I saw him, acknowledged that at one point he had himself been an orthodox Freudian, although his withdrawal from that sort of thinking was unclouded by any problems with Freud personally, since he had had virtually no contact with Freud. Nonetheless it is hard to believe that Fromm could easily forget how his *Escape From Freedom* had once been denounced as a betrayal – all hell broke loose over his innovating ideas. Karl Menninger, who wrote a blistering review of the book, tried to maintain in his last years that he could not remember what could have separated him from neo-Freudians like Horney, and Menninger even tried to cover his tracks by writing flatteringly to Thomas Szasz. (The kind of hatred Szasz could inspire among analysts took even Marcuse's breath away, and Marcuse was hardly a stranger to ideological hatreds.) But Menninger had, on the appearance of *Escape From Freedom*, done his best to discredit Fromm publicly. Horney, along with Fromm, Harry Stack Sullivan, and Clara Thompson, formed the psychoanalytic Left; people like Abram Kardiner, Sándor Radó, and Alexander were on the identical side of the anti-establishmentarian fence.

But left-wingers are notoriously difficult to hold together organizationally, and each of these people tended unnecessarily to differentiate their own publications from those of others. I suppose it is the fate of brave pioneers to have special difficulty in hanging together. Still, it is appalling in retrospect, thinking of the ideal of toleration,[31] to find Alexander criticizing Horney; and Fromm himself, who may well have later regretted tarring Otto Rank's use of 'will' with fascism, looks from a Rankian perspective now as someone who did not hesitate on occasion to stoop to conquer. Had Fromm ever functioned as part of a prestigious research university, his work would never have been as underrated as it is now; this attractive hypothesis has been advanced by as acute an observer as David Riesman.

Yet although Fromm was outside the clinical 'mainstream', and in her lifetime Helene Deutsch was very much a part of it, both of them were capable of taking the identical view of the writings of Otto Fenichel. Deutsch told me she thought Fenichel's famous textbook was the 'cancer' of psychoanalysis, and Fromm too thought that Fenichel, one of his opponents over *Escape From Freedom*, engaged in a kind of obsessive theorizing that meant the end of psychoanalysis. Sándor Radó, highly critical of Fromm, once reminisced that Fenichel, a former analysand of Radó's, had succeeded in his textbook in constructing 'a remarkable record of all the errors in psychoanalysis'.[32]

Fromm in his lifetime was notable for not being afraid to be alone, even in the face of the worst threats of heresy-hunting. And he generalized about how difficult it was for most people to risk his own kind of solitude. (Mill might have theorized about heresy, but he had less first-hand experience of it.) Fromm told me that he had had a 'brief' orthodox phase, from about 1926 until 1935; yet if one examines some of his papers in the early 1930s the seeds of later ideological trouble are already discernible. When I talked with Fromm, I tried to press him to elucidate in writing what the implications of his ideas were for practical issues connected with the conduct of psychoanalytic therapy. Fromm said he was going to do a book-length work on the matter, but never lived to fulfil that objective.

Freud, too, had not wanted to write much about technique, and I think only got into the subject in order to differentiate his approach from that of Adler and Jung.[33] Students have an excessive need for certainty and leap at every chance to be given rules and guidelines. Freud had not initiated the idea of training analyses; that represents a contribution of Jung, who doubtless thought that the fact that Freud had not been personally analyzed helped account for the kinds of troubles Jung had had with him. Only after Freud was already sick did didactic analysis become standard training for future analysts, even if in Paris today there are prominent analysts who want to do away with the practice of training analyses. Lacan's seemingly arbitrary ways of proceeding in certifying people as analysts are not really so different from Freud's own habit of personally anointing those to be sanctioned within the profession as qualified to treat patients. (For all the Lacanian interest in experimenting with time, little seems to be remembered about what Alexander had to say on the subject; nor was Alexander aware of how much he owed to Jung, although heresy-hunters would have been delighted to associate him with the Jungian 'deviation'.)

Before almost anyone else, Jung had gone to some lengths to show why the use of the couch had authoritarian implications; yet few in Paris today, for example, seem aware of the possible drawbacks to its therapeutic use. Fromm told me that he simply thought that the couch was not 'helpful', and he preferred having the patient sit in a chair. The problem with the couch, according to Fromm, is that 'nothing happens' therapeutically, and here Fromm turned to discuss his own 'unsuccessful' analysis with Hanns Sachs. Fromm never mentioned to me any other analysis that he underwent except that one with Sachs, although one researcher has now concluded that Fromm had something of a record in having had some four other analysts.[34]

Fromm thought that Sachs had excelled in making 'ludicrous' inter-pretations. (Helene Deutsch told me she thought Sachs was a poor therapist; she readily acknowledged how many of his prominent analysands seemed to appreciate him, but she felt it was at the expense of their relationship towards Freud.) Fromm said he was obliged by the injunction to free associate to be 'conscientious', and expressed from the couch just what sort of animal (a pig) Sachs reminded him of. Actually, Fromm said, Sachs bore more exact resemblance to an owl. But Sachs had responded to Fromm's observation by saying that Fromm's hanging his coat on a peg right beside Sachs's coat belied Fromm's own negative-sounding words. Fromm insisted to me that such an interpretation made no sense, since realistically there was nowhere else in the room to put his coat.

Fromm had met Sachs in later years when Sachs was established as the first training analyst in Boston. At that point Sachs had both a servant and a butler, the first butler Fromm had ever seen, or Sachs either according to Fromm. In those days Sachs had an abundance of Wasp upper-class patients, and Helene Deutsch told me how when she had moved to Boston, becoming the second training analyst there, Sachs had lamented about the difficulty of trying to conduct analysis without using rabbi stories. After about a year, Deutsch ran into him again and asked how he was doing without the rabbi tales; fine, Sachs said, he changed the rabbi into a minister, thereby 'baptizing' the jokes. Humour was an essential aspect of Freud's and other early analysts' own therapeutic practices, although little is written about this aspect of their clinical approaches.

Since I had been trained as a political scientist, and Fromm understood what sort of field work I was then conducting, he encouraged me to try and find out 'where the power lay' within the psychoanalytic movement. (Although much has been written about the so-called secret committee around Freud, I do not think he ever yielded the mantle of the authority of psychoanalytic leadership.) Fromm's third wife, who sat in on our interviews (and I seem to remember cats wandering around), wondered aloud where on earth the New York analysts had got their technique from, since the aim of neutrality and distance seemed so foreign to how Freud himself had proceeded. Her question was an excellent one, which I have thought about a lot. I concluded later that the Americans had come to Vienna in Freud's sick phase, and identified with the relatively distant, detached, dying Freud. But there was also hypocritical disguising of what Freud had actually been like, and this shared secret became a powerful bond among Freud's loyal disciples.[35]

Fromm, when I saw him, was astonished to hear about the change that had taken place in Anna Freud. He recalled her as a modest, shy, and retiring person, and seemed to have little idea about the political power she was capable of wielding. He knew that 'London' had been responsible for himself being dropped as a direct member of the

International Psychoanalytic Association (IPA), but somehow he did not link this expulsion with Anna Freud herself. Fromm correctly perceived that there had been a 'court' around Freud, and he wanted to be sure that I found out who were the most important figures there. (Although I have not examined the letters at the Library of Congress between Waelder and Anna Freud, it is a safe bet that his attack on Fromm got directly sent to her.)

Fromm mentioned Freud's mother's dream, which was reported by Lancelot Whyte, about the death of her famous son Sigmund.[36] When I contacted Whyte, he was not certain whether it had been a 'dream' of the old woman's or a waking vision; in any event Fromm made the shrewd point that when Freud's mother described how she had visualized the major heads of state of the European countries standing around her eldest son's casket, she was revealing a curious conception of him, and of herself. For how many mothers, and Jewish ones at that, if they had had such a fantasy, would have allowed the news of that calamity to cross their lips? Freud's mother obviously had an image of Freud as a powerful warrior, one that he himself shared; so that when he took the night train from Paris to London in 1938, old and sick, still he dreamt that he was arriving at the same place in England as William the Conqueror in 1066. Fromm had his own prophetic streak, which may have helped sensitize him to this side of Freud. And Fromm also had a special interest in exploring the primal tie to mothers, and how it can be coped with.

From Fromm's point of view, Freud's strongest point had been his 'honesty', but I think that this is rather harder to discuss than Fromm might have thought. Fromm was after all a representative of old German culture, whereas Freud remained a Viennese to his fingertips. For the Viennese, I am convinced, truth-telling was a complex matter, and Austrians rather sneakier than Germans. I am reminded of a story told me by a bookseller in pre-World War II Vienna when in 1938, after the Anschluss with Germany, he found that his concierge was flying a Nazi-party flag outside the building. This seemed a surprising partisan affiliation, so the concierge then took the Viennese bookseller up to his apartment; he opened a closet that was full of the party flags of every possible political group, from the monarchists to all the left-wing organizations. Whoever had come out on top would have been celebrated with an appropriate flag. One cannot exactly see that as old Viennese dishonesty, since none of them were, by North American standards, straight-shooters. Freud could talk out of both sides of his mouth, sending praise to an author while simultaneously asking a disciple to tear the same author's books to pieces.[37] North American straightforwardness would have seemed to central Europeans as barbarism. Freud's subtle capacities for artistic inventiveness turn up in the way he fashioned his case histories, which is likely to seem to many contemporaries now as falseness and an unscientific example of rhetorical partisanship.

Freud, as Felix Deutsch admitted privately, was a great 'fighter', and I think he had a complicated set of weapons at his disposal. Freud's disappointment with Jung meant that he never got over the loss of that most talented of all his students, and as one of Freud's pupils once remarked to me, all Freud's writings have to be understood in the light of the opponents he was trying to rebut. Kurt R. Eissler, like Freud before him, collected a set of his own stated 'war plans'. And Fromm himself could be embattled. He told me how Jung had been a 'destructive' force, and knew all about the most unfortunate sides of Jung's politics in the 1930s.[38]

But as knowledgeable as Fromm could be, he seemed to have little precise information about Jung's private life, or any of the sexual involvements with his patients that we have subsequently learned so much about. Fromm did know exactly who in Switzerland had immediately denounced Jung's collaboration with the Nazis in Germany. As we have alluded to, one of Jung's enduring contributions, despite his politics, was his interest in being more explicit in bringing together psychology and philosophy. Here Fromm aimed to be himself more systematic, and Jung, rather similarly to Erikson, was temperamentally, and perhaps culturally, incapable of the kind of theoretical clarity that Fromm was so good at.

I think that what Freud had going for him, and what helped him prevail against all his opponents, was not just that he was such a masterful writer, but that he succeeded in getting his own version of events, without contradiction, into the history books. Only years later, for example, long after their historic falling out, did Jung mention in a seminar in the 1920s what had happened between himself and Freud, and that text did not subsequently come into print until 1989.[39] Freud had a powerful sense of history, something that Fromm also shared, which is what prompted him bravely to contradict Jones's version of Freud. (At that time, when Jones's books were widely being hailed as definitive, only Bettelheim was willing to state publicly that Jones had failed to be properly psychoanalytic.) Fromm also published a

Foreword to Helen Puner's 1947 *Sigmund Freud*, a strikingly prescient early biography.[40]

My work on the historiography of psychoanalysis can be seen as fleshing out some points that Fromm had early on understood on the basis of his theoretical convictions. As courageous as Fromm had been in challenging Jones, he was unaware of the degree of hanky-panky that has afflicted Freud's texts. It turns out that not only had Freud's letters been tampered with, at least up until the time I published the unedited version of Freud's comments to Lou Andreas-Salomé after Tausk's suicide, but even the published versions of Freud's writings have also been altered, when it suited his students to do so. It is not only the case that much of Freud's correspondence has to be republished some day, but texts now in the Library of Congress indicate that passages have been cut from papers of Freud's that are treated as canonical in the professional literature. Readers should be alerted that unless something appeared in Freud's lifetime, it is likely that changes have been introduced by his editors after his death. Freud's letters are now appearing uncut, starting with the Freud–Jung correspondence in 1974. But we are only now learning about how his other texts have been tampered with.

The aim of re-translating all Freud into English, however, seems to me a misguided undertaking; the French translations of Freud, which are still not complete, have dragged into his works all sorts of words that have not been used for centuries. Worse still, purism about translations, which are all inevitably an act of interpretation, is apt to reinforce the idea that what we have with Freud is a new gospel. Instead of treating what Freud said as holy writ, it seems to me better to acknowledge that on central points he could be wrong. Here Fromm was one of the most important of Freud's critics, and fixing up translations, and re-editing Freud's writings, is not capable of correcting some more central problems – that is, just where Freud could be mistaken.

Fromm stoutly maintained that he himself did not believe in 'kowtowing' to free associations. He reported how in Berlin, during the time he was active there, it was commonly discussed how important it could be, from the therapists' point of view, to analyse dreams that analysts had when they fell asleep during sessions with patients. Fromm implied not only that analysts could get bored, but that such nonsense of trying to find the psychological significance in the content of the dreams of delinquent analysts reflected the early conviction that the truth about the patients was already known. Fromm was impressed enough by our encounter for him to tell me that he was eager to hear from me in the future, and over the years we exchanged a number of letters about what I had been finding out.

Unfortunately, it seems that a large part of Fromm's own correspondence has disappeared, at least what he kept in his files. Fromm's conviction about preserving his own privacy (and that of others) may deter scholars from appreciating the stature he genuinely deserves in the full-scale account of the history of psychoanalysis. Kohut and Donald Winnicott, for example, have both had volumes of their letters appear. Such documents are ready fodder for students of intellectual history, and to the extent that we have lost such material in connection with Fromm it is going to be harder to reconstruct his proper role. In Freud's case, for example, it has recently been discovered that there was an early draft of his paper on war and death, in the form of a lecture he gave to B'nai B'rith in Vienna under the title of 'Death and Us'.[41] It is going to take a long time before we come anywhere near exhausting the Freud primary sources, and only in the coming century are the sealed Freud Archives at the Library of Congress going to be made available for the inspection of neutral researchers. It might be better if scholarship devoted more of its energy to verifying the merits of what someone like Fromm had to say, rather than continuing to track down the intricacies, interesting though they may be, of what we can learn about Freud.

I am convinced that part of Fromm's strength came from a genuine identification that he made with Freud. For Fromm everything in psychology was supposed to be open to question, even if on some points even he may have been too credulous about what Freud (or Marx) had to say. It is one of the critical aspects of the history of psychoanalysis that to be genuinely like Freud means that one has to be independent. But this means that penalties are going to be paid, in that the crossing of trade-union boundaries entails that there are bound to be organizational squabbles. I have found, in some of my travels among psychoanalytic groups, that one dividing line has to do with those who read as opposed to those who do not; it is impossible to defend oneself against those who do not examine texts, not to mention against people who make no pretence of trying to be fair-minded. If one presumes already to hold the key to genuine knowledge, the ideal of toleration makes no sense. Fromm was, I think, being true to the best spirit of Freud as an investigator to the extent that Fromm tried to give expression to what he himself had experienced. That sort of outspokenness should be more important than any allegiance to organizational bodies. But Fromm's kind of independence is bound to come at a price, and not everyone is willing to pay the kind of penalty he did. Nietzsche's own isolation was about as extreme as anyone's in the history of ideas.

Too many in psychoanalysis have been willing to have twisted thoughts, and unclarified positions, in order to avoid the dangers of heresy. Both Paul Federn and Sándor Ferenczi were so intimidated by the risks of deviancy that their work suffered as a consequence; I wonder how widespread this phenomenon has been. The problem is that each of the many sects that have grown up within psychoanalysis has been relatively unaware of what others have been doing; and therefore it has been hard to establish all the continuities in the history of ideas that the historiography of psychoanalysis should be aware of.[42] It is no genuine tribute to Fromm, however, to try to assimilate his original ideas into the work of subsequent analysts, like the object relations school for instance, since these later people have been able to proceed with the mutual support of one another, running little ideological danger. That ideas might be in style now should not be taken by itself to enhance Fromm's pioneering, since that amounts to insulting him by looking through the wrong end of a telescope.

In my own experience, once I published *Brother Animal* in 1969 there was a special series of attacks on me. This was felt necessary because my first book, *Freud: Political and Social Thought*,[43] had been welcomed by powerful orthodox analysts. When I was interviewing Freud's pupils and patients, I think it was assumed by those I saw that somehow I would ultimately be controllable. Analysts are after all dependent on colleagues for referrals, and the unconscious ways people can be intimidated into conformity ought never to be underestimated. As a student of the history of ideas, with no clinical practice of my own to defend, there were no conceivable practical sanctions, aside from the possibility of hostile reviews, that could be exerted against me. Silence in the face of publications is always an effective device. Although it looked to orthodox Freudians as if I had betrayed the 'cause' from inside, which helps account for the anger of Eissler and Anna Freud,[44] I always felt secure in my own independent course. Unfortunately the more outsiders like social philosophers know about such internecine fighting, the more likely they are to continue to steer clear of the whole effort by psychoanalysts like Fromm to link up with the great tradition of political thought.

Implicit in my approach, as in the work of Fromm, was an ideal of objectivity; although the truth may be impossible to discover, I believe it is essential in all scholarship to proceed as if the standard of truthfulness is the ultimate recourse. Although it is unfashionable in many academic circles today to say this, still I would insist that putting a premium on our own subjective responses can endanger not just the pursuit of research but ultimately democracy itself. How I interacted with Fromm personally, and my own educational background, had a profound impact on what I happened to learn from him. I would not doubt that someone else, with a different set of concerns, would have come up with an impression of both him and his work that would be unlike my own. I am also not sure that I can prove that my own version of Fromm is in any sense definitive, and I would certainly be eager to agree that many others, far more knowledgeable about Fromm, are in a better position than I to write about his contribution. Simplistic scientism, the belief among some analysts that causes can be directly linked to effects, needs to yield to a less linear outlook that concedes the inevitability, and desirability, of allowing more leeway to legitimizing interpretations that are unverifiable. After all, what I am trying to accomplish here is just to start establishing some links between the social thinkers who preceded Fromm as well as some key writers who followed him.

I would insist that my own hesitancies, and awareness of how illusory objectivity can be, does not in any way imply that there does not in principle have to be such a thing as truth. A permanent danger of fascism exists in the modern world, and perspectivism or moral relativism, no matter how encouraged by Nietzsche's teachings or how attractive tolerance for diversity may seem, can be an invitation to the idea that might makes right. (The whole point in writing about Fromm now is to try to redress an existing imbalance in intellectual history as it has been received.) Giving up the standard of objective truth, which Fromm refused to do, can lead to deferring to whatever happens to be dominant at any time. Fromm, like other émigrés from Germany, was centrally concerned with the rise of fascism; I would argue that the success of Hitler in overcoming the Weimar republic is the single most important political event in twentieth century history. The Nazi near-revolution did not take place violently, but

Hitler's success occurred within the confines of the pre-existing republican political system. The fact that Weimar Germany could self-destruct is an essential part of why Nazism continues to be so troubling a turn of events.

Fascism, however, has many possible sources, some of them stemming from the way intellectuals think. Nietzsche-like playfulness about varieties of interpretations can lead some contemporary philosophers to think it is legitimate to make up things as they go along. I gather that in later years, long after Fromm wrote that paper against Rank, he had his doubts about the wisdom of reprinting the piece. Anyone like Fromm who witnessed the triumph of the Nazis is perhaps entitled to be supersensitive to ideas connected to 'will' that might sound congenial to a Hitlerian points of view. Fromm was right to denounce Jung's collaboration with the Nazis, although Jung's unfortunate anti-democratic politics, not to mention his anti-Semitism and political opportunism, do not mean that his psychological thinking cannot still have something vital to teach us. Dostoevsky was a defender of the Czar and the Orthodox Russian Church, and also anti-Semitic, as we have discussed, but that cannot refute his being one of the greatest psychological understanders of all time. The relationship between psychology and politics is a complicated one, and just because a thinker is sound politically, or that we find a figure attractive democratically and socially, does not mean that a profound psychology is necessarily embedded in a theorist's work. Fromm's own critique of American policies at the height of the Cold War (which I did not happen to share) helped damage his standing among the typically hard-nosed political scientists who on policy grounds grew to suspect the author of *Escape From Freedom*. (The extensive FBI dossier on Fromm is a tribute to how nonsensical J. Edgar Hoover could be; on the other hand, we now know that the Frankfurt Marxist Franz Neumann was for a brief period a KGB agent.[45] One cannot expect that the FBI could keep straight one such thinker like Neumann – whose widow Marcuse married – from someone like Fromm.)

Even though I would have disagreed with Fromm politically, he has something to teach us about the dangers of all sorts of collaboration. He was highly critical of Erikson's ego psychology, on the grounds that it embodied an implicit sort of conformism; and to some extent Fromm was right about Erikson, although, as we shall see, I think I learned a lot myself from contact with him. In university life right now in North America we are, I think, being swept up by a dangerous form of righteousness, called political correctness, which is a movement I consider seriously at odds with the ideals of the objective search for truth. Hannah Arendt and Karl Jaspers wrote to each other about what they considered the collapse of German universities at the beginning of the Nazi regime.[46] I only wish it were easier to be brave within today's university pressures, and to insist on the significance of merit alone as opposed to all the non-academic criteria that are being imposed on us. It is one thing to have courage within psychoanalysis, when I remain an outsider to the field; but I concede it is a lot harder, as a member of academic life, to assert the endangered qualitative priorities that are so precious to the life of the mind.

Although these observations about contemporary academic life may seem a digression, I admit that courage is harder to come by than may seem to be the case, and that Fromm is to be commended for the risks that he took, which after all involved not just his livelihood but the congeniality and support of traditional colleagues. I hope he found sources of sustenance in Mexico. It still seems to me remarkable how he was willing to stand up for what he believed in, as he could tolerate a kind of isolation that surely was not always easy to bear. He should be a model of independence and autonomy for us all.

One can hope that intolerances among the Left in psychoanalysis can be minimized; for it is those people, not the organization-types, who have had all the new ideas, although it is hard to detect which currently fashionable theories are to be attributed to identifiable earlier thinkers. How many Kohutians, for example, would feel comfortable with considering what Jung wrote about the self and processes of 'individuation', and yet why should that lineage cause so much concern? Donald W. Winnicott happily went about distinguishing the 'true' self from the 'false' one, even though any such philosophic-sounding talk would doubtless have offended Freud. Originality should not require a certified pedigree within psychoanalysis; some of the most interesting new thoughts have come from people whose names are apt to be anathema to orthodox analysts. I would be in favour of doing the best work one can, and claim Fromm's example even where he might have disagreed with the specific conclusions one arrived at.

In the history of psychoanalysis, and in intellectual life as a whole, it is too often the case that earlier figures get forgotten. Whenever I have been on a PhD board and met Marxist candidates, I have always tried to ask some questions about Marx's enemy Mikkel Bakunin;

because the fact that Marx won and Bakunin lost, within the struggles of the First International, says nothing about the merits of the points that each of them had to make. I was originally attracted to psycho-analysis because of the way in which its respect for failure was at odds with political science's tendency to glorify success. Whatever Freud's personal snobberies might have been, his system of thought paid the greatest respect to those parts of us that malfunction. In keeping with Freud's original standing as an outsider, it is striking how much of an uphill struggle it has been to establish the legitimate role that Fromm has played in the history of psychoanalysis; but that only makes me think that rectifying the situation, and paying him his due honour, is especially incumbent on us. Whatever legitimate disagreements there ought to be about what Fromm's legacy adds up to, I think few can deny that his responsible outspokenness, which I have called courage, should be a special beacon for us all.

This essay has probably done more to put Fromm in the context of the history of psychoanalysis than to spell out his special con-tribution to social thought, but I have been trying to expand the understanding of the implications of Freud's work. The reader will have noticed the reappearance of some of the issues – like conformism and individuality, as well as the fear of freedom – which we en-countered in treating the ideas of J.S. Mill, Nietzsche, and Dostoevsky. Fromm was a socialist as well as a Freudian, and even if we put aside his attempt to place Marx only within a sanitized form of humanism, it should be clear that his work adds up to a challenge for pre-existing liberal thought. Unlike Freud, whose moralizing was episodic and largely unspoken, Fromm tried to create a universal ethical system out of his union of Freud with Marx. No one can really hope to succeed at such a grand enterprise, but to the extent that Fromm came up with ideas that challenge how we think psychologically, socially, and politically, then he did something important not only to add to the tradition of social philosophy, but to establish the significance for political theory of such a central theorist like Freud. Although Fromm might have been surprised to discover that one of the central points he had been able to establish was the relevance of Freud, and the whole of the psychoanalytic tradition, for political thinking, I think it is to Fromm's enduring credit that he added so momentously to the vitality of Freud's heritage.

NOTES

1. Julien Benda, *The Betrayal of the Intellectuals* (Boston, Beacon Press, 1955).
2. Raymond Aron, *The Opium of the Intellectuals* (London, Secker & Warburg, 1957). See also Tony Judt, *Past Imperfect: French Intellectuals, 1944–56* (Berkeley, University of California Press, 1992).
3. Ludwig Binswanger, *Sigmund Freud: Reminiscences of a Friendship* (New York, Grune & Stratton, 1957), p. 9.
4. Neil G. McLaughlin, 'How To Become a Forgotten Intellectual: Intellectual Movements and the Rise and Fall of Erich Fromm', *Sociological Forum*, Vol. 13 (1998), pp. 215–46; Neil G. McLaughlin, 'Why Do Schools of Thought Fail? Neo-Freudianism as a Case Study in the Sociology of Knowledge', *Journal of the History of the Behavioral Sciences*, Vol. 34 (Spring 1998), pp.113–34. See also Daniel Burston, *The Legacy of Erich Fromm* (Cambridge, Mass., Harvard University Press, 1991). Pioneering early studies include notably Clara Thompson, with the collaboration of Patrick Mullahy, *Psychoanalysis: Evolution and Development* (New York, Grove Press, 1950) and Norman Birnbach, *Neo-Freudian Social Philosophy* (Stanford, Stanford University Press, 1961).
5. Erich Fromm, *Escape From Freedom*, *op. cit.*, p. 241.
6. *Ibid.*, p. 284.
7. *Ibid., p.* 139.
8. *Ibid.*, pp. 185–86.
9. 'The Ego and the Id', *Standard Edition*, Vol. 19, p. 50.
10. Fromm, *Escape From Freedom*, *op. cit.*, p. viii.
11. Isaiah Berlin, *Four Essays on Liberty* (London, Oxford University Press, 1969), and Michael Ignatieff, *Isaiah Berlin: A Life* (New York, Metropolitan Books, 1998).
12. Fromm, *Escape From Freedom*, *op. cit.*, p. 104.
13. Erich Fromm, 'Sex and Character', in *The Dogma of Christ, and Other Essays on Religion, Psychology and Culture* (New York, Holt, Rinehart & Winston, 1963), pp. 107–27.
14. Erich Fromm, *Man For Himself: An Inquiry into the Psychology of Ethics* (New York, Holt, Rinehart & Winston, 1947), Erich Fromm, *The Sane Society* (London, Routledge & Kegan Paul, 1956), Erich Fromm, *The Anatomy of Human Destructiveness* (New York, Holt, Rinehart & Winston, 1973).
15. See Paul Roazen, 'Review of Gay's *Freud: A Life For Our Time*', *Psychoanalytic Books*, January 1990; Paul Roazen, *Encountering Freud: The Politics and Histories of Psychoanalysis* (New Brunswick, New Jersey, Transaction, 1990), pp. 13–16, 263–64; Paul Roazen, 'Review of Gay's *Freud: Explorations and Entertainments*', *The Toronto Globe and Mail*, June 9, 1990.

POLITICAL THEORY AND THE PSYCHOLOGY OF THE UNCONSCIOUS

16. Erich Fromm, *Sigmund Freud's Mission* (New York, Harper Colophon Books, 1959).
17. Erich Fromm, *Marx's Concept of Man* (New York, Frederick Ungar, 1961), and Erich Fromm, *Beyond the Chains of Illusion: My Encounter with Marx and Freud* (New York, Pocket Books, 1963).
18. Max Weber, *The Protestant Ethic and the Spirit of Capitalism*, translated by Talcott Parsons (New York, Charles Scribner's Sons, 1930).
19. Ernest Jones, *The Life and Work of Sigmund Freud*, 3 volumes (New York, Basic Books, 1953–57). See also Ernest Jones, *Sigmund Freud: Four Centenary Addresses* (New York, Basic Books, 1956).
20. Paul Roazen, *Freud and His Followers* (New York, Knopf, 1975; New York Da Capo, 1992), Part VII, Chs. 5–6; Paul Roazen, 'The Freud–Jones Letters', *International Forum of Psychoanalysis*, October 1996 (in *Behind the Scenes: Freud in Correspondence*, ed. Patrick Mahony, Carlo Bonomi, and Jan Stennson, Oslo, Scandinavian University Press, 1997); Paul Roazen, *Oedipus in Britain: Edward Glover and the Struggle Over Klein* (New York, Other Press, 2000).
21. Robert Waelder, 'Historical Fiction', *Journal of the American Psychoanalytic Association*, Vol. 11 (July 1963), pp. 628–51.
22. Roazen, *Freud and His Followers, op. cit.*, pp. 39–46; Paul Roazen, *Meeting Freud's Family* (Amherst, University of Massachusetts Press, 1993), pp. 35–37, 168, 189–95. Ana-Maria Rizzuto, *Why Did Freud Reject God? A Psychodynamic Interpretation* (New Haven, Yale University Press, 1998), Chs. 10–11.
23. Paul Roazen, 'Psychology and Politics: The Case of Erik H. Erikson', *The Human Context*, Vol. 7 (1975), pp. 579–84; Paul Roazen, 'Psychohistorian as Mythologist', *Reviews in European History*, September 1976, pp. 457–65; Paul Roazen, *Erik H. Erikson: The Power and Limits of a Vision* (New York, The Free Press, 1976; Northvale, New Jersey, Aronson, 1997); Paul Roazen, 'Erik Erikson's America: The Political Implications of Ego Psychology', *Journal of the History of the Behavioral Sciences*, Vol. 16 (1980), pp. 333–41; Paul Roazen, 'Review of Friedman, *Identity's Architect: A Biography of Erik Erikson*', *The American Scholar* (in press); Paul Roazen, 'Review of *Ideas and Identities: The Life and Work of Erik Erikson*', ed. Wallerstein and Goldberger, *Psychoanalytic Psychology* (Spring 2000). See also Roazen, *Encountering Freud, op. cit.*, Ch. 8.
24. Erich Fromm and Michael Maccoby, *Social Character in a Mexican Village: A Sociopsychoanalytic Study* (Englewood Cliffs, New Jersey, Prentice-Hall, 1970).
25. Erich Fromm, *The Working Class in Weimar Germany: A Psychological and Sociological Study*, translated by Barbara Weinberger, ed. Wolfgang Bonss (Cambridge, Mass., Harvard University Press, 1984).
26. Roazen, 'Review of Gay's *Freud*', *Psychoanalytic Books*, January 1990, pp. 10–17.

27. Paul Roazen, *Sigmund Freud* (N.J., Prentice Hall, 1973; New York, Da Capo, 1987). Frederick Wyatt, *The International Journal of Psychoanalysis*, Vol. 57 (1976), pp. 488–91.
28. Herbert Marcuse, 'Critique of Neo-Freudian Revisionism', in Roazen, *Sigmund Freud*, *op. cit.*, pp.59–81.
29. Irving Howe, ed., *Voices of Dissent* (New York, Grove Press, 1958), pp. 313–20.
30. Quoted in Neil McLaughlin, 'Origin Myths in the Social Sciences: Fromm, the Frankfurt School and the Emergence of Critical Theory', *Canadian Journal of Sociology* (1998).
31. Paul Roazen, 'A Plea For Toleration', *Clinical Studies*, Spring 1997.
32. Paul Roazen and Bluma Swerdloff, *Heresy: Sándor Radó and the Psycho-analytic Movement* (Northvale, N.J., Aronson, 1995), p. 101.
33. Roazen, *Freud and His Followers*, *op. cit.*, Parts III, IV.
34. Ernst Falzeder, 'The Threads of Psychoanalytic Filiations or Psychoanalysis Taking Effect', in *100 Years of Psychoanalysis*, ed. Andre Haynal and Ernst Falzeder (London, Karnac, 1994), pp. 180–81.
35. See for example, Paul Roazen, 'Freud's Analysis of Anna', *op. cit.*
36. Lancelot Whyte, *Focus and Diversions* (New York, Braziller, 1963), pp. 110–11.
37. Roazen, *Freud and His Followers*, *op. cit.*, pp. 501–02.
38. Paul Roazen, 'Jung and Anti-Semitism', in *Lingering Shadows*, ed. A. Maidenbaum and S. A. Martin (Boston, Shambahla, 1991).
39. C. G. Jung, *Analytical Psychology*, ed. William McGuire (Princeton, N.J., Princeton University Press, 1989).
40. Helen W. Puner, *Sigmund Freud: His Life and Mind*, 2nd edition (New Brunswick, N.J., Transaction, 1992).
41. David Meghnagi, ed., *Freud and Judaism* (London, Karnac, 1993).
42. Paul Roazen, *The Historiography of Psychoanalysis* (New Brunswick, N.J., Transaction, 2000).
43. Paul Roazen, *Freud: Political and Social Thought* (New York, Knopf, 1968, 3rd edition, with new Introduction, New Brunswick, New Jersey, Transaction, 1999).
44. Roazen, *Meeting Freud's Family*, *op. cit.*, and Roazen, *Encountering Freud*, *op. cit.*, Ch. 6. See also Paul Roazen, 'What Is A Fact? Eva Rosenfeld', *Psychotherapy Review*, October 1999.
45. Allen Weinstein and Alexander Vassiliev, *The Haunted Wood: Soviet Espionage in America – the Stalin Era* (New York, Random House, 1999), pp. 249–51.
46. *Hanna Arendt/Karl Jaspers Correspondence 1926-1969*, translated by Robert and Rita Kimber, ed. Lotte Kohler and Hans Saner (New York, Harcourt Brace, 1992).

123

The Rise and Fall of Bruno Bettelheim

Examining Bruno Bettelheim should, like our look at Fromm, further explore some of the key political, social, and philosophic sides to psychoanalysis. Bettelheim's role in intellectual history has long been known to be a special one, but now it appears that his place is bound to remain every bit as contentious as that of any other figure in the controversial story of the development of Freud's school. Perhaps the height of Bettelheim's stature, at which time he was probably the most famous psychoanalyst in the world, came when Woody Allen cast him for the part of an interpreting psychiatrist in *Zelig* (1983). Ever since Bettelheim's suicide in 1990, however, his standing has been in a slump, and subsequent accusations against him by former patients have meant that the downturn of his reputation has deepened drastically.

Out of all his impressive body of writings, he will probably remain best known for his famous study on Nazi concentration camps. In 1943, while Bettelheim was associated with a little-known institution called Rockford College in Illinois, he published in a relatively obscure journal, after being turned down elsewhere, an article titled 'Individual and Mass Behaviour in Extreme Situations'. Here he had a chance, at a time when the general public was still unaware of some of the worst atrocities of the Nazis, to report on his own observations after having spent 'approximately a year'[1] at Dachau and Buchenwald in 1938–39. Dwight Macdonald republished in his journal *Politics* parts of Bettelheim's piece soon afterwards, and it has subsequently become a classic document in modern social science.

124

They were then camps, Bettelheim reported, 'for political prisoners',[2] and he detailed the ways in which he thought the inmates reacted oddly, by the standards of pure rationality, to their confinement. Bettelheim said he himself had survived the ordeal by having made the decision, as a psychologist, to protect the integrity of his personhood through observing and collecting data about how the camps affected the personalities of other prisoners. He distanced himself from what he experienced and differentiated his own response from that of others by the self-protective device of using his knowledge of depth psychology to interpret behaviour under the extremity of what only later came to be known as the Holocaust.

Although he reported that at the time 'extreme malnutrition' had 'deteriorated' his memory, Bettelheim recounted how he found two compatriots, one the son of a Viennese psychoanalyst, to share their thoughts and feelings with him. (The analyst's son has since reported that Bettelheim spent seven or eight months in the camps.) Bettelheim proposed that the 'initial shock' of incarceration had been hardest for the non-political middle-class political prisoners, who were 'a small minority', to resist: 'They had no consistent philosophy which would protect their integrity as human beings, which would give them the force to make a stand against the Nazis.' From this population came 'the several suicides' and these people were the ones responsible also for anti-social behaviour like cheating on fellow inmates and spying on behalf of the Gestapo.[3]

Bettelheim contrasted the behaviour of others with his own fundamental choice. Perhaps the most enduring sentence in all Bettelheim's work, for me, was how he summed up in italics 'his main problem' during the time he spent in the camps: *to safeguard his ego in such a way, that, if by any good luck he should regain liberty, he would be approximately the same person he was when deprived of liberty.*[4]

Prisoners adapted to the camp situation in different ways. (It will be recalled how Dostoevsky's own experiences in Siberia got immortalized in his *The House of the Dead*.) Bettelheim studied the dreams and fantasies of the inmates; readers at the time must have been startled to learn how impossible 'open resistance' was, 'as impossible as it was to do anything definite to safeguard oneself.' In passing, he commented that the 'few who had tried to fight back could not be interviewed; they were dead.' While everyday experiences that might have occurred in 'normal' life provoked a 'normal' reaction, he argued that paradoxically the greater the suffering in the camps the more apt people were to accept their lot as martyrs and not to resent it.[5]

Those who stayed in the camps more than a year became, in Bettelheim's terms, 'old prisoners', and were, he held, apt to change their attitudes towards families and friends in a way that he thought qualified them for being described as having 'transgressed to infantile behaviour'. Such people, he alleged, exhibited a wide variety of irrational responses. For example, they wanted to believe that in the outside world, which they had been forced to leave, 'their worldly possessions should be secure and untouched, although they were of no use to them at this moment'.[6] To think of change back home was too threatening.

More troubling, and here some have thought that Bettelheim was insulting his fellow sufferers, was his proposal that such old prisoners tended to adopt the convictions of their persecutors. *'They had learned to direct a great amount of aggression against themselves so as not to get into too many conflicts with the Gestapo, while the new prisoners still directed their aggressions against the outer world, and – when not supervised – against the Gestapo.'*[7] (This was another sentence that Bettelheim italicized.)

While Bettelheim and 'the few other prisoners who realized what was happening' held back and retained their autonomy, he complained about a mass behavioural pattern that he considered an example of regression into infantilism: 'ambivalence to one's family, despondency, finding satisfaction in daydreaming rather than in action'. By allowing themselves to be pushed by circumstances into 'childhood attitudes and behaviours', they 'became in this way more or less willing tools of the Gestapo'.[8]

It is hard for me to evaluate how Bettelheim's argument was then received. He was, of course, describing the perfectly dreadful, almost unimaginable circumstances of concentration camp life. But he was not talking about factories of extermination, since that part of Hitler's program had yet to be inaugurated during the period in the late 1930s when Bettelheim himself was imprisoned. The public has too easily been muddled over the extent of Bettelheim's personal experiences. William Styron in *Sophie's Choice* somehow relied on Bettelheim's authority about Auschwitz, when in fact Bettelheim had nothing to do with any of the death camps; he was already in the United States by 1939.

It is still memorable and shocking how Bettelheim in his 1943 article thought that a prisoner had reached 'the final stage of adjustment to the camp situation when he had changed his personality so as to accept as his own the values of the Gestapo'.[9] Anna Freud, in a book written while her father was alive and in the spirit of the work of his disciple Sándor Ferenczi, described the 'defence' of identifying with the aggressor,[10] and Bettelheim was giving concrete illustrations of this unconscious self-defeating process. For example, he said 'It was not unusual to find old prisoners, when in charge of others, behaving worse than the Gestapo. . . .' He maintained that not only did 'old prisoners' seem 'to have a tendency to identify themselves with the Gestapo' in regard to aggressive behaviour, but 'they would try to arrogate to themselves old pieces of Gestapo uniforms'. While rationally the old prisoners should have resisted their tormentors, Bettelheim was saying that instead they 'accepted their goals and values, too, even when they seemed opposed to their own interests'.[11] Bettelheim was appalled at what he observed, though it confirmed some of the worst of what psychoanalysis had taught about the human condition.

At the end of his paper, just before summarizing its findings, Bettelheim placed a paragraph that struck me, when I reread the essay long after first coming across it, as weird. For he seemed here to be trying somehow to retract, under pressure from his editors or out of conformity to contemporary sensibilities, the essential theoretical message of his piece, covering the tracks of his iconoclasm with words that might protect him from critics:

> After so much has been said about the old prisoners' tendency to conform and to identify with the Gestapo, it ought to be stressed that this was only part of the picture, because the author tried to concentrate on interesting psychological mechanisms in group behaviour rather than in reporting types of behaviour which are either well known or could reasonably be expected. These same old prisoners who identified with the Gestapo at other moments defied it, demonstrating extraordinary courage in doing so.[12]

In essence, however he may have tried to pull back at the last moment, the crux of Bettelheim's argument led in a different direction. When he went on to call 'greater Germany' a 'big concentration camp',[13] he meant to denounce how people collectively had failed to resist outside conformist pressures. Bettelheim was, in the spirit of John Stuart Mill, trying to uphold the liberal ideal of the individual as an autonomous and self-reliant entity, as opposed to what Bettelheim perceived as the degradation of the human spirit under the extremity of the Nazi system.

However critically others might have reacted to Bettelheim's article later on, at the time it did seem to register an important anti-fascist message. Bettelheim's publisher for many years, The Free Press of Glencoe, reported on a later book jacket that General Dwight D. Eisenhower had made 'Individual and Mass Behaviour in Extreme Situations' required reading 'for all military government officers in Europe'. It is known that when, at the end of the war, Eisenhower first saw the liberated camps, he was literally sickened, and insisted on the local townspeople being marched through them to see the horror for themselves. I do not know how he heard about Bettelheim's piece; a staff officer may have brought it to his attention. Alternatively, the impetus may have come from higher up; one story has it that Eleanor Roosevelt was involved in getting Bettelheim out of Buchenwald in 1939, and perhaps she took notice of his work. She stayed once with General Lucius Clay, head of the American military government in Germany, and it is known that he thought the world of her.

Growing up in the 1950s, as I did, meant that Bettelheim had not, in my own education, attained the general stature he had acquired by the 1980s; his writings were never included as part of my own required reading. As a Jew I was reasonably aware of the significance of what had happened in the concentration camps; on a trip through Europe as a teenager I had paid a silent pilgrimage through a small barren detention camp in the Netherlands used by the Germans during both world wars. And during my first year at Harvard College, in the spring of 1955, one of my best teachers showed us movies taken of the camps by liberating allied soldiers; these amateur-seeming black-and-white shots were all the more impressive for their immediacy and lack of professionalism, and as a college instructor myself I always showed first-year students some comparable film footage. But psycho-analysis, at least Bettelheim's use of it, was by no means central to my undergraduate reading.

During my first year of graduate work in political science at the University of Chicago during 1958–59, I heard a good deal about Bettelheim. He was then teaching on the Committee of Human Development there, and also since 1944 had been head of the Sonia

Shankman Orthogenic School for 'autistic' children. As it was first explained to me, according to the strict categories of classical psychiatry, children could not be labelled psychotic, since psychosis means the breakdown of an already well-integrated and functioning personality; autism was a way of referring to the most emotionally troubled sorts of youngsters.

I knew virtually nothing about the clinical side of psychoanalysis and even less about autism or Bettelheim's inpatient facilities for treating disturbed children. But I did learn of him as a graduate instructor. A young woman I knew made him sound like a classroom bully, capable of using psychoanalytic concepts abusively; evidently he could publicly interrogate students about their unconscious motives for objecting to this or that he might have said in his teaching. But what sank in to me, from secondhand, was that I did not myself understand the concept of the unconscious, or the implications it might have for social philosophy. That year I did a term paper on 'Freud and Political Theory' for a course, but it was as yet only a beginning on my part.

I am not sure how typical my own story may be; but since details do matter and carry conviction, my own experience can help a later generation understand how it was that Bettelheim succeeded in eventually becoming such an influential force. During a year of graduate work (1959–60) I spent studying political theory at Oxford, I felt distinctly frustrated by the difficulties in pursuing depth psychology there; although I was attached to Magdalen College, a great and ancient institution, the library there had not a single copy of any of Freud's books. While at Oxford I did read a new book by Alasdair MacIntyre on *The Unconscious*, and he later published a piece on both Bruno Bettelheim and Erik H. Erikson, which generated further interest on my part.[14]

In the winter of 1962, by then back at Harvard, I had bought and read Stanley M. Elkins' book *Slavery*;[15] this was a period when the civil rights movement was in its heyday, as American liberals began to wake up to how racist its history had been. (It was in 1962 that excerpts from James Baldwin's *The Fire Next Time* had scorched out of the pages of *The New Yorker*.[16]) Elkins' study, which has subsequently gone into a further edition, was persuasive by virtue of its comparative historical framework; he tried to show how slavery differed in Latin America from the United States, but he also relied on a number of psychological perspectives, one of them being

Bettelheim's, to account for the psychological characteristics of the slave system.

As a matter of course we had read in college several first-hand accounts of concentration camps, both those of Hitler's Germany and those of Stalin's Soviet Union; but here Elkins was arguing that Bettelheim's concepts could help explain what the pre-Civil War plantation South had been like and how it had succeeded in cowing American slaves. In many ways Elkins was a conservative in that he assailed the abolitionists for helping needlessly to destroy the Union. But his approach also seemed challenging and intellectually radical. The Cold War was still in full swing, and it was startling to think that American liberalism could have had ever had anything in common with Nazi totalitarianism.

For me Bettelheim's approach was buttressed by the kind of personal impact which Erikson, another non-medical analytic thinker, was then having at Harvard; his section in *Childhood and Society* on Hitler's youth helped change people's minds about the possibilities of a sophisticated use of psychoanalysis in social science.[17] Its central tenets no longer seemed as far-fetched as some of Freud's own efforts at social thinking, such as *Totem and Taboo* with its nineteenth-century sounding armchair anthropology.[18] By the 1960s Erikson was immensely influential, not only at Harvard but in the general culture; and Bettelheim cited him as authoritative.

If Baldwin's rhetoric had been arresting and Elkins's thesis about racial injustice forming an underside to American history had begun to sink in as part of psychoanalysis's importance for social thought, by the summer of 1963 Hannah Arendt's *Eichmann in Jerusalem* had become the central controversy on the minds of anyone concerned with political morality. She had covered for *The New Yorker* the trial of Adolf Eichmann after he had been snatched from Argentina by the Israelis. The tale she told of the destruction of European Jewry during World War II was in itself shocking enough; the morality of war-crime trials was another vexing question; but on top of everything else she accused the leaders of the Jewish councils of having helped make matters worse for their own people: 'The whole truth was that if the Jewish people had really been unorganized and leaderless, there would have been chaos and plenty of misery but the total number of victims would hardly have been between four-and-a-half and six million people.'[19] Arendt, who like Bettelheim also held a teaching position at the University of Chicago, had only disdain for psychiatry and could not, like him, call on the authority of science to support her point of view; Arendt's blaming of the victim (and her suggestion that as few as four-and-a-half million might have died) seemed even more unacceptable than Bettelheim's own detached, first-person account. In the midst of a tremendous row over Arendt, Bettelheim reviewed her book favourably for *The New Republic*.

Bettelheim's *The Informed Heart*, ignored publicly by Arendt, had come out in 1960, although I know I did not read it until one of my students, when I was already teaching my course on 'Psychology and Politics' at Harvard in the mid-1960s, asked me encouragingly why I was not assigning it. Here Bettelheim had expanded his original 1943 article, excluding some of the more technical concepts and extending his critique of conformity to modern mass society as a whole. In addressing himself to the concentration camps, he remained unremitting: 'Psychologically speaking, most prisoners in the extermination camps committed suicide by submitting to death without resistance.'[20] Or, as he still later put it, 'they had given up their will to live and permitted their death tendencies to engulf them'.[21]

Once again Bettelheim's argument was persuasive by virtue of its being an intellectual biography. He reported how, born in 1903, he had grown up in Vienna with the alternative ideologies of Marxism and psychoanalysis in the air; they were rival approaches to improving mankind's lot. The problem of reconciling Marx and Freud was one that was still alive in the mid-1960s. Marcuse, author of *Eros and Civilization*, was then approaching the height of his fame, partly achieved at Fromm's expense; as we have discussed, Marcuse had denounced Fromm as a 'neo-Freudian' revisionist. Bettelheim, although he and Marcuse came from opposite ideological origins, partly rose in stature as a part of the general debate over Marx and Freud. Bettelheim reported that he had first been decisively drawn to psychoanalysis, with its interest in the inner world of the psyche; it was after he had been placed in a concentration camp that he learned the power of external reality in affecting personality structure.

On being released from the camps, Bettelheim was able to integrate what he had learned from Freud with the lesson the Nazis had taught him. (Only in 1975 did I become emancipated enough to think of putting in print the realization that Bettelheim had failed to specify on what grounds he had been imprisoned and how he managed, apparently with hundreds of other inmates, to get released.[22]) If the environment could be used by the Gestapo to tear people down, then why, Bettelheim wondered, could it not also be used for constructive healing purposes? I had not yet read his books *Love Is Not Enough* or *Truants From Life*, which were accounts of his efforts at re-habilitating emotionally disturbed children at his clinic in Chicago.[23]

I had got, I thought, the gist of his message, and it was supportive of a belief I cherished, drawn from John Stuart Mill, about the viability of liberalism. Just as the Nazis had taken away self-determination from people in an effort to break them down, Bettelheim was proposing that severely troubled children needed to be given a special degree of choice within an environment that would be structured enough to ease them in dealing with their problems, and help counteract their earlier life with their parents. While it had seemed to me that it was legitimate for an outcry immediately to have arisen against Arendt, much as I admired all the other moral questions she had eloquently succeeded in raising, I thought Bettelheim had made a memorable and sound contribution to social science. At one and the same time he was defending the key liberal value of autonomy, and also being sensitive enough to be aware of the need to explain the realistic if opposite desire for conformity. Bettelheim, like Arendt, was helping to explain the appeals of tyranny.

Part of what I found so attractive in Bettelheim was his pronounced distance from conventional middle-class expectations. He had made a notable splash when a portion of *The Informed Heart*, in which he attacked the Anne Frank family for complacency, had come out ahead of time in a monthly magazine. Bettelheim's position was that the Franks had erred in reacting to the Nazi threat with an air of 'business as usual'. Anne had 'had a good chance to survive', Bettelheim con-tended, 'but she would have had to leave her parents'.[24] By sticking to their commitment to traditional family life, instead of separately going to live in disguise with welcoming gentile families, the Franks had ensured that when they were caught it would be as a group. Bettelheim was insisting that rational survival was at odds with conventional emotional beliefs, and his tough-mindedness was pro-vocative.

During the next few years I read more of Bettelheim. He was co-author of a book called *Dynamics of Prejudice*[25] in a series started by Fromm's former colleague Max Horkheimer. From the standpoint of liberalism, prejudice, including anti-Semitism and racism, was irrational; liberals had idealistically assumed that people listened to one another without any barriers but those set by the terms of an argument. Once the Nazis triumphed in previously democratic Germany, however, psychopathological theorizing to explain it seemed appropriate. Totalitarianism in general, and Hitler in particular, appeared to be so off course from what liberalism optimistically expected that psychoanalytic thinking in connection with the concentration camps came as curiously reassuring. One desperately wanted to think that the norm was democracy, and that other forms of authoritarian politics represented an aberration. Such an assumption about progress would have been in keeping with John Stuart Mill's beliefs.

Bettelheim's *Symbolic Wounds* (1954) struck me as a powerfully argued bit of theorizing that challenged the then prevailing psychoanalytic conceptions of the nature of male and female.[26] He was also questioning the traditional Freudian views on the relation of the individual to society. Instead of seeing human nature as the outcome of conflicts between primitive instincts, Like other revisionist analytic thinkers at the time, Bettelheim pointed to the key role of the ego's striving for integration; failure to achieve ego strength could account for the release of drives that might appear to others as instinctual in nature. *Symbolic Wounds* was original enough to have got Bettelheim in some hot water with orthodox defenders of Freud; by 1960 he acknowledged that his 'own breaking away from' the 'theoretical models' of psychoanalysis 'came only with the writing of *Symbolic Wounds*'.[27]

His *Dialogues With Mothers* (1962) also had cut athwart various pieties.[28] Instead of the reassurance so many popularizers seemed eager to be rewarded for handing out, Bettelheim was telling neighbourhood mothers of ordinary kids what they were doing wrong. He seemed to flourish on not needing to be accepted. And like many of us in the face of so-called experts about human behaviour, the mothers themselves appeared intimidated and awed by his superior knowledge. Arendt herself, in deriding how psychiatrists in Jerusalem had certified Eichmann's 'normality', referred to the proceedings as 'the comedy of the soul experts'.[29] That he could be considered normal proved to her not only the worthlessness of the categories of their reasoning but the collapse of Western culture as well. Evil became 'banal'. Whatever Bettelheim and she shared in common, clearly they were at odds over psychoanalysis. (They both may have shared with Fromm a European-émigré discontent with the state of American culture.)

For me personally, having in 1964 completed my Ph.D. dissertation on 'Freud and Political Theory', what became imperative was that I learn more about Freud as the founder of psychoanalysis; I was convinced he ranked with the giants in intellectual history. Books had taught one sort of knowledge about Freud but people could teach me something else. The secondary literature about Freud was hidebound with sectarian orthodoxy; and therefore I found conclusively inter- esting about Bettelheim that he had been brave enough to criticize in print Ernest Jones's authorized biography of Freud. In *The American Journal of Sociology* Bettelheim had dissected Volumes I and II of Jones's work; Bettelheim thought it an overrated study that com- municated a 'total misunderstanding of Freud's Vienna which was so important in shaping the man Freud'.[30] In those days, only Fromm, for example in his *Sigmund Freud's Mission*, was willing to risk sticking his neck out. In his other books Fromm was becoming more and more hortatory, and his political moralisms helped too many to discount his criticisms of Jones. Nobody had ever tried (as had been done with Fromm after *Escape From Freedom*) to excommunicate Bettelheim, though, and he kept after Jones. In *The New Leader* he published a review of the third and final volume of Jones's Freud biography as 'a dissenting opinion' from the lavish praise Jones had otherwise received. In the same weekly Bettelheim had appreciatively reviewed Fromm's *Sigmund Freud's Mission*.[31]

By the mid-1960s, when I was conducting interviews with those who had known Freud or could cast light on the early history of psy- choanalysis, it was suggested to me in Chicago by an old European analyst that I ought to see Bettelheim himself; he would have specific ideas about what was mistaken in Jones. In those days it seemed a scandal that, despite all his work with disturbed children, the only standing he had with the Chicago Psychoanalytic Institute was as a 'non-therapist member'. Organized psychoanalysis has had its features as a trade union, and membership categories continue to be jealously guarded lest outsiders be misled about the extent of anyone's licence to practice. But in Bettelheim's case he was obviously more engaged in therapeutic endeavours than almost anybody else in the world of psychoanalysis, which made his official title seem so peculiar.

I knew that Bettelheim had no real personal contact with Freud, although it was easy to anticipate that he had valuable thoughts about the development of the psychoanalytic movement as a whole. His reputation for being tough-minded did not make it easier for me to undertake to see him. I had taken the precaution of talking with a contemporary of mine who as a child had been a patient in Bettelheim's school. In fact this friend gave me an invaluable piece of advice that turned out to be essential to the success of my meeting with Bettelheim. Whatever happened, I had been advised, be sure to level with Bettelheim and tell him the absolute truth. I was prepared then for a formidable presence.

It so happened that Bettelheim kept me waiting outside his office for a good half an hour, in striking contrast to how punctual others had been with me; Freud was not only personally obsessional about time, but practising analysts have to be inclined that way because of the nature of their kind of work. At the beginning of the interview Bettelheim gruffly announced that his time would have to be accordingly brief since he alleged that I had been late; if he had been right, my offence would have been grave. Thinking of my friend's advice on how to handle Bettelheim, I screwed up my courage and firmly stated that I had been right on time but that he himself had been tardy. I had nothing to lose and he seemed rude. The result was that he checked his appointment calendar, straightforwardly acknowledged his mistake (without any effort to use charm), and the interview then proceeded on a sound human footing for the full time he had originally allotted me. In later years, this meeting with him stood out in my mind for how exceptionally brilliant and insightful he had been, about not only Freud but the whole history of psychoanalysis. And his stature grew for me as I saw many dozens of other people with whom to compare him. He tended to answer large questions with abrupt-seeming answers; for example, when I asked 'what had happened to Fromm' since his earlier work, Bettelheim simply responded that Fromm had 'gotten religion.' (In hindsight, knowing now how Bettelheim ended his own life, it has to seem curious that he chose with me to interpret the Viennese analyst Hermine Hug-Hellmuth's murder by her nephew as 'psychologically' a suicide.)

My next contact with Bettelheim was of a different sort; in 1969 I reviewed his *The Children of the Dream* for the Sunday *New York Times*.[32] Bettelheim had gone to Israel for a brief seven weeks in order to study kibbutz life. I had no doubt then, nor now, that he went there with his head crammed with theories. But he freely admitted that his report was personal and impressionistic. I was almost wholly uncritical because once again he seemed to me so full of ideas, and he sent me a nice thank-you note. A university press wrote to me suggesting I do a book about Bettelheim, but I am not sure I even answered the enquiry since I felt inhibited about undertaking such a project because of something indefinably unpleasant connected with Bettelheim.

I thought it a strength in Bettelheim that he did not take for granted the special virtues of middle-class life and that he made himself a critic of the standards of contemporary culture. The communal method of education described as having taken place on the Israeli kibbutz, although it involved only a small fraction of Israel's whole population, inevitably seemed to Bettelheim an extraordinary social experiment. He had at hand a modern example with which to reopen the ancient question of the extent to which people are responsible for creating society, or society in turn shapes its members.

Bettelheim's own experience with institutionally rearing children in Chicago was at odds with traditional claims that to raise children in groups is bound to be damaging to their mental health. To bring the kibbutz experiment even closer ideologically to Bettelheim, the founders of the kibbutz movement were relying on a variant of Freudian teachings. They wanted to abolish the powerful role of the Eastern European ghetto mother and allow the community itself to assume the overall functions of the direction and control of the lives of its children. Parents were to play only the most distant role in the upbringing of their children.

Bettelheim claimed to have found in the kibbutzim an absence of all the problems that most seem to distress young adults elsewhere, such as drug addiction and juvenile delinquency. Yet he was ruthless about pursuing the psychological consequences of kibbutz life. If the Israelis succeeded in getting rid of some of the worst aspects of the hostility and ambivalence between parent and child, which we unfortunately experience, they did so at a price; for they simultaneously did away with the advantages of middle-class culture, for example in destroying the intimacy and deep attachments of traditional family life. Bettelheim claimed that, among those who grew up as members of the kibbutz, he observed an emotional flattening out and fear of deep attachments, and he faulted them for being unable to be fully autonomous as feeling human beings. Whatever gains there were in kibbutz culture, Bettelheim was determined to point out the losses as well, especially when they were unanticipated ones, and that seemed in keeping with Freud's own essentially tragic outlook.

At the time I wrote my favourable review of *The Children of the*

Dream, I did not yet have any children of my own. Once I became a parent only a couple of years later, I grew a good deal more sceptical about Bettelheim's outsider approach to traditional family life, as well as Anna Freud's own criticisms of what she called 'biological' as opposed to 'psychological' parenting. Freud's whole school of thought endorsed the idea that neutral observers can know best what children need; and while it is sometimes true that under special circumstances a detached party can benefit from distance to make valid recommendations that natural parents may benefit from using, once I had my own experience as a parent I found it harder not to be suspicious of all pretences to expertness in an area of thinking so filled with conflicting ideological convictions. I could scarcely share the belief underlying Bettelheim's work and that of Freud's daughter Anna as well, that parents can be considered both bad and unnecessary. Bettelheim in particular, with his positive recommendations, seemed to share disquieting similarities with the kind of behaviouristic psychologizing propagated by B.F. Skinner. John Stuart Mill should have made me more sceptical about those intent on using psychology to do things for other people's own good.

It has rarely been noted how some of Freud's own child-rearing advice shared remarkable similarities with that of a contemporary behaviourist like John B. Watson. Despite what look like inherently incompatible differences, Freud and Watson had many cultural points of view in common. But Freud remained fundamentally committed to a biologistic orientation and never gave up his special commitment to the significance of our phylogenetic inheritance. And when he wrote about the meaning of Oedipus's crimes, after all he was illustrating the power of biological destiny; Oedipus fled from his foster parents in Corinth out of fear of parricide and incest.

Bettelheim's adaptation of psychoanalytic teaching came from his being used to dealing therapeutically with parents who were at the end of their rope. One assumes optimistically that on no other grounds would any parent ever agree to the stringent terms Bettelheim exacted: the parents had to agree that the children never return to their original families but instead remain at the school, if only at night, even after they were able to pursue a normal public education.

I have more and more come to question the legitimacy of our relying on generalizations for so-called normal children, when the theories in question are derived from dealing with parenting that has misfired. So often what is at issue are different moral and ethical considerations, like those which separated John Stuart Mill, Nietzsche, and Dostoevsky from each other, as well as their predecessors. No so-called experts can legitimately make judgments about social and political theory, much less preach about the state of our general culture. There is a limit that I think should be put to all different psychopathological schools of thought, entirely aside from the narrow question, which is still a fundamental one, of what one thinks about the ethics of treating small children by means of psychotherapy, when one knows how inevitably it has to involve an invasion of a delicate and precious area of privacy. I think it makes a difference whether such an intrusion is undertaken with humility and as a cautious last resort.

Again, these are questions and sceptical convictions that came to my mind only twenty years later. I do remember, however, not long after *The Children of the Dream* was published being distressed at seeing Bettelheim's emotional response to an anti-Vietnam war sit-in at the University of Chicago. Although I was strongly against that war right from the start, I did not believe in the propriety of such student tactics; but then I did not think any of these middle-class kids could fairly be called, as Bettelheim publicly did at the time, neo-Nazis. His description of student activists as 'very, very sick', 'paranoiacs', who were trying to 'beat down father to show they are a big boy',[33] seemed to me both crude and polemical, substituting clinical categories for strictly political ones. It looked like Bettelheim was reliving something inside his own head and not appreciating the special circumstances in America that he was, in reality, confronted with.

It was, and here I am confessing my own limitations, not life or experience but rather a book that finally undermined my confidence in Bettelheim. He had continued to publish about his orthogenic school; *A Home for the Heart*, for example, appeared in 1974.[34] I remember noticing that the pictures on Bettelheim's book jackets, where he smiled and looked friendly, seemed oddly incongruous with the man I admired and the fiercely bold spirit I thought I perceived there.

Terence Des Pres's *The Survivor* (1976) shook me out of my dogmatic slumbers, and Bettelheim's response to it finally succeeded in disillusioning me. For years I had been assigning *The Informed Heart* to my undergraduates, and then Des Pres came along challenging Bettelheim's whole thesis. I found Des Pres's *The Survivor* beautifully written and movingly argued, and although he did not enjoy the credibility of ever having himself been in a concentration camp, he relied on a range of first-hand literature in order to confront Bettelheim.[35]

Throughout *The Survivor* Des Pres criticized Bettelheim for having supposed that it was correct to have thought that the prisoners ever regressed to infantilism. Des Pres believed that the survivors should be viewed as reminders not of human weakness but of evil circumstances that were objectively powerful. Both the Nazis and Stalin's regime subjected prisoners to filth for the sake of humiliation and debasement. Des Pres argued that prisoner behaviour in response to such circumstances was not childish but rather a heroic response to dreadful necessities. He cited one camp where the inmates burned it down and found throughout the literature instances of people who somehow managed to maintain their inward sanctity. Resistance took subtle shapes, and Des Pres explored the way human dignity endured in the form of freedom from the entire control by external forces. Instead of blaming the victims for imitating the conduct of their captors, Des Pres highlighted how life's resiliency copes with the obstacle of absolute power. Survivors helped one another, engaged in acts of sabotage, and from Buchenwald made contact with the Allies for a bombing raid on SS parts of the camp.

Des Pres pointed out that Bettelheim was imprisoned during a special period when criminals among inmates wielded power. He disputed Bettelheim's notion that social bonding among prisoners was absent; nor was it true, Des Pres argued, that they did not hate their oppressors and did not sometimes revolt. According to Des Pres, Bettelheim had felt superior to his fellow sufferers, and his account was fatally marred by his egotistical obsession with autonomy that blinded him to the extent of the mutual support that existed within the camps.[36] Dostoevsky's ideal of human brotherhood was a reality that those over-committed to John Stuart Mill's liberalism could not see. In fact Bettelheim seemed to have had an almost Nietzschean disdain for the 'herd'.

If Des Pres's book took me by storm, I was equally stunned by Bettelheim's response. He published a long article in *The New Yorker*, ostensibly occasioned by the appearance of Lina Wertmüller's movie *Seven Beauties*.[37] Having read Des Pres's *The Survivor*, however, it was apparent to me that Bettelheim was only using the occasion of the movie as a suitable platform to get back at Des Pres. Much of

Bettelheim's article was taken up with Des Pres's book, although he begins and ends it by trashing the Wertmüller movie. Since Bettelheim later reprinted his piece in his *Surviving and Other Essays*, after he had won widespread acclaim for his National Book Award-winning *The Uses of Enchantment*,[38] I can leave it to the reader to weigh and assess the merits of Bettelheim's points against Des Pres. For myself, I thought Bettelheim was retracting, without acknowledging doing so, some of the most controversial parts of his 1943 piece. But Bettelheim's response to Des Pres, impassioned and eloquent as it was, bore no reasonable relationship to anything that I had read in *The Survivor*.

If Bettelheim could so distort Des Pres's text, how reliable could he be taken to have been concerning the concentration camps – a world that I had never seen? As disquieting as anything was the fact that at no point in his new article did Bettelheim let the reader know that he was in fact the central object of Des Pres's whole argument. The offence was, I thought, compounded by the fact that, given the place that Bettelheim had chosen to review *The Survivor*, Des Pres had no right of reply.

In 1979 Des Pres, who was to die prematurely, published an article called 'The Bettelheim Problem' in the quarterly *Social Research*.[39] This became his final retort. Des Pres now linked Bettelheim's theories about child-reading to the 'autistic and schizophrenic reactions' he had supposedly observed among adults in the concentration camps. Furthermore, Des Pres stressed how frequently Bettelheim as a therapist saw himself at odds with parents who were described by Bettelheim as psychologically the destroyers of their offspring.

Des Pres left friends and associates behind who admired what he had achieved. Alfred Kazin and others had reviewed *The Survivor* favourably; and recently Elie Wiesel, who praised *The Survivor*, wrote a preface to a collection of Des Pres's essays. (Des Pres, not long after the publication of *The Survivor*, got himself into an unusual form of literary scandal. He wrote a laudatory review on the front-page *New York Times* Sunday book section about *The Belly of the Beast* by Jack Henry Abbott; they were prison letters. Abbott had spent over twenty years in jail as a convicted murderer; Norman Mailer successfully helped get Abbott out of jail, and then in 1981, within weeks of being released from prison and right after the appearance of Des Pres's review, Abbott stabbed to death a young actor and playwright who was working in a New York City restaurant. Even before the famous

Leopold and Loeb trial of the 1920s in Chicago, at which Freud was asked to testify, Nietzsche, and Freud too, had been blamed for advocating normlessness.)

Although my own change of opinion about Bettelheim was striking, still I continued to assign his *The Informed Heart* alongside with Des Pres's book as an alternative reading. But my mind was free to reconsider even more of Bettelheim's thinking. I had begun to question the unspoken screening process that he had used, which might have helped select out for acceptance those patients for his school who were most likely to benefit from his particular psychological approach; that might help explain his implausible-sounding claim that eighty per cent of the children admitted to his facility had recovered.

Then, when I was on a panel with a famous neurologist at a professional conference, the subject of autism came up. I was informed in no uncertain terms that Bettelheim had been responsible for perpetrating a great deal of misinformation and consequent social damage. For the scientific evidence had become overwhelming that genuine autistic problems have to be accounted for by primarily organic factors. And therefore Bettelheim's own exclusively psychogenic approach to autism left many anguished parents with an unnecessary burden of guilt feelings.

While Bettelheim never explicitly retracted any of his earlier therapeutic goals, if one carefully watches a television series made about him in the mid-1980s, he can be seen deliberately skirting away from his initial claims to have been treating autistic children. But the average viewer will not be apt to notice the fine distinctions that Bettelheim was now making. Nor did the general reading public ever seem to realize how thoroughly Bettelheim's earliest pretensions had been discredited. In an autobiographical piece 'How I Learned About Psychoanalysis', which appeared in 1989, he was talking about having treated 'psychotic children',[40] even though this may remain a contradiction in terms, as well as beg the question of the biochemical basis of psychosis.

In reflecting on the slippery issue of terminology, I cannot help being reminded of how, when I interviewed Bettelheim, he mentioned that Dr. Annie Reich was 'a good friend' of his. Since she had once been married to Wilhelm Reich, I later interviewed her. She informed me in passing, and without any special friendly feelings but just when

Bettelheim's name came up, that he had never had any psychoanalytic training in Vienna but had worked there in his father's factory. Far from being any kind of friend of Bettelheim's, she must have known how damaging such a contention could be. In a 1988 interview, which only appeared after Bettelheim's death, he indicated that he had just started a training analysis when the Nazis first entered Austria.[41]

According to Laura Fermi's book on the emigration to America of the continental intelligentsia, Bettelheim's early career in Vienna was 'in aesthetics'.[42] If it had once been startling that he was listed as a 'non-therapist' member of the Chicago Psychoanalytic Society, in hindsight one has to wonder not only about his credentials for treating children, but how he could ever have got to be called any kind of psychoanalyst. In fairness to Bettelheim, I can think of other people in psychoanalysis who went on to practise, especially with children, without any formal training.[43] And unfortunately it is true that having graduated from a training facility is no guarantee of special insight-fulness. Still, his having only had personal analysis ought not, at least for someone of Bettelheim's generation in the field, to have been enough to have sufficed.

Nevertheless, for years Bettelheim's position in the general culture seemed to be preeminent. A translation of his *The Empty Fortress* sold more than 100,000 copies in France.[44] Despite whatever grounds for uneasiness about him there were, he remained much feared as a book reviewer. He handled books with unchallenged authority, and more than occasional acerbity, for the *New York Times*, the *Times Literary Supplement*, and the *New York Review of Books*.

In 1982 he published in *The New Yorker* what I regarded as a tendentious piece attacking the English translations of Freud, which then appeared as a book in his *Freud and Man's Soul*.[45] Bettelheim tried to blame the then medical monopoly of psychoanalysis in America on the translation of Freud's texts, while in reality the translators themselves had no medical qualifications. Bettelheim was using the occasion to make a valuable defence of humanism. But it was a piece of Jesuitical reasoning for Bettelheim to use as the epigraph to *Freud and Man's Soul* a passage from a letter of Freud's in which he says that 'psychoanalysis is in essence a cure through love'. That comment has to be understood as one of Freud's ironies; he meant that *patients* transfer emotional feelings onto their analysts, and through the analyst's rationally interpreting that form of transference (or unre-quited love) psychoanalysis can have a therapeutic impact. Bettelheim continued to publish; in 1982 he was author of *On Learning to Read*, and then in 1987 his *A Good Enough Parent: A Book on Child-Rearing* came out.[46]

I had heard through the grapevine that he had remained unhappy ever since his (second) wife died in 1984. But I was surprised on March 14, 1990, to read on the front-page of the *New York Times* that Bettelheim had passed away. At the age of eighty-six there could be no special shock about such mortality; but the story was complicated in Bettelheim's case because while I habitually regard the *New York Times* as authoritative, that same day the Toronto newspapers were claiming that he had committed suicide. On March 15 the *New York Times* ran an additional story, on an inside page, describing the particulars of Bettelheim's self-inflicted death on the fifty-second anniversary of the day the Nazis invaded Austria.[47]

Bettelheim had been in low spirits for some time and suffered from a variety of physical ailments. He had three children, two daughters and a son. Evidently Bettelheim, who after three decades at his orthogenic school retired in 1973 to California, had a serious falling out near his end with his daughter on the West Coast. He gave up his spacious apartment there and moved to a retirement home on the East Coast to be close to his other daughter. Things got no better for him. He left a note (addressed to only two of his children), took some pills along with alcohol, and placed a plastic bag over his head, asphyxiating himself.

I remember once when interviewing Eva Rosenfeld, one of Freud's former patients who was also a friend of the family, that the subject of Freud and suicide came up. It is true that Freud, after enduring a painful cancer of the jaw for sixteen years, which included numerous operations, finally instructed his personal physician that it was pointless at the age of eighty-three to struggle on further, and a lethal dosage of morphine was mercifully administered. If anything, Freud had been allowed to go on too long; his doctor remained resentful and had wanted to do something to help weeks earlier, but Freud's daughter Anna, who was a key decision-maker at the time, wanted her father to go on and on.

Eva Rosenfeld quoted to me Freud's sister-in-law Minna as having once proudly said of him: 'any ordinary man' would have done away with himself years ago. Eva said she thought that suicide was out of the question for Freud, since such a death would have meant that no one would ever take his books seriously. So when Bettelheim died, I did wonder whether he had not cared enough for his own publications. I had always thought that much of his work was written too flatly, as if he were not personally present in it; a writer needs to invest his work with a certain kind of narcissism. As chance would have it, I met someone just after Bettelheim's death whose wife, pregnant with their first child, was reading *A Good Enough Parent* at her bedside; the young husband was tactful enough not to alert his wife to the tale of the circumstances of Bettelheim's death. His suicide does cast a shadow over the admiration his work earned, especially since he did so contentiously say of the concentration camp victims that 'millions, like lemmings, marched themselves to their own death'.[48]

It seems to me hardly possible to establish that suicide is always morally wrong, especially in someone so elderly, and yet I do believe, when children are being left behind, that there ought to be a serious ethical presumption against it. I find myself in thorough sympathy with one of the sayings attributed to Ludwig Wittgenstein, three of whose brothers killed themselves: 'if suicide is allowed then everything is allowed. If anything is not allowed then suicide is not allowed.' The form of Wittgenstein's thought may have been an aphorism, like one of Nietzsche's, but I think the substance of what Wittgenstein was trying to say is at odds with Nietzsche's philosophical point of view.

It ought, I think, to be seriously troubling how many psychoanalysts have ended up as suicides (that physicians kill themselves more than statistically expectable is a separate matter). Why analysts should do so seems to me to pose a special problem, perhaps related to unrealistic expectations of what life can ideally be like. The list of those analysts who have committed suicide is sobering; among those who killed themselves are Edward Bibring, Paul Federn, Clara Happell, Johann Honegger, Max Kahane, Karl Landauer, Maud Mannoni, Monroe Meyer, Sophie Morgenstern, Martin Peck, Amanda Pichón-Rivière, Victor Rosen, Tatiana Rosenthal, Karl Schrötter, Herbert Silberer, Eugenia Sokolnicka, Karin Stephen, Wilhelm Stekel, and Victor Tausk. Given the frequency of medical cover-ups about suicides, it is reasonable to assume that there are even more such deaths among analysts than we already know about.

Perhaps it is a mistake to place Bettelheim's name in any such line-up of analysts who have killed themselves. The most charitable outlook might be to see him instead in the context of concentration camp survivors, who had to live out their lives as if, according to the image proposed by the historian Saul Friedlander, they contained 'shards of steel'[49] that would never heal. It may be a tribute to Bettelheim's strength of will that he managed to stave off for as long as he did what tragically appears to be an all too prevalent outcome for those who personally endured the Holocaust.

However Bettelheim's reputation may turn out to be affected by the way he chose to die, it was terrible to learn what we have been told about him since then. The *Washington Post* ran a long article on August 26, 1990, alleging that former patients at Bettelheim's school in Chicago claimed he was abusive and violent, screaming and hitting children (some of whom suffered from neurological deficits) in his charge.[50] *Newsweek* almost immediately ran a story about the matter, citing further evidence along the same lines.[51] It turns out that his eventual successor as head of the school put a ban on corporal punishment and installed shower curtains. (Bettelheim is said to have dragged a young woman by the hair from a shower, striking her.) The absence of shower curtains does seem to me to fly in the face of the liberal value of autonomy that he claimed to be trying to uphold.

For me one of the most striking aspects of the *Newsweek* piece was the weak defence of Bettelheim put up by some former staff members of his. It is not enough for a disciple (and former patient) to maintain: 'He was a son of a bitch. But he was also a genius.'[52] It is dreadful to think that such abuses could have been practised for so many years and that either no staff members had the courage to speak out or else patients who complained were not believed. One wonders how those who participated in running Bettelheim's facility could be legally or professionally not liable for what once went on.

An appalling account of therapeutic tyranny, by a former patient at Bettelheim's orthogenic school, also appeared in *Commentary*.[53] It would seem that psychoanalysis had allowed a Dostoevsky-like Grand Inquisitor to rule over his charges. The *New York Times* published a story similar to that in *Commentary*, and letters to the editor, again along the same lines, appeared both in *Commentary* and the *New York Times*.[54] A series of letters also appeared in the University of Chicago's alumni *Magazine*; although some wrote in Bettelheim's defence for what he had meant to them as a teacher and therapist, on the whole people were bent on repudiating him, demanding to know how the university had ever allowed such practices to go on, and questioning the propriety of going through with the idea of naming a centre in Bettelheim's honour.[55]

Presumably we have not heard the end of this. It was surely distasteful to have material of this sort appearing when Bettelheim was no longer around to defend himself. A splendid memorial tribute to him appeared in the *Partisan Review*, but the question of the physical abuse of children did not arise in it at all.[56] Nothing can, or should, be able to take away from the work Bettelheim published. He was original, challenging, and provocative; his books and articles deserve to be evaluated on their own merits. Instead, *Newsweek* ran a new story in 1991 about him allegedly plagiarizing his work on fairy tales.[57] I suspect that unless something more gets done soon on Bettelheim's behalf, and I cannot say who could be in a position to be able to do it, his reputation may never recover. At least one full-scale, balanced biography of Bettelheim has now appeared, but it was shortly followed by a muck-raking one that left his career in tatters.[58] One hopes that more such books will help put in perspective the distressing aspects to Bettelheim's career.[59]

It is normal and even obligatory for writers and thinkers to be reevaluated after they have died, and it is often the case that they go into an irreversible decline. In contrast, Hannah Arendt's own death in 1975 brought forth a paean of laudatory articles, and her stature has been climbing ever since. She may have despised psychoanalytic thinking, and omitted reference to Bettelheim when she wrote about the concentration camps, but rather like George Orwell who rejected Freud while freely making use of his psychology in *1984*,[60] Arendt's own works reflected our culture's involvement in the Freudian perspective. Bettelheim did as much as anyone to propagandize that outlook. Even if one sets Freud aside, the most anti-psychological texts usually conceal an unspoken line of psychological reasoning. Sir Isaiah Berlin intensely disliked Arendt's contribution, but he was at least as hostile to Freud as she; since his recent death too his stature has been rising. As I indicated earlier, Berlin's famous discussion of negative as opposed to positive liberty would benefit from an exploration along depth psychological lines. Berlin's endorsement of John Stuart Mill's sort of liberalism does not foreclose discussing further what Rousseau may have meant by 'forcing' people to be 'free'.

But with all these allegations about Bettelheim and his suicide to boot, one does not know what his contribution adds up to. While Arendt's ideas in *Eichmann in Jerusalem* kicked off an immediate storm of controversy, there has been so little tolerance of give-and-take within the field of psychoanalysis that few people even know how Des Pres had questioned Bettelheim. For myself, there was also the problem of how Bettelheim had chosen to handle the criticism by Des Pres; and then came the shock of Bettelheim's suicide.

Other people have bravely faced a difficult old age. Creativity, often with the help of denial, extends to helping cope with the problem of aging. Even Arthur Koestler's suicide seems to me not to tarnish his own work in the same way as it does Bettelheim's because one expects something different of a psychoanalyst, especially one who had written so disparagingly about the behaviour of other concentration camp inmates. It seems in keeping that Bettelheim evidently did not contact members of the Hemlock Society,[61] for that would be to have made the admission of human comradeship; but he used a technique (the plastic bag) recommended by Hemlock people. Bettelheim's death by asphyxiation meant, I am told, a particularly gruesome body would have been left for those who found it. (He may not have taken enough to drug himself sufficiently, for his partly clothed body was found in a hall as he evidently was futilely struggling to get the bag off.)

On top of everything else, the accusations of physical abuse of his patients leave my mind numbed, since I feel somehow complicit with him in having relied on his books in my classes for so many years. I would imagine that the stories about his conduct are bound to damage all residential psychotherapeutic treatment centres for children. In hindsight, a sentence of Bettelheim's about Carl G. Jung's misconduct in having had an affair with a patient, Sabina Spielrein, who went on to become an analyst, does sound like a rationalization of Bettelheim's own sort of delinquency: 'However questionable Jung's behaviour was from a moral point of view – however unorthodox, even disreputable it may have been – somehow it met the prime obligation of the therapist toward his patient: to cure her.'[62] In contrast to Bettelheim's viewpoint, a contemporary Italian analyst has written me: 'The eroti-cization of the process of transference and counter-transference is, more than anything else, an unconscious misalliance, collusion, that is set in motion in order to avoid the surfacing of a very aggressive transference. Only a badly trained analyst is not aware of the truth of such a mechanism.'[63] It can be hoped that Bettelheim's own apparent misbehaviour will attract interpretive attention in the professional literature.

Bettelheim had written so many interesting books that it had reinforced my predisposition in favour of non-medical analysts. Now I wonder whether perhaps Arendt, Berlin, and others within my field of political science were more sound than I like to think in being so dismissive of psychoanalysis. I am bound to feel betrayed, if only because I had in print been proud to point out some psychoanalytic precursors to Bettelheim's individual theses.[64] With a career like Bettelheim's in mind I have to worry self-critically whether my time devoted to studying the history of psychoanalysis has been well spent, or whether it might have been better directed at examining the works of thinkers like John Stuart Mill, Nietzsche, and Dostoevsky. (Dead authors are less likely to disappoint.)

There is enough smoke surrounding Bettelheim now that there is reason to suspect the existence of real fire. His fall would appear to be so precipitous as to be almost unprecedented. (A French writer I know waved aside all such considerations, on the grounds that it all had 'added' to Bettelheim's legend.) But Louis Althusser's reputation, at least in North American academic circles, suffered a similar negative fate when he murdered his wife. And I can remember being sadly disillusioned when it turned out that Erik H. Erikson had been guilty of an act of autobiographical bad faith about his Jewish ancestry,[65] but Erikson's glossing over his religious past pales in comparison with the apparently uncontestable charge of the abuses at Bettelheim's orthogenic school. The only vaguely comparable recent story of the decline of a substantial reputation that I can think of has to do with the posthumous revelation that Paul de Man as a young man in Belgium published anti-Semitic newspaper articles. In de Man's case his work had become central to a whole school of literary criticism, and defenders have arisen to launch years of debate over the controversy now associated with him. One can only wonder what we have in store for us concerning Bruno Bettelheim.[66]

NOTES

1. Bruno Bettelheim, 'Individual and Mass Behaviour in Extreme Situations', *Journal of Abnormal and Social Psychology*, Vol. 38 (1943), p. 417.
2. *Ibid.*, p. 418.
3. *Ibid.*, pp. 422, 424–27.
4. *Ibid.*, p. 431.
5. *Ibid.*, pp. 430, 434, 435.
6. *Ibid.*, pp. 439, 440.
7. *Ibid.*, p. 443.
8. *Ibid.*, pp. 444, 447.
9. *Ibid.*, p. 447.
10. Anna Freud, *The Ego and the Mechanisms of Defence* (London, Hogarth Press, 1937), Ch.9.
11. Bettelheim, *op. cit.*, p. 448.
12. *Ibid.*, p. 451.
13. *Ibid.*, p. 452.
14. Alasdair MacIntyre, *The Unconscious* (London, Routledge & Kegan Paul, 1958); Alasdair MacIntyre, 'The Psychoanalysts', *Encounter*, Vol 24 (May 1965).
15. Stanley M. Elkins, *Slavery: A Problem in American Institutional and Intellectual History*, 2nd edition (Chicago, University of Chicago Press, 1968).
16. James Baldwin, *The Fire Next Time* (New York, Dial Press, 1963).
17. Erikson, *Childhood and Society* (New York, Norton, 1950), Ch. 9.
18. 'Totem and Taboo', *Standard Edition*, Vol. 13, pp. xiii–161.
19. Hannah Arendt, *Eichmann in Jerusalem: A Report on the Banality of Evil* (New York, Viking Press, 1963).
20. Bruno Bettelheim, *The Informed Heart: Autonomy in a Mass Age* (Glencoe, The Free Press, 1960), pp. 250–51.
21. Terence Des Pres, 'The Bettelheim Problem', *Social Research*, Vol. 46 (1979), p. 625.
22. Paul Roazen, 'Psychology and Politics', *Contemporary Psychoanalysis*, Vol. 12 (1975).
23. Bruno Bettelheim, *Love Is Not Enough* (New York, The Free Press, 1950). Bruno Bettelhein, *Truants From Life* (New York, The Free Press, 1955).
24. Bruno Bettelheim, *Surviving and Other Essays* (New York, Knopf, 1979), p. 248.
25. Bruno Bettelheim and Morris Janowitz, *Social Change and Prejudice*, including *Dynamics of Prejudice* (New York, The Free Press, 1964).
26. Bruno Bettelheim, *Symbolic Wounds: Puberty Rites and the Envious Male* (New York, Collier Books, 1962).
27. Bettelheim, *The Informed Heart*, *op. cit.*, p. 32.

28. Bruno Bettelheim, *Dialogues With Mothers* (New York, The Free Press, 1962).
29. Arendt, *Eichmann in Jerusalem, op. cit.*, p. 22.
30. Bruno Bettelheim, 'Book Review of Jones's *The Life and Work of Sigmund Freud*, Vol. I & II', *The American Journal of Sociology*, Vol. 62 (1957), p. 420. See also Bruno Bettelheim, *Freud's Vienna and Other Essays* (New York, Vintage, 1991), pp. 39ff.
31. Bettelheim, 'Two Views of Freud', in *Freud's Vienna and Other Essays, op. cit.*
32. Roazen, *Encountering Freud, op. cit.*, pp. 269–72.
33. Jesse Lemisch, *On Active Service in War and Peace* (Toronto, New Hogtown Press, 1975), pp. 96, 137.
34. Bruno Bettelheim, *A Home For The Heart* (New York, Knopf, 1974).
35. Terence Des Pres, *The Survivor: An Anatomy of Life in the Death Camps* (New York, Oxford Press, 1976).
36. Roazen, *Encountering Freud, op. cit.*, pp. 272–74.
37. Bruno Bettelheim, 'Reflections', *The New Yorker*, Aug. 2, 1976, pp. 31–52; see also Bettelheim, *Surviving and Other Essays, op. cit.*
38. Bruno Bettelheim, *The Uses of Enchantment: The Meaning and Importance of Fairy-Tales* (New York, Knopf, 1976).
39. Des Pres, 'The Bettelheim Problem', *op. cit.*
40. Bruno Bettelheim, *Freud's Vienna and Other Essays* (New York, Knopf, 1991), p. 34.
41. David James Fisher, 'Homage to Bettelheim (1903–1990)', in *Partisan Review*, Vol. 28 (1990), p. 66. See also *The Psychohistory Review*, Vol. 19 (1991).
42. Laura Fermi, *Illustrious Immigrants: The Intellectual Migration From Europe, 1930–41* (Chicago, University of Chicago Press, 1968), p. 169.
43. Paul Roazen, 'Tola Rank', *Journal of the American Academy of Psycho-analysis*, Vol. 18. See also: Roazen, *The Historiography of Psychoanalysis, op. cit,*, Part V, pp. 205–15
44. Elisabeth Roudinesco, *Jacques Lacan & Co: A History of Psychoanalysis in France, 1925–85*, translated by Jeffrey Melhman (Chicago, University of Chicago Press, 1990), p. 623.
45. Burno Bettelheim, *Freud and Man's Soul* (New York, Knopf, 1982).
46. Bruno Bettelheim, *A Good Enough Parent: A Book On Child-Rearing* (New York, Knopf, 1987).
47. *New York Times*, March 15, 1990, p. 16.
48. Des Pres, 'The Bettelheim Problem', *op. cit.*, p. 644.
49. Quoted in Fisher, *op. cit.*, p. 9.
50. Charles Pekow, 'The Other Dr. Bettelheim', *Washington Post*, Aug. 26, 1990.
51. *Newsweek*, Feb. 18, 1991, pp. 59–60.
52. *Ibid.*, p. 60.

53. Ronald Angres, 'Who, Really, Was Bruno Bettelheim?' *Commentary*, October 1990.

54. *Commentary*, Feb. 1991, pp. 6–12; *New York Times*, Nov. 4, 1990, Nov. 20, 1990; see also *Society*, July/August 1991, pp. 6–9.

55. *Magazine*, Summer 1990, pp. 31-32, October 1990, pp. 3–4, December 1990, pp. 3–4, February 1991, pp. 5–6.

56. Fisher, *Partisan Review*, *op. cit.*, pp. 627–29; but see Fisher's article when reprinted in *The Psychohistory Review*, Vol. 19: 2, pp. 255–61, especially 259–60.

57. *Newsweek*, Feb. 18, 1991, p. 75; Alan Dundes, 'Bruno Bettelheim's Uses of Enchantment and the Abuses of Scholarship', *Journal of American Folklore*, Vol. 104 (1991).

58. Nina Sutton, *Bettelheim: A Life and a Legacy*, translated by David Sharp (New York, Basic Books, 1996), and Richard Pollak, *The Creation of Dr. B.: A Biography of Bruno Bettelheim*. See Paul Roazen, 'Review of Pollak's *The Creation of Dr. B.*', *Boston Book Review*, Sept. 1997.

59. See *Educating the Emotions: Bruno Bettelheim and Psychoanalytic Development*, ed. Nathan M. Szajnberg (New York, Plenum Press, 1992), and *Bruno Bettelheim's Contribution to Psychoanalysis*, ed. Paul Marcus and Alan Rosenberg, *The Psychoanalytic Review*, Vol. 81, No. 3 (Fall 1994).

60. Roazen, *Encountering Freud*, *op. cit.*, pp. 294–308.

61. Fisher, *op. cit.*, p. 4.

62. Bettelheim, *Freud's Vienna and Other Essays*, *op. cit.*, p. 80.

63. Letter from Roberto Speziale-Bagliacca, 1991.

64. Roazen, *Brother Animal: The Story of Freud and Tausk*, *op. cit.*, pp. xxxv, 175, 195.

65. Roazen, *Erik H. Erikson*, *op. cit.*, pp. 94–99.

66. D. Patrick Zimmerman, 'The Clinical Thought of Bruno Bettelheim: A Critical Historical Review', in *Psychoanalysis and Contemporary Thought*, Vol. 14 (1991), and Paul Marcus, *Autonomy in the Extreme Situation: Bruno Bettelheim, the Nazi Concentration Camps and the Mass Society* (Westport, Praeger, 1999).

Erik H. Erikson as a Teacher

Erik H. Erikson's current standing is less definable than at any time since the first publication of his classic text, *Childhood and Society* (1950).[1] Despite all the recurrent interest there has been in Erikson's ideas, he has attracted virtually no interest among political theorists, who seem to keep an eye out mainly on what is fashionable within academic departments of philosophy. Psychoanalysis has remained largely an alien tradition of thought within social theory, and few seem to realize how it fits into the history of ideas. In the course of my own research I often found the anachronistic assumption that Freud could be considered important because Erikson had mentioned him.

While he was once widely acclaimed as among the world's most eminent psychoanalysts, and in 1970 *Newsweek* featured him on one of its covers, now his work has become so much an accepted part of the intellectual scenery in the English-speaking world that little special attention gets paid to him. In Germany his book on Luther secured him some stature, but it is now out of print there; and in India his biographical inquiry into the origins of Gandhi's doctrine of non-violence aroused controversy, but the French are still largely unaware of the significance of his teachings.[2] Erikson's personal presence has long been unavailable to students likely to be attracted to his ideas. Born in 1902, Erikson had unfortunately for some time had a difficult old age before his death in 1994; deafness combined with an attention span that came and went, probably Alzheimer's disease, made a saddening picture for all of us who had known and admired a younger Erikson in control of all his faculties. An excellent recent biography about him may hopefully do much to revive interest in him.[3] A book of essays in his honour, and the first selection for a one-volume version of his writings, have also just come out.[4]

A special problem has beset Erikson's work in that he trained no devoted disciples. Partly this was a consequence of his artistic temperament; a man of his disposition, aware of the subtle nuances he tried to convey through his prose, was unlikely to seek to convert apostles to his way of thinking. It also needs to be said that for Erikson to have undertaken any sort of training in his own special approach would have risked the charge of psychoanalytic heresy. No matter how significantly Erich Fromm's *Escape From Freedom* had preceded *Childhood and Society* by almost a decade, Erikson always dreaded being associated in anyone's mind with Fromm's brave pioneering attempt to unite depth psychology with a social and ethical perspective. Erikson's tactic was to choose to ignore Fromm's works, while Fromm had only in passing alluded to what he considered the built-in socially conservative bias in Erikson's contribution.[5]

I remember how once at a meeting of the Boston Psychoanalytic Society Hedwig Hitschmann, the widow of an old Viennese analyst, privately complained about how Erikson had erred in giving a public lecture under the announced heading of 'Neo-Freudianism'. Erikson himself had not chosen the term (which Fromm himself did not like), but even so Mrs. Hitschmann questioned why Erikson had allowed himself to appear under such a rubric. Erikson preferred to consider himself under the more neutral-sounding designation 'post-Freudian', since it made him seem less a malcontent revisionist. Mrs. Hitschmann's observations were not well-meant, and amounted under the circumstances to an accusation of disloyalty; her husband had been present at the Vienna Psychoanalytic Society during the troubles Freud had had before World War I with Alfred Adler, and it is impossible to overstate the extent of the various faiths and fears within psychoanalytic sectarianism. Helene Deutsch was sitting among the small group of us there in one part of the room, and I suspect that Mrs. Hitschmann's remarks were aimed at Helene especially, since she had got on badly with Edward Hitschmann, although she was known to think highly of Erikson. Helene, however, brushed aside the invitation to be inquisitorial, and got rid of the problem of neo-Freudianism with the gentlest of remarks: 'That isn't Erik's way.'

This small incident took place in the mid-1960s. Around that time I was seeing Helene a lot for my general interviewing about Freud and his followers, and I knew that she admired Erikson for what she considered his immense inner charm. In her special vocabulary he had 'no elbows', which for her meant that however successful his career it had not been the result of pushing others aside. I also knew that she was grateful to Erikson, when she had recently been alarmed about one of her adolescent grandsons, for his willingness to comfort her. (Any clinician has anonymous clients, but it seems known that Reinhold Niebuhr was among those who sought Erikson's help.)

However controversial psychoanalytic purists might want to make him seem, Erikson was offered in the 1960s the position of training analyst at the Boston Psychoanalytic Institute, then a bastion of professional traditionalism. But he turned the offer down, not only because of his desire to conserve time for writing his own books. For to be institutionally affiliated with organized psychoanalysis, and become involved with training candidates as Erikson had once done in San Francisco, might have distracted him from what he was seeking to say. The result has been that disciples of Heinz Kohut's 'self psychology', or to cite those even further afield from Erikson's convictions, the apostles of Melanie Klein, have continued to thrive in the passionate quest to convey the concepts of their respective mentors, while Erikson has more or less diminished as an influence, despite the acknowledged stature of his texts, because he lacked an embattled school to proselytize for his teachings. Even the admiration that the now widely hailed Donald W. Winnicott had for Erikson has failed to get into the literature. (Fromm still has a following in Mexico, and the time he regularly spent in New York City meant he had disciples there too; the International Erich Fromm Society is today primarily made up of Germans.)

There is no doubt in my mind that Erikson had a distinctive point of view, and one that is worth commemorating, for the sake of both social thought in general and psychoanalysis in particular. Among other objectives, Erikson sought to bring back into Freudian thinking the key Christian concepts that Freud had sought to eliminate from Western thought; when he proposed a concept like that of 'mutuality', in which the actors in any situation strive to bring out the best in each other, he was trying to establish a standard very different from the old psychoanalytic goal of 'genitality.' But Erikson has to be held directly responsible for the diffuse state of his teachings. For despite the fact that he wrote on behalf of what he called 'generativity', and in contrast to how important he thought it was for an innovator to watch over his special field of inquiry, he did almost nothing to institutionalize his ideas. Here I have to be critical of him, since in some vague way I, like others, might have benefited had Erikson taken more care to promote his admirers.

I should say immediately that I was always a peripheral figure in Erikson's world, but I learned an immense amount from him, and I feel permanently indebted for his intuitive contributions to my own work, usually made in an informal setting. Erikson could be at his charming best at a chance meeting on a street-corner, where I had spontaneous questions to ask or new information from my research on Freud and his followers to communicate. Whenever I tried out an idea on Erikson, he invariably gave it back to me with an original twist from which I greatly benefited. When Anna Freud asked me in the mid-1960s from whom I had learned most about psychoanalysis, I was at a loss for words since the Boston Psychoanalytic Society was so down-at-the-heels in terms of the life of the mind, and yet I knew that she would not be pleased at my mentioning Erikson's name.

As much as I owe Erikson, he had a form of vanity which proved harmful to some of his students. I remember one case in particular. In the days when I knew Erikson I was a junior member in the Department of Government at Harvard; he was a University Professor who had been brought there by McGeorge Bundy in his capacity as Dean of the Faculty of Arts. In our department there was a couple, man and wife, who were experts on India, and significant helpers of Erikson in his early work on Gandhi. When they were coming up for tenure, always a touchy matter in a department where it was expected that nine out of ten candidates would not succeed in attaining a permanent position, the Chairman of my department reported to me what Erikson had to say about the work of the married specialists on India. There was a genuine streak of diffidence in Erikson, and apparently he had been a good deal less than generous in his praise of these two political scientists; he suggested that there were good points about their work, but also some flaws. Erikson should have had the tactical skills to know that such a lukewarm backing could only amount to a kiss of death for his supporters. They did in the end both land jobs together at a prestigious research university but their success owed more to the stalwart backing of John Kenneth Galbraith and David Riesman than to the wishy-washy support of Erikson himself.

I cite this example because it is consistent with a general retiring attitude on Erikson's part within academic life. He had known well enough how to get a series of important academic appointments for himself. But I think that he always felt uncomfortable in university life, having never had – aside from his psychoanalytic training – any sort of formal higher education in Europe. Therefore he remained, out of insecurity, unwilling to undertake the kind of useful networking that one expects a mentor to engage in. So students of his, who for example organized the teaching staff of his large undergraduate course, had to rely on others in the university, impressed at a distance by the work that they did for Erikson, to recommend them for academic jobs elsewhere.

Perhaps this is the point to describe what kind of immense impact Erikson was capable of having at Harvard. He had not been there during my undergraduate years at Harvard, 1954–58, but when I returned to do further graduate work in 1960 he was already established on the scene; he began, for example, to be asked regularly to publish in the quarterly *Daedalus*. I suppose it had an extra impact on me that I had spent that year at the University of Chicago, where Bruno Bettelheim was then holding forth, since Bettelheim – who for a time became even more famous than Erikson – was citing Erikson unquestioningly, about various developmental phases in the life cycle for example. I cannot forget the first occasion I ever saw Erikson, as I was leaving Widener Library (where he had his office) with an old college classmate of mine. Erikson, with his impressive shock of white hair, had been careful to make sure that the door was held open for us. 'That's Erik Erikson,' my friend whispered to me.

During the next years Erikson taught a large undergraduate lecture course on 'The Life Cycle'. The enrolment was limited to 250 students. Since seniors who were about to graduate had to be given preference for enrolling in the course, it turned out that the class was made up entirely of seniors. That meant that Erikson was lecturing to approximately one-quarter of the graduating class. (I feel obligated to confess a bit of sociopathic behaviour on my part; I was determined in the mid-1960s to learn as much as I could about Erikson's approach, and so I set out to audit his undergraduate course. At the first lecture, when the class was standing room only, Erikson asked all those who were not seniors to leave their seats, and I blithely ignored his request – which he silently noticed – in my effort to acquire knowledge of his work.) He was a remarkable lecturer, actually one of the best teachers I ever had. In contrast to some of my other role models, Erikson made it perfectly plain that when he spoke from the podium it was exactly as if he were discussing an issue in his living room. This meant that he could hold vast audiences, of a thousand people for example, and still retain the simplicity and directness of his usual conversational style of speaking; this was in contrast to the formal oratory of others in the social sciences. I wish for his sake that he had sustained more of this natural informal talent in some of his writing. For example, one of his greatest lectures every year, and it was renowned among the campus community, was on Ingmar Bergman's film *Wild Strawberries*. The students, somewhat to Erikson's chagrin, always identified Erikson as the old professor in the movie, while Erikson meekly insisted that he was in fact younger than that old gentleman. The lecture was quietly dazzling, filled with flashes of intuitive insight. He later wrote the lecture up for a published article, and unfortunately he insisted on looking at the film through the narrow perspective of all the stages of the life cycle that his full-scale theory postulated; the result was, I thought, a wooden literary performance, a pale shadow of Erikson at his unrestrained best in thinking out loud on his feet.[6]

I wonder if readers who come to Erikson's books without any prior personal contact with him get an adequate appreciation of just how original and bold a thinker he could be. Let me cite one personal example. When I first started out to interview Freud's patients and followers who were still alive in the mid-1960s, one of the earliest ones I encountered was the psychoanalytic theorist Robert Waelder. He was famous then as a pillar of psychoanalytic orthodoxy, the reader will remember him as a severe critic of Fromm's *Sigmund Freud's Mission*, and I was at the time rather naïve about the politics of the whole movement. I am ashamed to admit that I was then inclined to think that Erikson had dropped too much of the 'classical' psychoanalytic doctrine, which is partly why I was so eager to meet Waelder in the first place. (Waelder was prolific, with a special interest in politics, and apparently scholarly; he once had been the librarian of the old Vienna Psychoanalytic Society.) I cannot say that the lunch with Waelder was a disaster, but I certainly came away with a chastened conception of his true standing.

I found Waelder wholly lacking in the kind of intuitive strokes that Erikson was so blessed with; Waelder was a man whose mind was filled with pigeon-holes for categories. He arrogantly scoffed at what Erikson would ever be able to tell me about Freud's circle in Vienna.

(Erikson suspected that people like Waelder considered Erikson's ego psychology as merely 'the Americanization' of psychoanalysis.) As Helene Deutsch once said to me much later about Waelder, he knew about human emotions 'only by hear-say'. When I told Erikson at the same time that I had just met Waelder, Erikson must have been able to read my feelings from my facial expression, for his only response was: 'So now you know!' Never again would I be able to take seriously the kind of orthodox doctrine that Waelder and others were trying to promulgate; too much effort seemed to be going into clarifying and codifying Freud, as if epicycles were being adding to the Ptolemaic conception of the universe. Erikson was undertaking an altogether different sort of endeavour. I recall later being almost insulted when Erikson asked me what I thought about a particularly poor example of a political scientist using orthodox psychoanalytic theory for research. I thought that Erikson should have been more confident about my reaction being the same as his own. But he also may have been testing me. Erikson could have a gentle way of being challenging, as when he once asked whether I had read St. Augustine's *Confessions*; he was trying tactfully to steer me away from the texts psychoanalysts commonly thought about, back to one of the greatest of Freud's precursors in the history of self-exploration. If my political theory mentors had known of his immense respect for Augustine, perhaps they would have been less fearful of how I was damaging myself professionally by contact with Erikson.

At the same time Erikson could be irritatingly elusive in how he wrote. For example he once proposed in 1972: 'if vision is … the basic organizer of the sensory universe and if the beholding of one's person's face by another is the first basis of a sense of mutuality, then the classical psychoanalytic treatment situation is an exquisite sensory deprivation experiment.'[7] No one that I know of has ever followed up on what I consider an original idea; Erikson was implying that Freud's use of the analytic couch meant that patients were being unnaturally deprived of sights and sounds. And that 'sensory deprivation' might help explain many of the odder emotional reactions that take place in the course of psychoanalytic treatment, such as transference for instance. Yet by having referred to it as an 'exquisite' sensory deprivation, Erikson was carefully not directly challenging Freud the way Fromm had.

Erikson was helpful to my work in ways that I cannot easily itemize. He was, of course, a graduate of the Vienna Psychoanalytic Institute, with some memories of Freud to share; so he was a living example of that early generation of analysts that I was so eager to study. Like almost everyone else he was a bit sceptical that I would get the cooperation of all the people I needed for my work. But I do remember with clarity his response when I told him in a coffee shop that I had been interviewing Helene Deutsch; she had been, he told me, his first instructor at the Vienna Psychoanalytic Institute. I would have to be 'very careful' about how I used the material she gave me. Erikson may not have been politic enough in advancing the careers of his students, but he was constantly on guard about his position within psychoanalysis.

Not only did Erikson not want his work associated with that of Erich Fromm, but I do not recall his ever favourably mentioning Carl G. Jung. (In later years Erikson in print made some generous general references to Jung.) As far as I could tell Erikson seemed determined not to fall into the category of being a psychoanalytic rebel. As a matter of fact he leaned over backwards to try to romanticize Freud as the first psychoanalyst. Whether he was writing about Martin Luther in a spiritual crisis or Mahatma Gandhi creating his doctrine of nonviolence, Erikson repeatedly drew comparisons with issues in Freud's own life. (Thinking of how Freud had dissected the maxim 'love thy neighbour' it was pretty far-fetched of Erikson to make any comparisons between Freud and St. Francis of Assisi.) It is true, though, that when Erikson came to publish his own interpretation of Freud's Irma dream, he went through agony; he must have known how Anna Freud would be bound to react to his daring to interpret her father psychoanalytically.

Henry A. Murray, who later reported to me Erikson's crisis of conscience over the completion of his Irma essay, had in fact been one of those who first in America discovered Erikson's talent. Starting in the 1920s Murray (himself analysed by Jung) had been running a Harvard Psychological Clinic. Murray had a MD with a speciality in surgery, was socially well-connected, and rich enough to help out his clinic from his own pocket if that proved necessary. But Murray was also an inspiring teacher, in a different way from Erikson; he did not match Erikson's casual platform presence, but on an individual basis Murray put himself into his students to draw out their best talents, and was successful in building up an academic organization.

Unfortunately it did not long survive Murray's own retirement, and the study of clinical psychology at Harvard is weaker now than seventy years ago.

Murray spotted Erikson's unusual abilities in the 1930s, when Erikson first arrived in the States from Europe. Freud's disciple in New York City, A. A. Brill, had not been taken with Erikson, whose special qualifications then were in child analysis. But Murray, who never succeeded over a long lifetime in writing the biography of Herman Melville he yearned to produce, helped put Erikson on the map in Boston. By 1935 Felix Deutsch, when looking around in Boston with the idea of moving there himself with his wife Helene and their son, was astonished that Erikson was already established in the city as *the* child analyst.[8] Boston had such a powerful medical fraternity than it was all the more remarkable that Erikson, without any formal academic credentials, could succeed so swiftly.

Murray's own training had been eclectic; in addition to being analyzed by Jung, he had also been treated by the Freudian Franz Alexander. Murray was attempting to steer clear of the fanatics he thought were gradually taking over the new Boston Psychoanalytic Institute. (I remember in particular how he dismissed one of the leading early Boston analysts as a 'crackpot'.) All this independence on Murray's part meant that he lived an existence more daring and unusual than the local analysts; in addition to his first wife he had a long-standing mistress who was a co-worker.

Murray was an unusual free spirit, and he shared many of Erikson's own reservations about the orthodox psychoanalytic movement. In particular, Murray thought that Anna Freud had been an academic embarrassment when she briefly taught at Radcliffe College in the early 1950s. Murray shuddered when he related how people had to help Anna out in coping with the normal give-and-take of university life; imperious as she could be, she had a fragile side and old friends assisted her in meeting the unexpected challenges she encountered at Radcliffe.

Erikson, though he was to spend years of university teaching, was also not at home there. He publicly admitted to suffering from the kind of identity confusions he had made so popularly accessible in his books, but from what I could see his own relationship to Anna Freud was fraught with unresolved conflict. In the late 1920s she had been his analyst. I feel certain that Erikson's wife Joan was a key help to him there; she did not share the sycophantic reverence that was so

160

common in the circle around Anna Freud, and with both her feet on the ground Joan doubtless knew that Erikson could only succeed in being himself outside that magic enclave.

Erikson was, for a Freudian, remarkably bold in criticizing some of Anna Freud's ideas. For example, in a 1936 review of a book of hers he distinguished his own distinctive approach from that of 'Miss Freud':

> Following the traditional route of psychoanalysis the book says much about what may limit and endanger the child's ego; it says little about the ego itself. Correspondingly psychoanalysis has so far been useful to pedagogy primarily as a basis of criticism of cultural progress and the dangers it involves for children. So far as further studies may illuminate the ego, psychoanalytic insight will be able to help education in its most specific problem: the strengthening and enriching of the ego.[9]

Nevertheless Erikson remained tied to Anna Freud in a way that defies easy interpretation. She had analyzed him at an extraordinarily low fee, when he was unsure what professional direction he should take in his life. Up to then he had been a talented young man who liked to paint portraits. Within psychoanalysis he found a field where he could use his native intuitive talents in understanding small children, and yet write about them with artistry instead of the conceptual heavy-handedness that has marred so much of psychoanalytic literature. He said to me that he always thought that Anna Freud could never forgive him for having given up the practice of child analysis. When I saw her first in 1965, she was clearly not any kind of enthusiast on behalf of Erikson's work. He could even go to London, spend time with an old Viennese analyst in Anna's circle there, and not see her himself; he would anguish about how stand-offish to his work she could be. In private she complained that he had grown into a know-it-all. Yet he continued to send her his books, even dedicating one of them to her, although he surely knew how 'unintelligible' she found his original ideas. (Unintelligibility was the way her father had treated the ideas of heretics like Jung, Alfred Adler, Otto Rank, and Klein.)

Erikson succeeded in effecting something of a reconciliation with Anna Freud toward the end of her life. And when her intimate friend Dorothy Burlingham predeceased her, Erikson wrote a little memoir about Dorothy for Anna Freud's new journal at the Hampstead Clinic she and Dorothy had founded. This must have appeased a good deal of Anna's irritation with him.

Erikson had felt from the outset that if he were going to be original and fulfil himself, it would have to be at the expense of remaining in Anna Freud's orbit. And so he had left Vienna in the early 1930s; in Boston his success was meteoric. In Anna Freud's world Erikson would be considered a servant; but in Boston he found a ready reception for his genuine talents.

I can testify to how Erikson was viewed as a servant in Vienna based on a dramatic-seeming nonverbal exchange between Erikson and his wife at one of his faculty seminars. For years Erikson had conducted these seminars, intended for advanced graduate students and faculty. He ran the seminars more or less along the lines of a clinical case conference. The presenter would bring biographical material, everyone in the room would have a chance to comment on it, and at the conclusion Erikson would try to pull the various threads together. But Erikson was not bent on looking for symptoms; as W. H. Auden commented about Erikson, he was 'that happy exception, a psychoanalyst who knows the difference between a biography and a case history'.[10] It was always impressive to see how Erikson could listen and learn, and still extract something teachable for the rest of us. His wife Joan made it a regular practice to attend silently each of these seminars, and she seemed to take notes about all of the presentations.

One session was led by Richard Sennett on Frank Lloyd Wright, and Sennett quoted Wright as having once said that after he had students he no longer needed servants. Erik immediately cast a meaningful glance over at Joan that spoke volumes to me. I had understood Erikson to have once said that he had sometimes driven Freud in Dorothy Burlingham's car. Erik even had a memory of Freud's crying on such a ride; it must have been that the prosthesis for his mouth was pressing down on some tear ducts, since the weeping did not seem psychologically motivated. When I said in print that Erikson had once chauffeured Freud he wrote a clarifying 'memorandum' for the Freud Archives, which is now amidst Erikson's papers at Harvard's Houghton Library. It turns out that Erikson did not learn to drive a car until he came to America, although he did accompany Freud in a chauffeur-driven car from Semmering to Vienna and back. Erikson had reason to be touchy about the role-playing of being a servant, for one of Anna Freud's child analysands, and a pupil of Erikson's at the same time Erikson was in treatment with Anna, has published a dream he had at the time in which Erikson was associated with being a chauffeur.[11]

I felt proud at being asked by Erikson to make the first presentation at that year's faculty seminar; he indicated to me that he felt wary of what some of the other participants in the class might be up to, implying that he had confidence in me. I brought for my talk, which I worked at carefully beforehand, some material connected with Freud's struggles with Adler and Jung before World War I, and how distressed Freud felt afterwards about the fate of his brain-child, psychoanalysis. Erikson concluded, tentatively, that what I had brought was really a 'generativity' crisis, central to Erikson's work then on Gandhi; I immediately agreed, saying that that was why I had brought this particular episode, and Erikson responded with a gracious 'thank-you'. (Although Erikson never made much of being a theorist – as a matter of fact he rather pretended not to be good at abstractions – his concept of generativity, characteristic of middle age, was intended as an addition to his own earlier interest in identity as a key part of adolescence. But then his whole notion of the life cycle was designed to get away from early psychoanalysis's concentration on the Oedipus complex.)

When I knew Erikson he was determined to fulfil the direction his own work had already taken him. In those days *Childhood and Society* was generally considered a masterpiece in modern social science, and I still think it ranks as his greatest single work. When *Young Man Luther* came out in 1958 I was a little disappointed, since I naïvely expected psychoanalytic psychology to be able to be more definitive; the concept of 'psycho-history' was one of Erikson's most memorable contributions. But in later years I came to admire the methodological subtlety of the Luther book, in that Erikson was trying to look at a historical subject from a variety of theoretical vantage points. (While Fromm had taken a rather negative view of Luther, Erikson was determined to see in the Protestant Reformation a peak of introspective self-examination. These differences between their approaches to Luther came up when they met once in Mexico.[12])

It did not then seem to me at all strange that Erikson should be so interested in Luther. I took it for granted that he had a profound commitment to Christian values; I even once spotted a crucifix in his Widener office which his other Jewish graduate students seemed to block out of their sight. I recall him once complaining that the problem with teaching psychoanalysis to undergraduates was that they took away too pessimistic a version of life; when I replied by asking whether he assigned Freud's *Future of an Illusion*, since that book contains Freud's utopian side in an anti-religious tract, Erikson acknowledged with a wry smile that he did not in fact use that book in courses. As a theorist he sought to be pro-religiously optimistic.

Erikson was trying to find in psychoanalysis an ethics which would support, rather than challenge, his Christian faith. And I am afraid that I must have seemed a bit of a pain to Erik, since it was so easy for me, trained as a political theorist, to handle conceptual problems. Erikson did not want to learn from me, for example, about any theoretical similarities between his own work and Melanie Klein's. I thought they both were highlighting a religious dimension in human experience, but Erikson simply waved her name aside. She had of course been for years a great rival in child analysis to Anna Freud's own approach, though I thought Erikson's dismissal of Klein seemed an independent decision of his own. While he was trying to correct some of the negativistic imbalances in psychoanalysis, making Freudian theory more healthy-minded, Kleinianism stood for a perpetuation of some of the darkest strains in psychoanalytic thinking. (She talked about psychosis being part of normal personality development, and made famous such at first-glance frightening concepts about early childhood as the 'depressive' and the 'paranoid' 'positions'.[13])

In keeping with that early published book-review challenge of Erikson's to Anna Freud's book on children, Erikson was concentrating on promoting the significance not of pathology but of the concept of ego strength. This notion was designed to emphasize the synthesizing functions of the ego, how a variety of contradictions and tensions could be successfully integrated by a healthy ego. Erikson was proposing to change the psychoanalytic approach to normality; instead of looking at problems in terms of what in a person's character had been denied or cut off, he wanted to turn towards how much conflict someone was able to incorporate and integrate. Instead of trying to isolate signs of failure, Erikson was determined to try to concentrate on the sources of success. And so he was proposing to study the whole of human development, from earliest childhood, in the light of the growth of the ego, which Erikson thought had stages like Freud's view of libido. The concept of the identity crisis became Erikson's most famous one, yet even here he emphasized how the term crisis could mean a turning point either for good or ill. And in describing the course of the ego's enhancement, society played, in his view, a largely constructive role. Religion was only one example of how a social institution was capable of encouraging ego strength.

Although I certainly felt the importance of Erikson's involvement in religious issues, it never entered my head that he might be Jewish. He did, I now realize, point out to me that one of the central defects in Ernest Jones's official biography of Freud was that Jones did not understand the Jew in Freud; but that comment seemed to me more a critique of Jones than to be something substantive about Erikson himself. It came then as a bombshell to me, as well as to others who had once lived in the Cambridge community, to read in 1975, in a front-page article in the *New York Times* Sunday book review section written by someone who had scarcely known Erikson at Harvard, that Erikson had been disguising a Jewish family background.[14] One knew from Erikson that his stepfather was Jewish but nothing that he had written autobiographically had described any kind of conversion experience to Christianity. Later I found out that Erikson had had a bar mitzvah, and that his mother and stepfather, with other family members as well, had left Germany for Palestine before World War II.

Erikson certainly was notable for having devoted much attention in his theories to the significant role of mothers. If, as I then presumed to be the case, Erikson was born illegitimate, and his mother brought him for help to that Jewish physician, Homburger, who then married her and gave the boy his name, against whom was the name-changing on Erikson's part, once he got to the States, directed? I think he was not just repudiating the stepfather; rather, his relationship to his mother seems to be more the crux of the issue. (Erikson kept the Homburger identity by the letter 'H.' as a middle name, but Anna Freud and others in that early circle always continued to refer to him as Homburger.)

My own feelings about Erikson underwent a temporary sea-change when I read the *New York Times* allegations about him; rather, I waited and hoped (in vain) that Erikson would publish some sort of reply. He knew I was writing a book about him since it had been announced on my most recent book-jacket; and so he sent me a 'memorandum' to clarify the religions of his parents. It was not a personal letter but a document that might have gone to others as well, and it did little, I thought, to put to rest the original piece in the *New York Times*. At that time I had already completed a first draft, inadequate to be sure, of a little book about Erikson's ideas. I knew that I had to rewrite the manuscript anyway, but doing so under such circumstances meant that I probably was more critical of Erikson's work than I should have been, or than looks justifiable by the standards of the beginning of the twenty-first century, when Erikson's stature is by no means as secure as it seemed in 1975.

One of the central points of Erikson's psycho-historical principles was that an observer should acknowledge some of the elements in his own interaction with his research. Yet there is a notable case of a Jewish boy in *Childhood and Society* which is described by Erikson with as much distance and dispassion as if he were giving an account of a Sioux or Yurok child. (For his time it was unusual as an analyst for Erikson to have done anthropological field work with such Indian tribes, and he had memorable contact with both Margaret Mead and Ruth Benedict.) In his autobiographical reflections Erikson had been guilty, I believe, of a kind of existential bad faith, yet that should not permanently affect how his achievement is evaluated.

I will never forget a dinner party Erikson hosted at a time when he and I were both writing something about the recently released Freud-Bullitt manuscript on Woodrow Wilson. There were just the four of us, my wife and I with the Eriksons. Erikson had told me beforehand that it might just be a 'cold supper', for it was on a Sunday evening, but it turned out to be a full hot meal. He began the dinner by toasting: 'No more undiscovered Freud texts!' That evening Erik and I spoke candidly, and then took different lines in print. Anna Freud was, along with her loyal cohorts, pleased with the position Erikson adopted in *The New York Review of Books*, dissociating Freud's hand as much as possible from the final manuscript.[15] At dinner Erikson said, when I told him what I knew of Anna Freud's initial reaction to the release of the manuscript on Wilson, that he could not understand how she had not at once seen the more of defects in the text. Erikson was mainly worried, as he admitted, that his own efforts at 'psycho-history' would be damaged by the polemical nature of the Freud-Bullitt precursor. When I wrote to Anna Freud at that point about the forthcoming book, her reply indicated that she would be, in answering my questions, essentially duplicating what Erikson had independently asked her.

As an outsider I had my own difficulties dealing with Anna Freud, since she was the guardian of so much primary source material; but I always found something distinctly odd about Erikson's attitude toward her. When I once asked him at a party at his house if he knew who had analysed her, he denied any knowledge on the subject. One would have thought he would naturally have always been curious about his own therapist's analyst, but I guess it is impossible to over-estimate the power of taboos among the early analysts. When I told him that it had been her own father who had undertaken her analysis, I was startled by his immediate response: 'I always suspected incest!' Now in some sense what Freud and Anna were engaged in, violating all known psychoanalytic rules of procedure, was a form of spiritual incest. Still, for Erikson to jump from being unaware of the name of Anna's analyst, to such a stark and unlikely possibility, does show the degree to which some of the deepest emotional undercurrents in Erikson had remained analytically untouched.

I believe it was that same night at Erikson's house that he jokingly warned Joan about me: 'Watch out what you say!' On one occasion or another Joan had told me how Heinz Hartmann had once felt he had to give her a private dressing-down about her lack of the proper awe toward Freud, and psychoanalysis. (In those days Hartmann was considered the Prime Minister of psychoanalysis, but Joan was scath-ing about how when Hartmann and Erikson were once on the same lecture platform, Hartmann seemed content to be talking to himself.) But although Joan was far more emancipated and free-thinking about psychoanalytic politics than Erik, it nevertheless was what I heard from him that always registered the most with me. I think I identified with his struggle to find what was valuable and worth preserving in psychoanalysis, even if much of the received so-called knowledge had to be discarded.

I would not want to give the false impression that my own work ever mattered in any great way to Erikson. I was surprised, and more than a little appalled, to hear later that Joan and Erik had read aloud to each other my book about him. They did regularly read to each other at night; but it had never once occurred to me that I should send them a copy of my book, since it was in no sense an authorized one, and I knew how sensitive to criticism he could be. When he re-published his original essay on the Freud-Bullitt book on Wilson, changing his argument rather strikingly in the direction I had myself first adopted, I took the trouble to itemize carefully in public exactly which points he had deleted in a piece that he tried to claim was identical to his original one.[16] I gather that he was distressed at this exposure. He was obviously entitled to change his mind, and I was pleased that he had moved closer to my own thinking; but I thought it opportunistic for him to claim merely to be repeating an original essay. Erikson not surprisingly objected to many points in my book about him, but I have it on excellent authority that he did reluctantly volunteer the conclusion that I had successfully placed his work within intellectual history.

Throughout the many years I was at Harvard I was never important enough for Erikson to have invited me to be one of his teaching assistants. But then he could not have known that I had been sternly warned by at least one of my Government Department mentors that if I knew what was good for me I would steer completely away from Erikson, and David Riesman as well. Cultish pressures existed then, and now as well, among political theorists against people like Erikson and Riesman. If only I had had more courage (or time), I would have become better acquainted with both Erikson and Riesman; but the preoccupations of pursuing my own writing were the central deter-minants of my decisions. The platform for my research was that lecture course I taught on 'Psychology and Politics' and also a gradu-ate seminar on 'Political Psychology', which never got accepted as suitably hard-headed subjects for a political science field which was then becoming increasingly behaviouristic and scientistic.

One aspect of Erikson did trouble me throughout the 1960s, and I came back to this in an article about him that I later published in 1980.[17] I was then concerned with the political implications of his ego psychology, and I still cannot understand how he chose to remain so silent during the worst of the Vietnam war years. This was particularly true since at the time, at a large faculty meeting at the height of a university crisis where we voted by standing, Erikson and I seemed to be on the same side. I recall being at a luncheon with Marcuse in those days when we both admired Erikson, although Marcuse did think that Erikson could be 'too nice'. Marcuse said Erik, when asked to sign anything of an anti-war declaration, would always beg off on the grounds that he did not 'know enough'. (Marcuse himself suffered from no such inhibitions, and could write about Freud's theories without any interest or understanding of the clinical side of psychoa-nalysis. Fromm was fully justified in thinking that Marcuse had just dabbled in psychoanalysis.) I am relieved to hear that an examination of Erikson's papers shows that he was much better connected with the White House than I ever would have expected, and that he did what he could to get Lyndon Johnson to back off from Southeast Asian military action. It would be in keeping with Erikson's temperament if he chose to use his influence informally and without fanfare.[18]

Some day a full-scale study of Erikson and his circle may be completed: David Rapaport, Robert Lifton, Robert Coles, Carol Gilligan, and many others will play a far greater role than I in the story that needs to be unfolded. Erikson succeeded in attracting people around him who behaved protectively about his person. I suppose this essay of mine is part of that tendency; for it is on behalf of the cause of making sure that Erikson's unusual contributions to psychoanalysis, social science, and political theory do not get needlessly neglected that I am offering this personal memoir.

De Gaulle is said once to have declared that old age is a ship-wreck, and it is a pleasure to record how Erikson's creativity extended to planning for his retirement years. After leaving Harvard the Eriksons lived for some years outside San Francisco; they later returned to Cambridge in 1984, where they moved into an unusual group setting. The Eriksons bought a house with two younger women who could help take care of the aging couple. One old friend of theirs reported to me what a real joy it remained to visit with the Eriksons, which meant to me that they had succeeded in coping with the final stage of the life cycle with the best possible resolution. I was to continue to be impressed by Erikson as a teacher. But the details of the arrangement for the house in Cambridge turned out unhappily for the Eriksons; the care-taking they had counted on inadequately materialized, nor had it really been an enforceable part of their agreement. The Eriksons finally took a financial bath on the house; Erik's own decline – whether Alzheimer's, senility, or some precipitate of a sulphur drug he had had to take in connection with an infection connected to prostate surgery – meant that prior to his death in 1994 he needed nursing home care. Well before Joan's own death in 1997 she was embittered by how she felt about the inter-generational housing they had idealistically planned on.

The Eriksons had authorized a fine biography of Erik which appeared in 1999. He had succeeded in constructing a set of theories about the development of the individual life cycle which complemented Fromm's own ideas about the relationship between personality and social structure. Both Erikson and Fromm had shared a certain kind of social idealism, which meant that their ideas were directed toward elucidating concepts of what it might mean to be human; Bettelheim's focus on the psychology of concentration camp life had also directed us to the question of the nature of fundamental psychological processes. Although Erikson can be accused of sometimes having a Pollyanna-ish air to his theorizing, and Fromm (along with French analysts who followed Jacques Lacan) objected to how Erikson's kind of ego psychology could be used for advocating conformist adaptation, Erikson did offer socially challenging ideas; his concept of 'pseudo-speciation', for example, was designed to highlight how we can try to elevate ourselves by putting other groups down. And his notion of 'negative identity', everything in a person that one strives to avoid or live down, indicated that his view of ego development was not designed to be without conflict or tension.

Although Erikson lacked the conceptual clarity of either Fromm or Bettelheim, his example of artistically trying to overcome the inherited negativism within Freudian theory did an immense amount to help emancipate people from the narrower constraints of Freud's theories. In Erikson's efforts to concentrate on the strengths people bring to emotional problems, without dwelling just on deficits, he was linking up with the great tradition of political theory which had always been keenly interested in concepts of human nature. Erikson was not just inventing hypothetical possibilities; for through the use of biographical subjects, such as Luther, Gandhi, as well as others, he was trying to show how problems that prove debilitating clinically can also, in the lives of unusually creative people, become enriching. So I think that Erikson, like Fromm and Bettelheim, can be seen as adding to the tradition of political theory as exemplified by John Stuart Mill, Nietzsche, and Dostoevsky.

NOTES

1. Erik H. Erikson, *Childhood and Society* (New York, Norton, 1950; 2nd ed., New York, Norton, 1963).
2. Erik H. Erikson, *Young Man Luther: A Study in Psychoanalysis and History* (New York, Norton, 1958). Erik H. Erikson, *Gandhi's Truth: On the Origins of Militant Nonviolence* (New York, Norton, 1969).
3. Lawrence J. Friedman, *Identity's Architect: A Biography of Erik H. Erikson* (New York, 1999). But see Erikson's daughter's harsh critique of him: 'Fame: The Power and Cost of a Fantasy', *The Atlantic*, November 1999, pp. 51–62.
4. *Ideas and Identities: The Life and Work of Erik Erikson*, ed. Robert S. Wallerstein and Leo Goldberger (Madison, Conn., International Universities Press, 1998). Robert Coles, ed. *The Erik Erikson Reader* (New York, Norton, 2000)
5. See Friedman, *op. cit.*, pp. 162, 200, 239, 240, 422. Erich Fromm and Michael Maccoby, *Social Character in a Mexican Village*, *op. cit.*, pp. 20n–21n.
6. Erik H. Erikson, 'Reflections on Dr. Borg's Life Cycle', *Daedalus*, CV (Spring 1976).
7. Erik H. Erikson, 'Play and Actuality', in *Play and Development*, ed. Maria W. Piers (New York, Norton, 1972), pp. 138–39.
8. Roazen, *Helene Deutsch*, *op. cit.*, p. 280.
9. Roazen, *Erik H. Erikson*, *op. cit.*, p. 22.
10. W. H. Auden, *Forewards and Afterwards* (London, Faber & Faber, 1973), p. 79.
11. Peter Heller, *A Child Analysis with Anna Freud* (Madison, Conn., International Universities Press, 1990), p. 369.
12. See Friedman, *op. cit.*, pp. 273–74.
13. Paul Roazen, *Oedipus in Britain: Edward Glover and the Struggle Over Klein*, *op. cit* . See also Edward Glover, *An Examination of the Klein System of Child Psychology* (London, The Southern Post, 1945), also in *The Psychoanalytic Study of the Child*, Vol. 1 (New York, International Universities Press, 1945).
14. Roazen, *Erikson*, *op. cit.*, pp. 95–99.
15. Erik H. Erikson, 'The Strange Case of Freud, Bullitt, and Woodrow Wilson: A Dubious Collaboration', *The New York Review of Books*, Feb. 9, 1967, pp. 3–5.
16. See also Roazen, *Erik H. Erikson*, *op. cit.*, 13, 202–03.
17. Roazen, *Encountering Freud*, *op. cit.*, pp. 152–60.
18. Friedman, *op. cit.*, pp. 361–62.

Conclusions

Beneath all the controversies in Freud's lifetime, and side by side with his own social speculations which fit rather readily within traditional political theory, went a growing body of psychological thought. It is possible, of course, to over-estimate what it is that psychoanalysts have come to agree on; yet I think despite all the famous controversies within the school Freud started, at least certain central questions have come to be more or less agreed upon as legitimate inquiries. So even though Freud may have forged his ideas out of his own autobiography as well as clinical work, in the hands of successive generations of thinkers his work could be used for purposes very different from those like his own. And it is by examining these successors of Freud that one can get a rather better idea of the implications of his ideas than just by reading some of his own most explicit 'applications' of his ideas to social thought.

When one thinks of people like Fromm, Bettelheim, and Erikson it is hard to over-estimate just how remarkably productive a group Freud succeeded in having around him. These three writers were in Freud's own time all on the margins of psychoanalysis; yet subsequently, both in America as well as elsewhere, they became famous as pundits. The common pull on all their ideas was to venture from the purely psychological, both descriptive and explanatory, towards the moral and philosophic.

Each of these three post-Freudian writers had his beginnings fairly strictly in the world of science, and yet they all felt pulled into larger questions; once they had arrived there it becomes clear how much they had in common with the three thinkers we started out with. Fromm, Bettelheim and Erikson were as interested in the problems of freedom and authority, self-development and self-frustration, as were ever the traditional figures in political philosophy.

In dealing with any of the main writers working within the broad confines of the Freudian tradition, it is always necessary to watch out for where the line has been crossed between empiricism and ideology. For often psychoanalytic writers will be purporting to write about 'is' questions, connected with how things happen, when in reality they have already moved over into the realm of ethics and morality, or what are known as 'ought' matters. It should be impossible, for example, to detach the problem of symptomatology, or the general question of what we might mean by the 'healthy', from a social and normative context. Although most clinicians are not readily prepared to talk about what ideally they might have in mind for their psychological patients, some such general conception is logically necessarily behind all their work.

All post-Freudian writers, and even main-line political theorists, take for granted a core body of psychological suppositions. From the point of view of the history of ideas, these three thinkers – Fromm, Bettelheim, and Erikson – are of course by no means on the same level as people of the historic stature of John Stuart Mill, Nietzsche, and Dostoevsky. The depth and complexity of the writers that we started out with, in terms of their respective critiques of Benthamism, puts them on a more elevated historical plane than any such near-contemporaries of ours such as Fromm, Bettelheim, and Erikson. And yet from the point of view of today's social science, and in particular political thought, these three post-Freudian writers have had an enormous impact of their own.

It is necessary, in thinking about these three post-Freudians, to distinguish between psychoanalysis as a trade-union organization and as an intellectual theory. Curiously enough, none of these three writers had a medical degree, which in a way fulfilled Freud's conviction that the future of his field lay outside the strict confines of medicine. Fromm, after the ruckus associated with the publication of his *Escape From Freedom* in 1941, was considered *persona non grata* within orthodox psychoanalytic circles. When he was cut from direct membership of the International Psychoanalytic Association (IPA), he had to settle for being merely an associate member of the Washington

Psychoanalytic Society. At various times he had been allied with such psychoanalytic thinkers as Harry Stack Sullivan, Clara Thompson and Karen Horney, and left a lasting legacy of influence within the William Alanson White Institute in New York; but also in Mexico he was able to found his own school there. Once Fromm had been attacked by people like Karl Menninger and Otto Fenichel for the supposed heresies of *Escape From Freedom*, he had walked into the revolutionary tradition in psychoanalysis first started by Adler and Jung.

Fromm explicitly repudiated many of Freud's central ideas, and expressed his preference for Marx's formulations. As time went on, he became more and more a moralist, and less a social scientist. But a late book like his *The Anatomy of Human Destructiveness* demonstrated the continuing power of his conceptual mind. Fromm's brand of ethical preaching seemed to become increasingly rather sentimental, and he always aroused great antagonism among the 'loyalist' Freudians. Fromm's pacifist political views did not endear him to political scientists, whose field has always thought of itself as a place where only hard-nosed views are in style. So that in the late 1960s for example, during the height of the Vietnam war, some political scientists felt comfortable talking about the 'modernization' of south-east Asia, and its rapid 'urbanization'; this sort of euphemistic terminology was a cover for the real war that was taking place there. The whole tradition of depth psychology, first started by Freud, has seemed to political scientists too 'soft' and 'subjective', altogether too 'weak' for the preferences of mainstream political science, which oddly enough still seems implicitly attached to the models of human behaviour which ultimately derive from Jeremy Bentham.

Now liberalism has always had a formalistic side, so that liberal thinkers have tended to place a high value on rules and explicitly set-out regulations. Freedom is not, however, as John Stuart Mill was one of the earliest within liberalism to point out, just a matter of such constitutional guarantees. Nowadays we have the phenomena of what are known as 'hate crime' and 'false news', and the issue is still an open one about just how much circulation of ideas should be possible. If for instance someone working in education were to be teaching that the Holocaust never took place, or that it was responsible for a minimal number of European deaths, would we allow such a person to go on educating the young? Despite all our commitment to the free exchange of ideas, some thoughts do seem beyond the pale; and every society has its notions of national security, and what amounts to endangering the survival of the state through violations of norms establishing certain secrets — in connection with atomic weapons or missile defences, for example. Freedom may be the central value of our society, but liberty could not exist without certain limits; trying to define those restraints is part of what a political theorist does.

The doctrines about individuality and self-development that arise in the context of clinical psychoanalysis are not just the everyday, working stock-in-trade of psychologist clinicians; but also the vast majority of psychiatrists, psychiatric social works, marriage counsellors, and lawyers share in the knowledge of these ideas as well. Post-Freudian social thought is more directly relevant to contemporary political science, and certainly more plausible to most, than Freud's own explicit attempts at social philosophy like *Totem and Taboo*, *Group Psychology and the Analysis of the Ego*, and *Moses and Monotheism*.[1]

In the hunger for meaning created by the decline in religious faith that Nietzsche had heralded with his aphorism that 'God is dead', people have sought refuge in a variety of secular religions like that forwarded by Freud. Psychoanalysis has served multiple ethical purposes, and Fromm, Bettelheim, and Erikson can be representative of only a range of the ideas that came up within modern depth psychology.

But our earlier discussions can help highlight some of what has been missing in post-Freudian social thought. The greatest thinkers, like Nietzsche and Dostoevsky for example, were more attentive to the inescapable contradictions in moral life. Tolstoy may have objected to honouring Dostoevsky on the grounds that he was 'all struggle', yet privately Tolstoy could write to his wife: 'To live an honest life you have to ... struggle endlessly, and suffer loss. As for tranquillity – it's spiritual baseness.'[2] Curiously enough Freud had written rather similarly to his own fiancée:

> I am very stubborn and very reckless and need great challenges, I have done a number of things which any sensible person would be bound to consider very rash. For example, to take up science as a poverty-stricken man, then as a poverty-stricken man to capture a poor girl – but this must continue to be my way of life: risking a lot, hoping a lot, working a lot. To average bourgeois common sense I have been lost long ago.[3]

Freud's programme of 'risking a lot, hoping a lot, working a lot' communicates a kind of spiritual intransigence that appears to be missing in the more modulated tones of someone like Erikson. Fromm may have been more aware of the tensions between opposites that we inevitably have to cope with, but like Erikson, he sought to construct a set of universal ethics which would harmoniously encompass all past religious systems. Bettelheim's concentration camp imprisonment left him permanently marked with a sense of tragedy.

Even though looking at these post-Freudians can point out how psychoanalysis fits into previous political theory, Freud himself can often sound right in keeping with some of the most characteristic thoughts of Dostoevsky, as for example when Freud wrote: 'You cannot exaggerate the intensity of people's inner lack of resolution and craving for authority.'[4] Although many of Freud's ideas have been vulgarized in their various popularizations, it is after all a distinction afforded to few writers. It would be hard to find a more commanding figure in contemporary intellectual life. To repeat, I think he is one of the greatest psychologists of all time – and certainly no one else in the twentieth century has done more to alter the way we think about ourselves. We might demonstrate this by adopting a standard suggested by Henry James in another context: 'The way to judge him is to try to walk all around him – on which we see how remarkably far we have to go.'[5]

To follow Freud within the context of the history of political theory is not to romanticize his standing. Psychoanalytic thinking can highlight key aspects of the work of people like John Stuart Mill, Nietzsche, and Dostoevsky, at the same time as Freud's own work gets put in better perspective. Through examining what post-Freudianism has to contribute to social thought we can get a better idea of the implications of Freud's thinking. Even if it turns out to be true that there is little new under the sun within intellectual history, its study can only strengthen and enhance our own thinking. Little conflict ought to exist between looking at the classics at the same time as contemporary writers; the great traditions of the past only become more vital in the light of recent intellectual developments. The history of ideas can best succeed in its objective of broadening us if we approach it through questions that are uppermost in today's concerns. The nature of human psychology is endlessly fascinating, and I have presented all the writers here in the spirit that they should be taken as a good beginning.

To be fair, we should be on our guard against ever allowing our knowledge of the personal foibles and limitations of recent thinkers to undermine the merits of their ideas. Of course, it complicates things to see how anyone can fall short of their own standards. But it would be an unbalanced comparison to take people about whom we think we know so much, and put them against distant writers whom we necessarily understand at least partly through the legends which a rich literature has built up. It takes the passage of time to know who deserves to rank where in intellectual history. So how the present interacts with the past has to remain an uncertain undertaking.

Trying to become better educated is a goal it would be hard to disagree with. It becomes easier to read around in intellectual history if one starts off from a given focus. And concentrating on various concepts of human nature can take one pretty far in terms of the vast tradition of the history of ideas. The more one knows about post-Freudianism, for example, the likelier it is that past great figures are going to come alive. It has been my long-standing hope that by studying comparatively recent psychological thinkers one can be drawn back to the intellectual giants in history. Depth psychology can thereby help lure us as students into what has all along been so vital in political philosophy.

NOTES

1. 'Moses and Monotheism', *Standard Edition*, Vol. 23, pp. 7–137.
2. Kelly, *Toward Another Shore*, *op. cit.*, p. 85.
3. *Letters of Sigmund Freud 1873–1939*, *op. cit.*, p. 85.
4. 'The Future of Psychoanalytic Therapy', *Standard Edition*, Vol. 11, p. 146.
5. *The Portable Henry James*, ed. Morton Dauwen Zabel (New York, Viking Press, 1951), p. 474.

Index